W·W·HOLDEN

William Woods Holden, 1818–1892

W·W·HOLDEN

A POLITICAL BIOGRAPHY

BY EDGAR E. FOLK

AND BYNUM SHAW

JOHN F. BLAIR, PUBLISHER
WINSTON-SALEM, NORTH CAROLINA

CATALOGING IN PUBLICATION DATA ON PAGE 285

FOR MINTA HOLDING FOLK

PREFACE

The pages that follow present the first detailed examination of the full life of William Woods Holden ever published. Holden was a political editor of the old personal school, and his Raleigh *Standard* was the most powerful newspaper in North Carolina in the nineteenth century, to be surpassed in influence and prestige later only by the *News and Observer* under the editorship of Josephus Daniels—who knew Holden.

A great deal has been written—much of it uninformed—about Holden's impeachment as the state's Reconstruction governor, but almost nothing has been published about the years Holden spent in the antebellum South as a persuasive molder of public opinion and as a maker of public servants. This volume follows that development in detail. In that respect it is based in large part on a very careful analysis of the pages of the *Standard* contained in a study by Dr. Folk, *W. W. Holden, Political Journalist*, covering the years 1843 to 1865. On publication of this volume, that manuscript will be turned over to the North Carolina State Archives, where it will be available to scholars wishing to see a more expansive treatise.

Chapters four and six follow the earlier study very closely and have been published in slightly different form in the *North Carolina Historical Review* (Vol. XIX, No. 1, pp. 22–47, and Vol. XXI, No. 4, pp. 294–318). The authors express their gratitude to the North Carolina Department of Cultural Resources for permission to include that material in this volume. Thanks go as well to the archives section of that department for ferreting out the photographs that appear in these pages.

Historians have not been kind to Holden, partly because they were prejudiced, partly because they simply did not understand the man, partly because they were careless in their research. The *Dictionary of American Biography,* that mainstay of college term papers, carries an absolutely savage notice accusing Holden of "the most brazen corruption, extravagance and incompetency." As late as 1914, even the prestigious Columbia University Press, in its Studies in History, Economics, and Public Law, was accepting the word of Southern historians that the Ku Klux Klan, which brought Holden down, was actually a benevolent force in bringing law and order to the South after the Civil War, and that it was "more sinned against than sinning."

This is an attempt, after a century of malignment of Holden, to set the record straight.

Holden was neither an incompetent nor a rapscallion, as he was described by his politically motivated enemies. That he was the first American governor to be impeached and convicted says more of his Klan-influenced prosecutors than it does of him.

The work here presented has been evolving for more than forty years, and it would be impossible now to thank all those who contributed to it. Holden's relatives were generous in providing original material. In particular, for the sake of history, a half sister bared the secret that haunted Holden all his life but that has been available to no other biographer. The authors are in her debt, and the bibliography shows indebtedness to many other sources. Regrettably, neither Holden's personal papers nor those of his contemporaries reveal much about his private life, and we have resisted the temptation to deal in conjecture.

To the library of Wake Forest University must go special thanks for allowing us to pore for so long over the three-volume transcript of the impeachment proceedings. Only eight hundred copies of that transcript were published, and most of them have been lost.

And, quite naturally, we must thank our wives, Mrs. Folk for living in Holden's shadow off and on for some years as she typed the original chapters with their profusion of footnotes documenting every fact and statement, and Mrs. Shaw for invaluable assistance in collating the source material and for typing the final version.

Lastly, we appeal to the reader to accept the material presented here as we have compiled it—as earnest seekers after the truth concerning a formidable figure too long held up to ridicule and scorn.

Edgar E. Folk
Bynum Shaw

W·W·HOLDEN

ONE

THREE DATES, one of them uncertain, wrote the destiny of William Woods Holden, the powerful nineteenth-century editor and Reconstruction governor of North Carolina whose political foes seized upon the mood of the times to destroy him as a public servant and as a man. The first two need only to be registered here, as they must be dealt with more fully. The first, taking place in March, 1818, not far from Hillsborough, North Carolina, was a simple matter of biology. The second was political, a bitter reverse occurring late in 1858. The third was fraternal, the founding on December 24, 1866, in Pulaski, Tennessee, of an organization that came to be known as the Ku Klux Klan.

The six former Confederate soldiers who concocted the Klan had no inkling that their innocent club would become an "invisible empire" mustering four hundred thousand members as it fanned out across the South like wildfire in a cruel and lawless attempt to preserve white supremacy in blatant defiance of Reconstruction legislation. It is doubtful that the founders of the Klan knew W. W. Holden; surely he had never heard of them. Yet they set in motion the wave of night riders whose atrocities Holden sought to combat, only to be dragged down for his efforts.[1]

Historians of both North and South have attempted, almost without exception, to give a patina of respectability to the covert activities of the Klan. The Reconstruction South has been viewed as an anarchic wasteland overridden by carpetbaggers and scalawags who beguiled the freed blacks into orgies of looting, murder, rape, and arson. It was against this alleged violence that the white-robed Klansmen rode out with their firebrands and muskets to strike fear into the hearts of the former slaves and their sympathizers.

In its most virulent form, Klan logic was a hysterical reaction to a deep-seated fear that the freedmen would rise to such positions of power and influence that white men—and white women—would be forever subjugated. Rumors of black violence circulated so widely that large numbers of respectable Southerners joined the riffraff that was the backbone of the Klan—the while denying that any such organization existed.

It existed, and it existed as a powerful force in the cotton lands of North Carolina. Holden, governor through a twisting chain of chance developments, sought to defeat it, and it defeated him.

Before the Civil War Holden was editor of the Raleigh *Standard*, the state's most powerful Democratic paper and one of the best newspapers in an era of a politically oriented journalism. He was a kingmaker of sorts, but because he was not an aristocrat, but was born, as he often said, "in obscurity," he was not universally admired. When, in an acrimonious convention in Charlotte in 1858, he was denied the gubernatorial nomination, his affection for the party abated.

Nevertheless, his editorials in the period of North-South crisis were strongly secessionist, and as a delegate to the secession convention he voted with the majority for a clean break. When hostilities broke out, however, he was quick to sense that the South was fighting a lost cause, and he became active in the peace movement, openly criticizing both Confederate President Jefferson Davis and North Carolina Governor Zebulon B. Vance, whom he had helped put into office.

At the war's end he was summoned to Washington by President Andrew Johnson and designated provisional governor. At the same time he was president of the state's Union League Council, an organization of Northern origin that espoused Republican principles and, in expanding southward, fattened its ranks by the inclusion of Union sympathizers and blacks, who constituted a large new voting block.

His association with the Union League helped Holden win the governor's chair on the Republican ticket in 1868, and, working with a Republican legislature, he was free for a short time to follow the dictates of law and his conscience in combatting the Klan. When Negroes were convicted on trumped-up charges in Klan territory, Holden used his pardoning power. The Klan responded by hanging its victims, thus taking them beyond the reach of Holden's redemption.

Holden resorted to public decree. On October 12, 1868, he issued a proclamation warning that intimidation of Negroes would not be tolerated and condemning the erosion of civil authority. To the Klan, the proclamation was just so much paper, and it was equally undeterred by an 1869 act of the legislature making it felonious to travel masked or in disguise.

In January, 1870, however, Holden was given the authority to meet the Klan on its own terms. Through legislation known as the Shoffner Act, the governor was empowered to declare a state of insurrection in any county where the constituted authorities were unable to preserve law and order. The measure also authorized Holden to use military force in the preservation of peace and the protection of all citizens.

In that act the Klan saw a real threat, and it marked T. M. Shoffner of Alamance County, the law's author, for death. Among his would-be executioners were the Alamance County sheriff and all his deputies. The vendetta was aborted, however, when a Klansman who was a friend of Shoffner's alerted the legislator, who escaped to Indiana.

As a substitute for Shoffner, the Klan descended on Wyatt

3

Outlaw, the black who headed the Union League in Alamance. He was taken to the courthouse square and hanged, and his body was decorated with a legend: "Bewar, ye guilty, both white and black."[2] Outlaws's "guilt" was having rounded up the black vote in Alamance County in the 1868 election, delivering it to the Republicans. A retarded Grahamite named William Puryear witnessed the Outlaw hanging and lacked the sense to keep quiet about it; he was found drowned in a millpond, a rock tied to his neck.

In Caswell County, just north of Alamance and, like it, a budding Republican stronghold, the Klan killed two men and whipped twenty-one others during a six-week period in the spring of 1870. One of those murdered was a state senator gathering information on illegal activity for the governor's office.

Under the circumstances, Holden felt compelled to meet force with force, and it was for his use of military power to restore order that a hostile legislature convening in November, 1870, moved quickly to try him for abuse of his office.

The eight charges, framed, as required by the state constitution, in the House of Representatives, accused Holden of unlawfully declaring the counties of Alamance and Caswell in insurrection; of illegally imprisoning a Democratic editor; of organizing a militia without legal authority; of abetting that force in what the legislators deemed to be various crimes; and of tapping the state treasury to pay his men.[3]

As the beleaguered Holden, who never wanted anything more than to serve the people of his state, began to prepare his defense, Klansmen all across the state were united in one reaction: "It serves the bastard right."

TWO

THE WORD "bastard," whether used as an epithet or as a term for illegitimacy, was not in Holden's vocabulary. He preferred to refer to his "unpretending origin." He used the euphemistic term many times but never bothered to explain it. Nor did his enemies make a point of it until it became a handy weapon in the political arena after Holden had become one of the most prominent men in North Carolina.

The facts of Holden's birth were established long after his death in interviews with a half sister, Mrs. Henry Murdoch of Hillsborough.[1] Holden's mother was identified as Priscilla Woods (hence the middle name), who lived near Hillsborough with her mother. She bore this son in her youth and lived in the same neighborhood for half a century afterwards, being given a house and some land by her child after he came into affluence.

Except for these skimpy details, nothing more of the woman—of her personality, of her mentality, of her physical characteristics—has been preserved. As a genetic legacy Holden may have received much from her or little; certainly she produced a son born to distinction. It is astonishing that here, after more than 160 years, their names are linked in public print for the first time.

On his father's side Holden was of English extraction. Late in the eighteenth century, a Thomas Holden came from England to Massachusetts and thence to Orange County, North Carolina, where he became a farmer near Hillsborough.[2] A son, also named Thomas, forsook farming to acquire a gristmill, which he operated five miles east of the town. Advertisements he inserted in newspapers, notably the *Hillsborough Recorder*, bear testimony that he attained some success in this business.[3]

It was this Thomas Holden, the gristmill owner, who fathered William Woods Holden, born in November, 1818, in a cabin probably not far from the mill. A year or two later, Thomas Holden married Sally Nichols, and the two became the parents of ten children.[4]

These details of Holden's birth are related because they had profound effects upon his life, influencing both his own mind and the thinking of others about him. In later years, as a successful editor, he wrote of his "inheritance of ignorance and poverty,"[5] manifesting pride in his ability to overcome such handicaps.

More than once he expressed contempt for those who spoke slightingly of his birth and who, he said, "would 'punish' me on account of my origin, and because I had the energy and ambition to struggle upwards in life, who, if they had been born in the condition I was, would have been there yet."[6] While he had genuine respect for the success other men attained by their own efforts, he was always irritated, a grandson recalled, by "undeserved pretension to political, literary or social superiority. There can be little doubt that a certain spirit of class consciousness remained ever with him throughout all his active years, manifesting itself especially when he was battling those whose claims to political preferment were founded no little on their family heritage."[7]

A great irony of Holden's life is that when he himself had achieved eminence by becoming the foremost editor and leader of the Democratic Party in the state, he was denied the governorship largely on social grounds. By insinuation and innuendo the word had been passed, and he did not become the state's chief executive until war had left his enemies momentarily powerless.

In his later life Holden seldom referred in detail to his youth, and one can only infer what it must have been like from a few hints he let fall and from a few contributions of others. For six or seven years he lived with his mother, no doubt in humble circumstances. Then he was taken to live in his father's home. There he was treated like the other children, and they regarded him as a brother. It was not until the youngest, Margaret, was in school after the Civil War that she learned from the malicious tattling of schoolmates that William was only a half brother.[8]

As an adult he wrote once of recollections of youthful skating excursions, of hunting by the moon and torchlight, of whipping another boy at school, and of being whipped in return by "the master."[9] But the carefree days did not last long, and Holden could not have had more than three years of formal education. That would have been in a "subscription" school, public schools not yet having been established in North Carolina.

At the age of nine or ten Holden left school to become a printer's apprentice under Dennis Heartt, editor of the *Hillsborough Recorder*, which Heartt had established in 1820. Although quaint by today's standards, it was for many years one of the more important journals in North Carolina. "The latest news from China," Holden recalled years later, "was printed once in three months; the Northern news, brought to Hillsborough by the triweekly stage coach, was condensed and printed once a week."[10] Otherwise the four-page paper, with five columns to the page, was filled with advertisements (given three columns of the front page), stale news clipped from other papers, poetry, fiction, and history. Heartt was "a good scholar and wrote well,"[11] Holden tells us, but he rarely took sides editorially on any issue—a policy from which Holden judiciously departed when he took up his own pen in later years.

One of the first things young Holden learned was how to get

out a paper under adversities, a necessary lesson for prospective editors. In the *Recorder* shop, he once recalled, a "double-pull Ramage press was used, with buckskin balls for inking the forms. Printing was executed under many difficulties. Types were costly and were used for from ten to fourteen years. The forms were sometimes underlaid with damp paper to bring out the impression. Mr. Heartt engraved the head of his paper, and with leaden cuts of various kinds illustrated his articles and advertisements. He made his own composing sticks of walnut wood, lined with brass."[12]

Heartt, who had been born in Connecticut in 1783, was a Whig, though not a violent or especially vigorous party man. It was an oddity of fate that he should have trained the man who became the chief instrument of the overthrow of the Whig Party in North Carolina and the most robust editor the state had known. Holden always had much admiration for Heartt, although he remembered that in the apprentice days "there were many features in his character and conduct which I could not then understand." Fifty years later, however, he could say that "in reviewing the past I have seen him in his true light, and I declare . . . that the best man in all respects whom I have ever known was my old master and teacher Dennis Heartt."[13]

One of the duties of an apprentice was to deliver the newspaper; and the historian William K. Boyd relates that on a chilly morning, when Holden was making his rounds, he came to a house on the outskirts of town where he was invited into the dining room to warm himself. At the table he saw a well-dressed young man who was a student at the state university at Chapel Hill. Holden, then about twelve, was poorly clad and barefooted. At the behest of the mistress of the house, the young man gave the ragged newsboy a buttered muffin. As he slowly savored the bread, the boy stared at the college student and thought how happy he would be to have the same opportunities. Pondering over the vicissitudes of chance in life, he resolved

8

to keep pace with the older boy despite the disparity in their conditions. Not quite forty years after that crisp morning, Holden was elected governor over Thomas S. Ashe, the young man who gave him the handout.[14]

On Christmas morning, just after his fourteenth birthday, another incident occurred that Holden subsequently took delight in relating—how he acquired his first dollar. As carrier of the weekly *Recorder* to the residence of William A. Graham, one of the town's most prominent lawyers and later governor, United States senator, and candidate for vice president, Holden presented to Graham a Christmas address composed, as Holden later described it, of "certain verses of very questionable poetry." In exchange the boy was given silver coins amounting to a dollar. Thirty years later Holden remembered how he had prized the silver and taken care of it.[15] He used the story to illuminate how he had capitalized on his meager opportunities while another Hillsborough native, John W. Syme, born to affluence and, in maturity, one of Holden's chief journalistic competitors, failed as an editor.

On July 4, 1834, Syme, Heartt, and Graham were speakers at Hillsborough's celebration of Independence Day. On that day, as far as the circumstances can be reconstructed, Holden suffered one of the most humiliating and deeply resented experiences of his youth. Without permission, he took the Fourth as a holiday and was flogged by an older boy, who acted as shop foreman. In his anger at this treatment Holden ran away—a serious breach of his apprenticeship. A biographer relates that "Mr. Heartt, according to custom, advertised in his paper threatening with the penalty of law those who would harbor the runaway, and offered a five-cent reward for his apprehension. By chance Holden saw the notice, secretly returned by night and changed the form of the *Recorder* so that when the next issue appeared the public was notified that the newspaper and its editor were for sale, and both might be had for the sum of fifty cents. At the

9

same time that he altered the type, the [fifteen-year-old] boy scratched upon the desk the words, 'from this day I will be a man'."[16]

While these and other legends of Holden may be apocryphal, they are at least characteristic. The boy soon returned to the *Recorder* shop, made his peace with Heartt, and in time became warmly friendly with the youth who had beaten him, so that the two, Holden remembered, had "many a hearty laugh"[17] over the incident.

As he grew older, young Holden became more and more restless in his position as printer in the quiet little town of Hillsborough. He was "poor and unknown and very ambitious," and he felt "the restless longings after fame which canker and corrode."[18] With the consent of Heartt, Holden at the age of sixteen left the *Recorder* and Hillsborough and walked the thirty miles to Milton, carrying with him a small bundle of belongings. In Milton he was employed for a time by Nathaniel J. Palmer, editor of the *Milton Spectator*. Then Holden went to Danville, Virginia, only to return after a short while to Hillsborough, where he again entered the *Recorder* office. He remained a few months, withdrawing to serve as clerk in a store in the town.[19]

He was still restless, unsatisfied, and out of his discontent grew a resolve—to tackle Raleigh, the state capital, in his immaturity the giddiest height he could conceive of.

THREE

O N THE NIGHT OF October 7, 1836, William Woods Holden, not yet eighteen, boarded the stagecoach that ran from Greensborough through Hillsborough to Raleigh. In the coach were a number of boys about his own age, students at Caldwell Institute in Hillsborough. In Holden's pocket were seven silver dollars, and he had gone $150 into debt to buy a fine gold watch and a new broadcloth coat.[1]

The trip to Raleigh was uneventful and would not be worth mentioning except that fate rode the route. Thirty years later, when Holden had become, in turn, the outstanding editor of the state and the first governor in the United States to be impeached, he recalled that the lawyer managing his prosecution was one of the students and that a colonel of the special troops he had hired, leading to his downfall, was another of the boys on the stage. The future prosecutor was Thomas Sparrow, later a Princeton graduate; the future colonel was William J. Clarke, who fought both in the war with Mexico and in the Civil War.[2]

Holden's recollection fifty years after his arrival in Raleigh was that the city of 1836 was quite small, with a population of about 1,000 whites and an equal number of slaves.[3] The city had been laid out as the state's capital after the General Assembly in 1788 had voted to establish the seat of government as near as possible to the state's geographic center. A thousand acres had been bought to carry out that purpose. The capitol in which the assembly had met since 1794 was destroyed by fire in 1831, and a new building was begun two years later. This capitol was being built when Holden arrived in Raleigh, and in conjunction with its construction a horsedrawn railway to a nearby quarry had been established. On Sundays Raleigh burghers were sold tickets on the rail line in order that they might profit from the fresh-air ride.

Otherwise, Raleigh had no railroad, no waterway, no major industry. Its chief business was that of government. It did have, however, a kind of merchant aristocracy. In 1830 Jordan Womble had opened a grocery store on Hargett Street that stayed in business for almost six decades. James Litchford, with a shop near the rectory of Christ Church, was the leading tailor, C. D. Lehman ran a drugstore, and Neal Brown operated a "wool hat" factory. For the accommodation of travelers, Edward Rigsbee had opened the City Hotel. Wesley Whitaker manufactured pianos. J. E. Lumsden ran a bathhouse, which he said would be "kept open from sunrise till candle-light, and where hot and cold baths could be procured at reasonable rates."[4]

The completion of the new capitol (still standing) in 1840 and the simultaneous arrival of the first steam locomotive in Raleigh (running the Raleigh-and-Gaston route), called for a joint celebration beginning June 10 and lasting three days.

Since much news of a political nature was generated in Raleigh, three newspapers flourished there, despite the small size of the town. These papers were the *Register* and the *Star*, both Whig, and the *Standard*, the Democratic organ. The oldest of the papers was the *Register*, first issued on October 22, 1799, by Joseph Gales, and continued by the Gales family for nearly sixty years as one of the most influential papers in North Carolina.

Gales had published a paper of the same name at Sheffield, England, but because he expressed in it certain opinions sympathizing with the French Revolution he was forced in 1794 to flee to Holland to avoid arrest. He arrived a year later in Philadelphia, where his ability to report the proceedings of Congress in shorthand gained him favorable attention. When he decided to leave Philadelphia because of the yellow fever, he was persuaded by Nathaniel Macon and other North Carolina leaders to locate in Raleigh.

The *Star*, the paper on which Holden found employment, had been founded in November, 1808. After passing through several hands, it was acquired in 1835 by Thomas J. Lemay, a native North Carolinian who had been trained in printing in the *Star* shop. Holden said later of Lemay that he "was himself a good English scholar and was very successful as editor and State Printer. He was the friend of my youth, a just and good man."[5]

The *Standard* was the baby of the trio. It had been established in 1834 by Philo White, a native of Whitestown, New York, who had edited the *Western Carolinian* in Salisbury from 1820 to 1830 and then had held a post in the United States Navy for several years. As editor of the *Standard*, White was elected state printer, receiving $900 a year in that capacity. In 1836 he sold the paper to Thomas Loring and went back to the navy. Loring, described by a contemporary as a "fat friar,"[6] made a rather timid party editor, and Holden was to witness an increasingly bitter fight between Loring and the Democrats who normally would have been his supporters.

When he went to work for the *Star*, Holden had no way of knowing that the *Standard* was to make his reputation. The youth was not a regular journeyman printer, for he had not learned to lock up forms or do job printing, but he was able to set type swiftly. He remained in the *Star* shop five years and boarded in the home of Lemay, the editor. His pay was $8 a week, a fair wage for the times. He worked "from sun to sun in the summer time, and from sun up till nine in the winter, and frequently all night during the sessions of the Legislature."[7]

Yet his energies were not entirely exhausted by the long shifts, nor was his ambition satisfied with merely being a swift compositor in another man's shop. Two bits of evidence support these conclusions. First, he tried to buy an interest in the *Star* and become associate editor after two or three years; second, when he failed to raise the necessary capital, he started reading law at night after his work at the *Star* was finished. At some point between 1838 and 1840 (Holden could not remember the exact year a decade and a half later) Holden held a conference with Lemay, after which he wrote a letter to William A. Graham requesting a loan with which to buy the *Star*.[8] Graham, who had given Holden a dollar for his Christmas verses, replied that he could not supply the money. Thus did fate intervene once again in Holden's life: had Graham been able to accommodate Holden, thus offering him the possibility of becoming a full-fledged Whig editor, Holden probably would never have had any interest in becoming editor of the leading Democratic organ a few years later. If that had happened, the history of North Carolina over the next few decades would have been quite different.

After the refusal of the loan, Holden turned more seriously to the study of law in the evenings, encouraged by Hugh McQueen, who became associate editor of the *Star* in 1839, and by Henry Watkins Miller, a young lawyer. Miller lent him books and told him what to read, and Holden developed a passion for Blackstone.[9] On January 1, 1841, a little more than four years after arriving in Raleigh, Holden received his law license, standing at the top of a class of twenty taking the examination. He planned at first to open a practice in Western North Carolina, but when that did not work out, he applied for a position as reporter for the State Supreme Court. If Thomas Ruffin, then chief justice, ever sent a reply to his petition, it has not been preserved.[10] In any case, he did not land the job.

Undaunted, Holden decided to set up practice in Raleigh, and on the front page of the *Star* of September 1, 1841, and thereafter on the back page for several months, there appeared an announcement describing him as

William A. Graham, governor of North Carolina 1845–1849

WILLIAM W. HOLDEN,
ATTORNEY AT LAW,
AND GENERAL AGENT AND COLLECTOR,
RALEIGH, N. C.

In the *Star* of December 28, 1841, there appeared a further announcement, that W. W. Holden, attorney at law, had removed his office to "No. 5, in the new building of B. B. Smith, Esq., where he always may be found, when not absent from the city on professional business. Collections of any amount promptly and faithfully attended to."

In the spring of the following year Holden was appointed general assignee in bankruptcy for Wake County, a post he held for nearly a year.[11] In February, 1844, he was succeeded by William J. Clarke,[12] one of the boys from Caldwell Institute whom Holden had met on the stagecoach that first brought him to Raleigh.

No doubt Holden could have had a successful career at the bar, perhaps thereby attaining his later ambitions at far lighter cost to himself. His examination spoke well for him; he had won enough business to set up a new office, and he had been entrusted with the bankruptcy proceedings of the county. Furthermore, he was achieving some prominence in the public life of the city, by no means a liability to a young attorney. He was assistant marshal in the Fourth of July parade in 1841 and was one of several orators selected to speak briefly at a hotel dinner that evening. He was chairman of a committee to request James B. Shepard, one of Raleigh's leading citizens, to be speaker at the July 12 celebration of the second anniversary of the Mechanics Association, a social organization for craftsmen.

On that occasion Shepard graciously proposed a toast: "William W. Holden: a high-toned, liberal and enlightened gentleman: the Mechanics are proud of him, while every class must appreciate his exalted worth."[13] Holden responded with a toast that in hindsight, was particularly prescient: "The Mechanics—when they shall speak throughout the Union as they ought to speak, aristocracy and the unjust distinction it engenders, will sink beneath the level of contempt and indignation."[14]

The following year Holden was the principal speaker, and the entire front page of the *Star* of August 10, 1842, and half of the second page were devoted to a transcript of his address. In keeping with the oratorical custom of the times, his speech was flowery and pretentious, quite different from the simple, straightforward style he adopted later. But he was then only twenty-four and still quite self-conscious. A short extract shows how he belabored the language:

...Fortified by the principles of a sound and practical philosophy, and sensible of his tremendous responsibilities as a citizen of two worlds, the possessor of high intelligence now weighs everything in the scales of justice and virtue, and estimates human greatness, not by the number of cities the aspirant for renown may have demolished, nor yet by the gore he may have spilt, but by the amount of permanent and substantial benefit he may have contributed to confer upon mankind. Thus estimated, how little is Napoleon, and how great are Watt and Fulton![15]

Meanwhile, on Nov. 3, 1841, Holden married Miss Anne Young, a niece of William Peace, the man for whom Peace Institute, a Presbyterian school for girls in Raleigh, was later named. Miss Young had been educated by private teachers and her family stood high socially in North Carolina. After the marriage, William Peace went to live with the couple. This union did several things for young Holden, not the least of which was to improve his social acceptability. Undoubtedly it gave him a higher degree of self-confidence than he had had before, and it fixed his residence in Raleigh, so that he remained under the eye of political leaders. And when at last another opportunity came to purchase a paper, it provided him with security that enabled him to borrow the necessary money.

Holden was advancing not only professionally, socially, and publicly but politically as well. On February 21, 1842, he served as secretary of a Whig meeting held in Raleigh to plan for the state convention two months later.[16] The *Star* of March 9, 1842, announced that Holden was one of the duly appointed delegates from Wake County to the state meeting, a rally which was to show the Democrats "what it is to hold an old fashioned RE-PUBLICAN CONVENTION."[17] Henry Clay was invited, but he sent his regrets.

Holden did not cut much of a figure at the convention. In newspaper accounts of the meeting his name appears only in the list of delegates. The record does not show him making a speech, offering a motion, or doing anything except attending the sessions, listening and learning. The convention nominated Clay for the presidency, and Holden, who had a high regard for the Kentuckian and who at times wrote contributions to the *Register* under the pseudonym "A Looker On," thought the selection "but spoke the wishes of a large majority of the people of this country."[18]

It is easy to look back and point out what the Whigs did not do to hold in the party the young man who became instrumental in overthrowing them in North Carolina. They might have made him the loan that would have permitted him to become editor of a Whig paper. They might have insisted more strongly upon the coming of Clay, whom Holden so much admired, to North Carolina in 1842. They might have entrusted Holden with party responsibilities that would have provided an outlet for some of his restless energies and a hope of someday realizing his still nebulous ambitions.

But he was only twenty-four, and the party was under the control of older men who had already achieved state and national reputations for leadership—men like John M. Morehead,

George E. Badger, William A. Graham, Edward B. Dudley, and Willie P. Mangum. It would have required a degree of foresight not given to mortals for them to invite this young man into their inner councils, to ask his advice, or to single him out for unusual favors.

It is also possible that nothing they might have done would have changed the future course of events. It seems clear now that two forces were working to make Holden, a Whig delegate in 1842, the editor of the official Democratic newspaper in 1843. One of these was a change that was subtly at work in Holden's political thinking. The other had to do with the troubles being experienced by Loring in his editorship of the *Standard*.

To understand these forces it is necessary to look briefly at the situations of the dominant parties and the general political climate. Since the remodeling of the state constitution in 1835, the state had been Whig by decided margins. The revision, which had been the subject of controversy for many years before it was accomplished, was necessitated by a dramatic shift in the state's population. People were crowding into the Western section, which had larger counties, but they were being outvoted in the legislature by the East, which was made up generally of smaller counties. Under the old system each county, regardless of population, was allowed two members of the House and one senator.

Naturally, the Eastern counties were opposed to the calling of a convention to consider altering the constitution. When the question finally was submitted to the electorate, the East was so solidly against the measure that in some counties only four or five persons voted for it; conversely, the West was so strongly in favor of it that in some counties only one or two negative votes were cast.

The vote on the amendments recommended by the convention was divided in the same way along regional lines, with 26,771 in favor and 21,606 against the proposals. The amendments provided that the state should be partitioned into fifty districts, each entitled to one senator. This deprived the East of ten senators. Representation in the House was to be based upon population, and that cost the East thirty-five members. In addition, the election of the governor, for a term of two years, was, for the first time, placed in the hands of the people.

These developments were significant for the Whigs because their party was particularly strong in the West. They had built up a tradition of being the party in favor of internal improvements by the state, of railroads, canals, and turnpikes that would bring the East and West into closer touch. These improvements would especially benefit the West, since they would provide markets for Western products and would afford cheaper transportation of Eastern goods.

The Democrats, on the other hand, were inclined to follow Nathaniel Macon, who spoke at the constitutional convention against government aid for internal improvements; it was basic to Jacksonian democracy to oppose such central action. Democratic theory called for rigid economy in government and a philosophy of individualism that left much to personal enterprise. Some Democrats, even some Democratic editors, favored internal improvements subsidized by the state, but on the whole, before Holden took over the helm, the party was fairly unified in its opposition.

In 1835, in the last General Assembly under the old system of representation, the Democrats had a majority, and they elected Richard D. Spaight governor over William B. Meares. In accordance with the old governmental system, Spaight was to serve one year, but his successors were to have two-year terms. In 1836, the year Holden moved to Raleigh, the opposing candidates were Spaight and the Whig Edward B. Dudley. The latter was elected by a majority of 4,043, although the Democrats saved the state for Martin Van Buren in the presidential election by putting forward an electoral ticket headed by Macon. With the Whigs growing in power, Dudley two years later was opposed

John Motley Morehead, governor of North Carolina 1841–1845

by John Branch, who had been governor for three terms under the old system. Dudley won by a majority of 14,156, and the Democrats lost both houses of the legislature.

In 1840 John M. Morehead was the Whig candidate for governor, and Romulus M. Saunders the candidate of the Democrats. Both candidates were from the West, and both announced themselves in favor of common schools and internal improvements, although Saunders hedged his support by announcing that he would not countenance going into debt to provide these improvements. The North Carolina campaign, quite logically, was strongly influenced by the national political fervor that swept a Whig, William Henry Harrison, briefly into the presidency.

Holden was later accused of being an "active participant" in the Whig campaign of 1840, but he vehemently denied it. He confessed, however, that "we were present, it is true, on many occasions, at the log cabin, and we witnessed the October scene; but like hundreds of others, we went for the purpose of seeing and hearing, and much—very much were we edified." [19]

Morehead won the gubernatorial election with a majority of 8,581, and later Harrison received the electoral vote by a popular majority of 13,141—a testimony to Whig strength. Two years later Governor Morehead sought reelection, and the Democrats nominated Louis D. Henry. Federal matters, rather than state, played a large part in the campaign. The conflict between President John Tyler and Whig leaders, which left him without support and almost a man without a party, cut into Morehead's appeal, and he won by a majority of only 3,532, far below his earlier lead. At the same time Democrats took control of both houses of the General Assembly.

This recapitulation is necessary because the events chronicled gravely influenced the position of Thomas Loring, editor of the Democratic newspaper in Raleigh, the *North Carolina Standard*. Democrats of considerable influence found fault with Loring's editorial support of party candidates, and with good reason. In 1836 Loring, rather than work himself into a partisan lather, had confessed in print that Dudley, the Whig, was the "one whom we personally love and esteem." This was apostasy, and it was compounded in 1838 when Loring proposed that the Democrats offer no opposition to Dudley, because his administration had been satisfactory and because a political contest would divide the state at a time when the South should be united.

Dissatisfaction with the *Standard* in 1840 was based not so much upon anything Loring did as upon the general ineffectiveness of the paper in combating the "emotionalism" of the Whigs. Loring was not a vigorous writer and lacked the verbal whips required in such a situation. In the presidential campaign he was so inept at belittling Harrison that his editorials won support for the Whig candidate. Loring was, in fact, opposed to the vituperative language commonly used by editors of his time, and in 1837 he had been instrumental in getting a newspaper convention in Raleigh to adopt resolutions disapproving "personalities and indecorous language" and condemning the tendency to violate "the sanctity of private life."[20]

Between the state and national campaigns in 1840, Loring announced that he would be absent from Raleigh for a brief period and that the *Standard* would be edited by Henry I. Toole, a younger man who exhibited the quality some Democrats found most lacking in Loring, enthusiasm. This taste of fresh editorials was so palatable to members of the party that it provoked greater discontent with the permanent editorship of Loring. By February, 1841, Loring had heard so much criticism that he offered the *Standard* for sale. All his materials and his subscription list were priced at $3,000, the *Star* reported, adding, "If a sale is not effected by the middle of April, Mr. Loring will continue in the establishment."[21]

Having given his critics a chance they declined to seize, Loring then took up the matter with Toole, who wrote a letter to

23

the *Standard* declining the offer to buy the paper. He said he had been connected with the *Standard* previously only on impulse and did not want a permanent association. Toole admitted that there was prejudice against Loring, which, he said, stemmed from the impression that the paper was controlled by William H. Haywood Jr., who at times not only ignored his party but opposed it on matters of principle. "Such an impression is injurious to both of you," Toole wrote. "My brief connection with the *Standard* enables me to say that the impression is erroneous."[22]

The legislative session of 1841–42 developed further dissatisfaction, which was described, with reasons for it, in an open letter to Loring sent to the *Standard* in 1845 by "Dark Corner." Until the latter part of 1841, the writer said, Loring was looked upon as a Democrat, "the advocate of a strict construction of the Constitution, as contended by the Virginia and Kentucky Resolutions of '98 and '99—the champion of the Rights of the people, and the opponent of Federalism in any and every form; in other words you were a professed disciple of the immortal Jefferson, the great Apostle of Liberty and founder of the Democratic Republican Party." It was subsequently felt that Loring abandoned these principles, the letter went on, and the dissatisfaction "spread in all sections so fast that opposition was seriously spoken of, you denying that the party had any claim upon either yourself or your Press, or that you were under any obligation to the party, on the ground that your connexion with the Standard was a private enterprise." The writer said people thought that Loring "aspired to assume control of the party—to dictate to them what they should or should not do."

Loring responded truculently to "Dark Corner," saying that he had not "mustered up so high a sentiment as contempt" for the opinions expressed in the letter.[23]

Already, however, Loring's independence had plunged him into financial difficulties: Democrats would not support his paper, and even those on the subscription list would not pay. In

January, 1842, Loring said he was carrying 2,000 names on the list, whereas a little more than a year later there were only about 800 paying subscribers.[24] In five and a half years, Loring said, he had lost $6,000 and stood to lose $4,000 more.

Loring's position was also affected by the intraparty conflict between the adherents of Martin Van Buren and John C. Calhoun, which developed rapidly in the latter half of 1842. The *Mecklenburg Jeffersonian* bewailed, "It is useless to conceal the fact, that the Democratic party in this state has been rent asunder by rash and ill-advised counsels, and is in imminent danger of a complete and final overthrow."[25] Yet each faction stubbornly maintained its position, refusing to make any conciliatory move.

Loring ran counter to the wishes of a vociferous portion of his party when on February 8, 1843, he placed Van Buren's name at the head of the *Standard*'s editorial columns as the Democratic candidate for president. Some other Democratic papers had already hoisted Calhoun's banner, and it was to combat this wing of the party that Loring took his action, saying that he was not willing to have Calhoun "or anyone else crammed down our throats."[26]

As long as he was editor, Loring clung to his position, regardless of division within the party and regardless of growing factional spirit. "To restore Mr. Van Buren is not merely to do justice to an injured and slandered patriot," Loring argued, "but to vindicate measures of high importance to public welfare, and to sustain truth in opposition to error."[27]

By the first of 1843 even the Whig *Star* "could approve the expression of our neighbor of the *Standard*; that he is not the organ of a party, but of principles."[28] The Whig *Register* saw a growing apostate interest in banks, while Joseph W. Hampton, editor of the Democratic *Jeffersonian*, accused Loring of being influenced by the banks. Loring replied to Gales of the *Register* that he had "uniformly expressed the same views," and to Hampton by flatly denying the charges.[29]

25

It was the issue of bank favoritism that probably brought the quarrel between Loring and his opponents to a climax. Gaston H. Wilder, speaking in the General Assembly, accused Loring of having allowed a loan of $1,300 by the Bank of State to influence the *Standard*. Although friends came to his defense, Loring himself replied in a bitter editorial that irretrievably alienated him from the apparently dominant wing of the party. Even those close to him thought he was too immoderate in answering Wilder and had destroyed the public concept of him as "cool, calculating and clear headed."[30]

In the aftermath, Democratic leaders met in Raleigh to discuss a possible successor to Loring. James B. Shepard, who had had his eye on Holden for years and had often befriended him, proposed Holden's name. Although "the suggestion was received with derision," Shepard persisted and won over his associates.[31]

According to legend, for which there is no documentation, Shepard thereupon took Holden out walking near the site of the later Federal Cemetery and offered him the editorship of the *Standard* with his own backing and that of other powerful Democrats for whom he had been authorized to speak. Holden was surprised and at first demurred, pointing to his record of more than ten years on Whig papers and his work with the Whig party. But Shepard, who obviously knew his man, was persuasive and finally gained his point. Holden returned to the city once more decided upon a journalistic career, this time as the chief spokesman of the Democrats.[32]

The historian William K. Boyd, in an account of this transformation, says that "a satisfactory explanation of Holden's change of political affiliations has never been made by friend or enemy."[33] Certainly it is true that in later years Holden's enemies used this crossroads decision to assert that he was a political opportunist—often in much stronger phraseology.

A careful study of Holden's personality, however, suggests

26

that he was by nature out of harmony with the increasingly aristocratic tendencies of the Whig Party in North Carolina. It was only by the accident of having worked first in the *Hillsborough Recorder* office and later in the *Raleigh Star* establishment that he was allied with the Whigs in politics, while in personal philosophy he was widely at variance with them. He must have had this brought home to him at the 1842 Whig convention, when, contrary to all the inclinations he revealed later, he remained entirely silent.

For one thing, Holden was broadly democratic, his early environment and experience having given him a sympathy for the common man and repugnance for such an attitude in the Whigs as he described later:

It required some nerve to be a Democrat from 1840 to 1850. The leaders of the old Whig Party, in possession of the State government, and sustained as they were by the various corporations, presumed upon their power, and treated the Democrats generally with disdain and arrogance. They carried this insolence—for we can with truth call it nothing else—even into social life; and the impression was sedulously sought to be produced that it was not "respectable," to be a Democrat. This was especially the case in Raleigh, the seat of the State government and the centre of the old "Whig Clique."[34]

It appears reasonably certain that his conversion from Whig to Democrat was not accomplished suddenly in a night stroll and that Shepard would not have proposed his name at the meeting of Democratic leaders unless he was aware that Holden had been undergoing a change in his political thinking. There is, in fact, no shred of evidence to connect Holden with the Whig party after the convention of April, 1842. Rather, we have from his own pen a disclaimer. "The truth is," he wrote, "... we were never a party man until we took charge of the *Standard*."[35]

On the surface there was little reason for Holden to switch parties for the ulterior motive of obtaining such a newspaper as the *Standard*. He was going from the dominant to the subordinate party (Democrats were in a minority of some six thousand to eight thousand) at a time when it seemed that the relative positions of the two parties in the state could not be reversed. He would have to go into debt $2,000 to buy the paper, and he could not be sure of getting his money back. He was purchasing a paper that was not a financial success: the *Standard* had a subscription list of about eight hundred[36] and an advertising patronage averaging about half a column for each of its four pages; at the same time the *Register* was giving both its front and back pages over to advertisements and was running a column or two of advertising on the inside pages. Loring, unable to please the warring factions of the party, had been running the paper at a loss (with about $12,000 in unpaid subscriptions on his books), and he was an experienced editor, whereas Holden's experience had been confined to setting type or writing for the papers of others.

In spite of this dubious outlook, Holden approached Duncan Cameron, president of the old Bank of State, and obtained a loan upon the endorsement of William Peace. With the money, Cameron also gave the young man some advice: "You will find that the surest, if not the quickest and most permanent and certain road to power in this country, is that of the press. It may not be so now, but in my judgement in future years it will be so . . . My advice is, as you have chosen the press, to abandon all idea of the law."[37]

The young man took both the advice and the money. He at once closed the deal with Loring to take over the *Standard* with the first issue in June and gave up all thought of practicing law. His last legal work was serving as administrator of the estate of Joseph Peace, brother of William, a year later. But from the spring of 1843, he devoted his unusual energies to journalism— and politics. The two words were closely akin.

The *Standard* of May 31, 1843, bore the usual line under the masthead, "Thomas Loring, Editor and Proprietor." The next issue, June 7, carried the line, "William W. Holden, Editor and Proprietor."

Thus unobstrusively, with the change of a few letters in type, a revolution in North Carolina journalism—and politics—was launched.

FOUR

T HE REVOLUTION was not immediate, nor was Holden's ability to bring it about even imagined when he took over the paper. Loring did little to help, introducing Holden to his readers with no undue show of enthusiasm. Holden, he said, "has the important advantage of being a practical printer, and is in every other way well qualified to fill the station he has assumed. He is a young man of great moral worth. . . ."[1] The same could probably have been said of a hundred other "practical" printers across North Carolina, but Loring left a lot unsaid, probably because he honestly did not recognize in Holden the qualities that were to make him a giant among the state's editors.

He had not only the business acumen to reanimate the ailing *Standard* but also an innate political sense that was to make him an important agent in reinvigorating the Democratic Party, leading it by audacious methods out of its defeatist attitude and giving it the expectation of success. Holden's equipment for his task included such important tools as enthusiasm for his work, respect for the editorial profession, aggressiveness, a background of comparatively wide reading, a forcible style, the abilities to persuade and to receive attention, a knowledge of human nature based on understanding of the common man, aptitude in catching currents of thought, and a ready grasp of situations, which often let him arrive at an understanding of conditions while others were still floundering in vagueness and doubt. All these were important instruments in building the editorial career he sought for himself; some of them were possessed in varying degrees by other editors in the state, but none of his contemporaries enjoyed all of them to the extent that Holden did.

In June, 1843, however, so little was known of Holden's genius that the announcement of his entrance into the editorial ranks created less commotion than many minor moves he was to make later. Most editors, including Thomas J. Lemay of the Raleigh *Star* and Edward J. Hale of the Fayetteville *Observer* (with whom Holden was to break more journalistic lances than with any other editor), did not comment at the time, waiting until they saw the first of his issues. Heartt, in Hillsborough, was surprised and a little hurt by the action of his former apprentice. The *Greensborough Patriot* thought the Whigs had got the best of the bargain in the exchange of Loring for Holden. The *Mecklenburg Jeffersonian* thought that under Holden the *Standard* would be edited with "decided ability." The Raleigh *Register* set the Whig tone in trying to treat the matter lightly; it threatened to reprint a eulogy to Clay that Holden had contributed to that paper under a *nom de plume*.

Holden characteristically seized upon this latter in his first issue of June 7, giving an indication of the type of warfare he intended to wage. He thought the *Register* would have done better to attack the soundness of principles in his salutatory than to indulge in personalities. Yet he promised to return all abusive language "with compound interest," and added that "we warn those who have avowed a determination to *put us down*, that victory is not always for the artistocratic and the wealthy, and that we shall be found, on all occasions, battling for correct principles where blows fall heaviest and thickest." He gave the *Register* full permission to reprint the eulogy on Clay, "but we leave it with the Editorial fraternity throughout North Carolina to say, whether the Editor of the *Register*, in disclosing the names of private correspondents, for party purposes, or for any other purpose, has not grossly violated one of the fundamental rules of the profession."[2]

The first issue and its reception indicated several things about the future of Holden's journalistic career: he could command attention from fellow editors. His paper would not be among those which were glanced at each week and tossed aside. His editorials could provoke replies, thus advertising the *Standard*, its editor, and the Democratic Party. This assured that his views would become, in time, possibly the most widely known of any man's in the state. Other editors felt it necessary to answer him when they might have ignored similar statements from another. Holden's newspaper audience consequently was many times larger than the circulation of his own paper. He was ready with apt rejoinders to all attacks, and he was likely to strike at some Achilles heel, as illustrated by his imputations of unethical conduct on the *Register*'s part, thus minimizing the force of otherwise legitimate charges. This faculty was to make him a dangerous and feared antagonist.

One of the first features that Holden, in his exuberance, experimented with was a series of dramatic sketches bearing the title "Mysteries of Coondom Unveiled." The purpose was to ridicule Whig leaders, most of whom were readily recognizable: George E. Badger as "Whiskerando," John Morehead as "Ajax the Second," Weston Gales as "Great Western," and Thomas Lemay as "The Little Blower of the Little Whig Trumpet." The feature was intended also to give Holden a little advertising, as he pretended that the chief purpose of the "coon caucuses" was to take steps "for putting down the *new* editor of the *Standard*." The Whigs were supposed to fear him because he knew so much about them and was bold enough to parade his knowledge in print. The sketches were attributed to "a friend of ours, who knows a thing or two, and who is generally wide awake when others think him fast asleep."[3] This anonymity

George E. Badger, United States senator from North Carolina 1846–1855

permitted Holden to talk about himself frankly and without modesty.

So the young editor had his fun with the "aristocratic" Whigs. At the same time, one may speculate, he was doing a little "whistling in the dark" in the sketches to keep up his courage as he carried the fight to such distinguished antagonists and was puffing his own importance to impress both them and his Democratic readers. But this was just the sort of thing of which Loring, who, as another editor said, ran his paper "with industry and ability"[4] but without aggressiveness, was not capable; and it was perhaps the powerful weapon the Democrats needed in dealing with the "arrogant" Whigs. Holden, by rushing in as older men had hesitated to do, showed that the entrenched party, even if apparently impregnable, could at least be attacked and that the discouraged Democrats could enjoy the assault. It was a good lesson for both Holden and his party.

The passing weeks brought evidence that Holden's methods and style were refreshing to at least some of those Democrats who had found much to criticize in Loring, for the *Standard* carried a number of letters expressing approval. Nevertheless, Holden would recall later, the *Standard*'s subscription list stood still for six months, neither advancing nor receding from the 800 mark while members of the party watched and weighed the work of the young man. At the end of that period, in which there were no elections or other events to stimulate circulation, Holden could "perceive a sudden and great quickening in my subscriptions,"[5] and the promise that he was to be successful brought deeper tones of self-assurance to his editorials.

Meanwhile, the *Standard* was engaging in more and more verbal duels with other papers, with the *Star*, the *Register*, and especially the leading Whig organ, the *Fayetteville Observer*. Although the quarrel with the *Star* was concerned with mere peccadilloes, it brought personal thrusts and became so uncompromising that Holden and Lemay could not both remain in

34

the Edenton Street Methodist Church, whereupon Holden withdrew.[6] Badger and other prominent Whigs also belonged to that
congregation.

The duel with the *Register* was of a different type. There had
not been the personal relations between Gales and Holden to
turn sour. Gales for many years had been the outstanding editor
in Raleigh, and he was less inclined to treat as an equal the
young pretender who could publish a paper that made people
talk about it and its owner. The early tactics of Gales were more
those of a superior seeking to squelch an irritating upstart. He
was particularly vexed by the energetic approach of the *Standard*
in the first election after Holden became editor, the contest in
the summer of 1843 between Henry W. Miller, Whig, and
Romulus M. Saunders, Democrat, in the Fifth Congressional
District. The Whigs were complacently looking to the election
of Miller, and Gales was indignant at Holden for not following
the lead of Whig papers in letting the election come quietly. But
if the Whigs thought they could make Holden, like Loring, follow the patterns they themselves adopted for campaigns, they
were to be disabused from the start. Holden, they were to learn,
went his own way, made his own plans and pursued them to the
end regardless of protests and regardless of how disagreeable
his plans were to opponents. With Holden's support, Saunders
was elected, eliciting from the Whig *Highland Messenger* an
expression of grudging admiration for the *Standard* editor: "We
like the fellow. . . . He fights like a man, that is, he does his best,
and if he had only a good cause, would make a formidable
antagonist."[7]

Thereafter, for several months, the *Register* continued to dan-
gle the threat of reprinting Holden's eulogy of Clay, and Holden
continued to answer that Gales was "welcome to all the professional *honor* he has won by revealing the name of a private correspondent."[8] Then the shoe, or a similar one, was on the other
foot, and the *Register* yelped as loudly about ethics as had the

Standard. Holden published correspondence between Gales and Colonel John H. Wheeler, state treasurer, concerning Gales's accusation, and his later acknowledgement that he was mistaken, that Wheeler had used an official check to pay off a personal account. Gales was deeply grieved at "this intrusion of a *private* affair into the public prints."[9] The *Greensborough Patriot* likewise lectured the *Standard* and the *Jeffersonian*, which had copied the article from the *Standard*, so that the affair, which really was between Holden and Gales, became something of an interparty matter.

It was similar publicizing of a private affair that first made the *Fayetteville Observer* notice Holden. The *Standard* accused Hale, the Fayetteville editor, of borrowing $10,000 from the state literary board, the board that handled public school funds. Hale complained that Holden would not publish a letter protesting that the transaction consisted merely of Hale's signing a bond for another person, who had taken out the loan. "We protest this lugging into the newspapers the private pecuniary transactions of private individuals," Hale said. "Even when truly stated they are wrong, often injurious to the individual thus dragged before the public, and always distasteful to the character of the paper making use of such a weapon."[10] Apparently the Whigs did not understand that Holden had learned "the use of such a weapon" from them. It might be noted here, however, that these were the last times that Holden was ever accused of using the tactic of invading privacy.

The fall of 1843 brought no elections in the state to provide subject matter for newspapers, and many issues appear somewhat lean. The intermission permitted Holden to adjust to his position as editor, to gain his political bearings so that 1844 would find him ready, he said, to "SPREAD ourself, when the battle begins to roar,"[11] and to win his place in the councils of the party. At a meeting of Wake County Democrats in Raleigh on November 2, 1843, to prepare for the state party convention there the following month, Holden was entrusted with four appointments: he was secretary of the meeting, member of the resolutions committee, member of the committee to make arrangements for the state meeting, and delegate to the convention.[12] At the state convention on December 14–15 he was also singled out for appointments. He and William H. Bayne were made secretaries of the meeting, which was attended by 146 delegates representing 31 counties, and, more important, he was elected one of the 22 members of the executive committee which acted for the convention between campaigns and in large measure guided party affairs.

At that first convention Holden attended he met another young man also making his initial appearance. A little less than fifteen years later the two were to oppose each other in the bitterest fight for the gubernatorial nomination that a Democratic convention was to see before the Civil War. The young man was John W. Ellis, who cut such an impressive figure that he was called upon by the delegates for a speech. Holden was much struck by the Rowan County representative and reported that "the style of his speech was eminently classical and beautiful, and the substance was sound, sensible and practical."[13]

When the spring of 1844 brought the most exciting political event of the decade to Raleigh, the long-deferred visit of Henry Clay, Holden felt confident enough to treat this trying ordeal with some face-saving for himself and his fellow Democrats. Two months before the visit he rebutted the argument of the Whigs that Democrats ought to unite with them in extending the hospitality of the state and the city, and in the *Standard* immediately preceding Clay's arrival, Holden demanded that the statesman meet squarely the problem of the annexation of Texas, calling "upon his Whig friends here to have this question answered when he makes his speech in this City. We want no dodging on his part, or on the part of his friends."[14] What influence this demand had upon Clay's decision to write his

Henry Clay, member of the House and Senate, secretary of state, candidate for the presidency, statesman

famous Raleigh letter to the *National Intelligencer* on April 17 (in which he opposed the annexation of Texas without Mexican consent) is impossible to say. Perhaps the distinguished visitor saw or heard of the demand of the young Democratic editor. The *Standard* also tried to throw a damper on the enthusiasm of the throngs that jammed Raleigh to greet Clay, the paper's accounts contrasting sharply with those of the *Register* and *Star*; but, all in all, Holden could squeeze little solace out of the Whig triumph, and forty years later he expressed his regret that "that accursed thing, party spirit,"[15] led him to the lengths he went in vilifying Clay.

During the presidential election campaign of 1844 Holden lost Lemay of the *Star* as an adversary and gained Hale of the *Observer*. The *Star* simply withdrew from the fisticuffs, and at about the same time the *Observer* took up the tilting. But it was not long before Hale became too exasperated for polite boxing. "Of all the vile, unscrupulous, blackguard sheets published in the United States," he exploded, "we doubt if there be one that will compare in these particulars, with the Raleigh *Standard*. Acting notoriously upon the principle of never retracting one of its thousand falsehoods, and never abandoning one, however often refuted, it is perfectly callous to public opinion, and occupies itself wholly in devising and collecting foul slanders."[16]

Such language is not to be taken too seriously. Even Hale, except in his passing mood, could not have meant it as it sounded literally, and an examination of the files of the *Standard* discloses nothing to warrant it. Such outbursts were more or less common when an editor found a disputant gaining some envied advantage. Neither wrath nor space was wasted upon those editors whose columns were fallow and doing little damage to the opposing party. The influence of an editor might in some respects be judged by the number of diatribes he inspired.

A year later Holden decided that Hale overstepped the wide bounds allowed by usage when the *Observer* said, "People talk about Mr. William W. Holden in a very ugly manner hereabouts. . . . No man of any party regards or respects him. Those he acts with constantly fear him—they know not how soon in the very thickest of the fight he might turn his weapons; while the uncharitable Whigs actually loathe him, as being diseased with a vile moral leprosy, *that has not left a single virtue unconsumed* amid his thousand meannesses and vices."[17] Holden replied quietly that he had "no hard words for Mr. Hale," but that "we shall strike the Observer from our exchange lists."[18] If that action was taken, it was soon reversed, because the scrimmaging of Holden and Hale was hardly interrupted.

It should be observed here that Holden, although he was peculiarly adept at provoking his editorial opponents, was unusually forbearing in returning their cutting epithets. "We can say as many hard things as most men, when we choose," he told them, but "we are willing to meet the Whig Editors upon the platform of decency and courtesy, and discuss *principles* with them as long as they desire it . . . but we cannot consent to do injustice to our readers, or sink the character of the public Press, by indulging in personalities."[19] The truth was that Holden did not need such tactics, and he realized also that "a disputant who loses his temper admits his own weakness or that of his cause."[20]

Two journalistic features of the "grand battle of 1844," with James K. Polk as the Democratic nominee and Henry Clay the Whig nominee for president, stand out in the files of the *Standard* and other papers. Democratic appeals to state loyalty and pride in the candidacy of a North Carolina native were met by the Whigs with imputations that Polk, as the *Fayetteville Observer* said, was descended from "a recreant branch of noble stock,"[21] and that his grandfather, Ezekiel Polk, a captain in the Revolution, deserted the American cause to place himself under the protection of Lord Cornwallis. Holden and the Democrats quickly dug up refutations in the form of letters, affidavits, and excerpts from newspapers in various places, with the result

Edward J. Hale, editor of the *Fayetteville Observer*

that the Whigs dropped the matter. Then, just before the election, Holden stormed in public anger over another Whig maneuver, the sending out of a "secret circular" by the Whig Central Committee in Raleigh. Very probably similar circulars had been used in previous elections and had passed unnoticed by Democratic editors, who did not see in their exposure the campaign possibilities that Holden saw. Certainly, similar exposés were to be made in almost every important election in the next decade, and warnings against circulars were to become familiar to voters; but no exposure created quite the excitement of this first one that alarmed Holden. As a matter of fact, the circular was in the form of a confidential letter addressed by the central committee only to members of the Whig party, emphasizing the necessity of doing all they could to win the election and pointing out the so-called falsehoods of the other party. It would seem a legitimate and natural letter to be disseminated, persisting in some form into modern times, but Holden was quick to get his own central committee to denounce the circular and to publicize the matter in a way to turn it to some advantage for the Democrats by imputing underhanded methods to the Whigs. What influence the *Standard*'s charges had upon the electorate cannot be determined. On election day Clay received 32,939 votes to 29,549 for Polk in North Carolina. However, Polk carried fifteen of the twenty-six states and won by an electoral vote of 170 to 105. Holden was as gleeful over the defeat of Clay as if North Carolina had contributed to it. He declared that for Whig Raleigh "the day of its deliverance is drawing nigh" because the "strong-hearted, open browed working-men are flocking to our standard."[22]

Just how nearly right Holden was in this latter statement, possibly even he only surmised and did not know. In these years he was feeling his way, perhaps following instinct and inclination more than cold logic and reasoning from facts. Even so, he was infusing new life into the Democratic Party as he hammered at Whig policies: their "extravagance" in giving state aid to internal improvements, their class government (as he considered it), their opposition to the annexation of Texas, and their aversion to a war with Mexico.

Soon after the congressional elections of 1845, when the Democrats won six seats to three for the Whigs, with two of these latter being decided by close margins, Holden took stock of the condition of the *Standard* and of his own position as editor. He admitted that "in the outset we were young, as we still are, and inexperienced, and lacked very much of that peculiar tact, knowledge and discretion, which are so important to an Editor: but we trust we have not been found wanting in zeal, integrity and perseverance." As for the future, "if industry and assiduity in our profession can atone for our defects, both of manner and matter, we promise our readers all that can be asked from one, who, however feeble and humble, brings to the discharge of his duties that enthusiasm, and that confidence in the honesty and soundness of his principles, which can know no diminution or abatement." [23]

He told his readers that the *Standard* had nearly doubled its circulation in the preceding two years (on November 26, 1845, the paper had 1,400 subscribers) and "is at present as firmly established and as prosperous, perhaps, as any paper at the seat of government." [24] Yet he thought it advisable to postpone, at least until the campaign of 1848, acceding to requests for publishing a semiweekly issue, offering as reasons: first, his belief that Raleigh was not "sufficiently commercial in its character to give impetus to another semi-weekly or to sustain two when in operation, to say nothing of the political influences existing against us in the City"; second, his judgment that many subscribers preferred a weekly to a semiweekly paper and that the subscription list was not large enough for division. A few weeks later, however, he at least tentatively changed his mind and asked those who would subscribe to a semiweekly to send in their names. [25]

The response evidently was not sufficiently encouraging, for it was not until five years later that he began the semiweekly *Standard*.

Some of the zeal and enthusiasm of which Holden spoke led him to begin early in the fall of 1845 to try to get the Democrats organized for the coming election for governor, a contest in which they had been embarrassingly defeated five times in a row. He urged the members of the party to hold county meetings as a prelude to the state convention early in 1846, and these appeals bore fruit in a large number of meetings over the state and in a representation at the convention of four more counties than in 1844. The convention reduced the number of members of the central committee from twenty-two to thirteen, with the smaller circle including Perrin Busbee, Kimbrough Jones, and Holden from Wake County. Then the convention ignored the consensus of the county meetings by unanimously selecting Green W. Caldwell, superintendent of the United States branch mint at Charlotte, as its nominee for governor. Caldwell, taken by surprise, immediately declined to run, and Holden thereupon made his first trial at governor-picking. He saw to it that a Wake County meeting proposed the name of James B. Shepard to the central committee, which, by a majority of one, declared him the nominee.[26] Because many other counties had recommended Walter F. Leak, a quarrel ensued, with Leak refusing to abide by the action of the "Raleigh Clique" and with both candidates starting on speaking itineraries. Finally, both agreed to submit their respective claims to the central committee, which again named Shepard, whereupon Leak withdrew, and county conventions and Democratic papers attempted to repair the damage that had been done the party by the quarrel.

Holden at this time was inclined to be rather sanguine in his views of affairs, and indeed the situation did look auspicious for the young Democratic editor. In the White House was a president, Polk, whose message Holden could endorse in "every

44

word, letter, semi-colon and comma."[27] The Democrats had defeated the Whigs in the congressional elections and looked forward to the campaign for governor. Holden himself had been nominated for the legislature as a candidate from Wake County, and he was achieving more voice in party councils. He had demonstrated that to an important degree he could already impose his will upon the party. The Mexican War, a partisan issue, was actually in progress. The *Standard*'s circulation was growing. Almost everything looked possible, even the election of a Democratic governor—Holden's own sponsor and close friend—despite the debilitating squabble over the nominee.

The editor's hopes proved false in Shepard's case. Whatever chances Shepard had had were wiped out just before the election when William H. Haywood, Jr., a respected North Carolina Democrat in the United States Senate, unexpectedly resigned in resentment over pressure brought to bear on him to support a new tariff measure the Democrats had introduced in Congress. His attitude, denounced by a group of Democrats as "sickly sentimentality and delicate conscientiousness"[28] was disastrous for Shepard, who had made national issues an important part of his campaign. On election day he received four thousand fewer votes than the Democrats had polled in 1844, while William A. Graham gained nine hundred more than his total of two years before. The Democrats also lost both houses of the legislature. They elected Holden and their other two House candidates in Wake County, but the editor was given a taste of that antagonism which was to embitter his life. During the campaign, Holden at no time used the *Standard* to advance his candidacy and, in fact, made no reference to it other than keeping at the masthead the names of himself and the other Democratic nominees. The Whigs trained their guns upon him, however, and after the election he congratulated "the Editor of the *Register*, the Federal leaders about Raleigh generally, and Mr. Badger in particular, upon the utter failure of all their efforts . . . to defeat our election to the Commons in the good old County of wake."[29]

Holden never explained why he wanted to serve a term in the legislature. Perhaps it was for the experience and the closer view of legislative machinery that membership in the House would give him. He and his fellow minority members watched the organization of both houses by the Whigs, the election of two Whig senators, the passage of a bill to redistrict the state for Whig advantage, and Whig recalcitrance regarding the Mexican War, as an odious preamble was attached to an appropriation bill for volunteers. Holden's record consisted largely of voting against these nominees and measures. The only legislation he sponsored was a resolution calling for a committee to find means of providing a building in Raleigh for the deaf and dumb. By the end of the session, he had had enough of politics from the inside—at least for the time being—and had determined not to run for reelection.

As the fall of 1847 approached, bringing near the time to plan for the biennial party convention, Holden began to assume more and more the duties of tactician for his party. He was twenty-nine years old and had been editor of the *Standard* four-and-one-half years. The larger part of his life since he was ten years old, however, had been passed in the offices of one party newspaper or the other, and he was more the veteran political journalist than his age indicated. His quick mind had caught many errors made by Whigs and many Democratic campaign mistakes. At the time the Whig Party appeared more nearly impregnably entrenched than ever before—it had constructed railways with state aid, established a public school system, initiated a policy of professional care for physical defectives, and had convinced both the state and the Democratic Party that Whigs alone were friends of internal improvements; its presidential electors had won in the past two campaigns, its majority in the congressional delegation apparently had been assured under the new redistricting, and its candidates for governor had won by substantial majorities for more than a decade.

But Holden saw several flaws in the Whig philosophy, and he seized upon them. One defect, in fact, was the reason he had given for withdrawing from the party five years before: the Whig Party was essentially aristocratic; its spirit and many of its policies seemed to him not consonant with the nature of the plain people. Holden mantained his sympathy with these masses throughout his life, contending for the common man, whether in politics, in education, or in regard to rights in war. There was something in the oligarchic rule of North Carolina that was irritating to his nature. Every little while one runs across in his *Standard* a tribute to the laboring man, as, for example, one beginning: "He is only a Mechanic. Sir, you are mistaken. He is a *gentleman*. Do you doubt it? Look at him. He is industrious, honest, and intelligent."[30] Since these plain people were in the majority, though inarticulate, the duty of the Democratic Party, as Holden saw it, was to give them voice and secure their allegiance. That was one of the first problems. Another was to convince the state that the Whig Party must grow more and more sectional as the slavery question came to the fore. And a third was to show that the Whig version of internal improvements was not the only one, nor the proper one, for the state.

In December, 1847, Holden started plans for the elections of the following year. He wrote David S. Reid, who as the representative in Congress from the Third District had proved himself an able man and who was Holden's choice as nominee for governor. Both in his letter to Reid and in the *Standard*, Holden expressed the opinion that winter was too early for the Democratic convention. He offered as reasons the bad travel conditions, the fact that the courts then were in session, and his opinion that "we always lose by long campaigns. The adversary has time to rally—to bring out . . . his politicians and merchants—to circulate his documents and 'revolutionary circu-

47

David Settle Reid, governor of North Carolina 1851–1856

lars'—and to put his presses—two to one to ours—fully to work. A short campaign—a Chapultepec fight [a two-day battle in the Mexican War] is the sort for us."[31] He suggested that April, about three months before the election, was the proper time for the convention. This suggestion later prevailed both in resolutions at county meetings and in the final decision of the central committee.

Holden's statement to Reid that the Whigs had two newspaper presses to one for the Democrats led the editor to analyze the situation for his readers. He pointed out that of the thirty-five papers published in the state, twenty-one were Whig, ten Democratic and four were religious and politically neutral. "Our political friends in all parts of the State," Holden said, "ought to look to this, and exert themselves to build up new Democratic papers and strengthen the old ones."[32] It happened that one of these old papers, the *Standard*, in fact, had just gone to the expense of putting on "a new dress" and naturally would appreciate additional patronage. Since it was always a noteworthy occasion, commented on by other papers, when a journal acquired "a new dress," changing the body type face, Holden took opportunity to chat with his readers, reviewing his years in the editor's chair, analyzing the present both as it concerned the paper and the country, and looking into the future. Part of the editorial is noteworthy as Holden's first statement on the problem that was to call forth many strong editorials in the *Standard* in the next decade, the slavery question, "the only issue which rises to disturb us, and to threaten serious consequences."[33] As for the editorship, he admitted again that inexperience might have made him commit errors and have some "unpleasant collisions," but he apologized for all injustice or offense to "any honorable opponent." He was happy to say that "we have been constantly sustained by accessions to our list," and he appealed to readers to help in extending the circulation and influence of the *Standard*.

In February, as was their custom, the Whigs held their convention, which Holden characterized as "a sickly and feeble affair,"[34] and nominated Charles Manly for governor. The Democratic convention two months later was rather poorly attended, with only twenty-five counties represented, in spite of the fact that it had two distinguished visitors, Stephen A. Douglas and Sam Houston. Their presence caused as many Whig frowns as Clay's visit four years earlier had occasioned Democratic scowls. Holden was so much struck with a talk by Douglas that he forgot his journalist's duty to take notes. The visitors listened to the report of the resolutions committee, for which Holden was generally given credit, although the committee had thirteen members. Reid was nominated on the recommendation of the committee, but the report made no mention of the question that came to be the chief issue of the campaign, free suffrage.

Reid had been detained at home by illness, and it was left to Holden to notify him of his nomination. The editor at once wrote a letter pointing out the situation in the state, with suggestions for the conduct of the campaign.[35] On the same day he published in the *Standard* an editorial highly praising the nominee. But to the disappointment of party leaders in Raleigh, Reid wrote Holden that he probably would decline the nomination, adding that if he should run he wanted to make "equal suffrage" an issue.[36] Subsequently he wrote a formal letter to the central committee flatly refusing to be the candidate. This letter was held in type in the *Standard* office while a messenger was sent to Reid urging him to reconsider. Upon this appeal Reid accepted and soon came to Raleigh to discuss campaign strategy. He insisted that the major issue should be free suffrage, and Holden assured him "that the *Standard* would zealously advocate the measure."[37] To the astonishment of the Whigs, then, these two young men conducted a contest under the "new banner inscribed with the seductive motto of 'Free Suffrage,'" and "to the North Carolina politicians . . . the announcement was like a clap of thunder in a clear sky," as Manly, the Whig nominee, later described it.[38]

Manly was, of course, wrong. The free suffrage idea, doing away with all property qualifications as a prerequisite for voting, had been brought up sporadically in North Carolina for a dozen years, although it had never been submitted to the electorate. The supposition that Douglas might have given Reid and Holden the suggestion as a campaign gimmick has no evidence to support it, and its improbability is indicated by the circumstances of its announcement a month after the convention. It was not necessary for the idea to come from an outsider or from the "charnal house of Washington City tactics," as Manly asserted.[39] Reid said that he himself had pondered over the question for many years and once had even tried to introduce it in the legislature. He denied unequivocally that he had talked or corresponded with anyone outside North Carolina about making it the central thesis of his campaign.[40]

Free suffrage was just the kind of issue that Holden could, indeed, "zealously advocate" and into which he could pour boundless enthusiasm. Here was a measure that would erase another class distinction and would put the common man more clearly on the political plane of the landed gentry. In an editorial Holden said that he, like Reid, had long favored the change in voting, which, he said, had been adopted in every state except North Carolina.[41] To spread Democratic propaganda on this and other issues he offered the *Standard* to new subscribers for five months for $1, and he threw himself wholeheartedly into the campaign.

Until the start of actual jousting by the candidates, the Whigs had no inkling of what was in store for them. As Reid traveled to New Bern to meet Manly on May 10 in the opening debate, which the latter presumed would be devoted wholly to national issues, editor Gales bespoke the confidence of the Whigs by expressing mock compassion for Reid: "We suppose, from all we can learn, that it required some hard 'coaxing and driving' to bring MR. REID to the 'scratch'—but he at last screwed up the courage and has entered upon the task of 'Love's labor lost.' ... We hope, however, that our friend, MR. MANLY, will deal tenderly with his opponent, and not tear his blushing honors entirely from his brow."[42]

The real picture was far different. The nonplussed Manly heard his rival, toward the end of his speech, spring the free suffrage proposal, following it with a call on Manly for an immediate reply. But the Whig nominee was too surprised to respond, and he asked to be allowed until the next debate to consider the issue.

One might suppose that Holden, as one of the few persons to know something of what would occur in New Bern, would have arranged to have a prompt report of the debate, possibly from a special correspondent if he did not go himself. A week after the debate the *Standard* carried a brief mention of it, saying that Reid proposed free suffrage and that Manly took notes but made no reply. Another week later the *Standard* reprinted from the *Newbern Republican* a fuller account of the discussion. A reader of today, unaware of the stage of journalistic progress in North Carolina at that time, may wonder at this tardy report, but Holden was not expected by his readers to do more than he did. Possibly they and other editors would have wondered at his undignified partisan zeal, at his unseemly haste, if he had. The day of special reporting was not to come to the state for many years. And so the *Standard* continued to give "all the facts and discussions of the campaign" as they were picked up days later from other papers in places where the candidates met. Except for the time factor, however, one may follow in the columns of the *Standard* the progress of the campaign remarkably well. Holden did yeoman service in behalf of Reid and the party.

After a second meeting of Manly and Reid a few days later in Beaufort, Holden reported that Manly had declared himself opposed to extending the suffrage and to "the abolishment of the present odious and unjust distinction."[43] In his *Memoirs* Holden says that the stand of Manly "sealed the fate of the Whig party in North Carolina, and I so announced in my next paper." The first part of this statement contains much truth, but in the latter part Holden was mistaken. On May 18, before the *Standard* reprinted the account of the New Bern discussion, Holden left for Baltimore to attend the Democratic National Convention, and no such pronouncement is to be found in the paper. Upon his return to Raleigh, he could see that "the leaders of the Federal party in this State are evidently alarmed at the force and eloquence with which Col. Reid advocates free suffrage before the people."[44] He wrote in a letter to Reid: "The suffrage question is still working well. We continue to hear of changes in your favor, but none for Manly. . . . The truth is, the enthusiasm is all on our side."[45]

If ardor was all on the side of the Democrats, indignation was on the side of the Whigs. They protested, with Manly, that the State Democratic party platform, which was supposed to set forth the party's foremost principles and policies, said nothing on this matter "so suddenly sprung upon the people." Yet, the *Register* said, "This demagogical cry is seized upon by most of the Loco Foco organs of the State, and re-echoed and endorsed by them all, as *the* great question of this campaign."[46] Both Gales and Lemay labeled it a dangerous agrarian doctrine, and Gales was certain the people "are not to be humbugged by any such specious or new-fangled claptrap."[47] Lemay wrote a long editorial giving labored reasons for opposing the "odious" doctrine.[48] Loring in his *Wilmington Commercial* asserted that free suffrage would lead to "the desecration of the Bible and the abolition of matrimony" as well as to the annullment of the commandment, Thou shalt not steal.[49]

Holden and Reid, skillfully playing their advantage, answered all arguments patiently or impatiently, as the occasion demanded. Through the campaign they tried to contend that free suffrage was not even a party issue, but was a question that transcended party lines, although only the Democratic nominee happened to favor the principle. The Whigs, caught off guard by the new progressiveness of their opponents and seeing, as Holden said, that the issue was "producing a powerful impression upon the public mind,"[50] attempted to belittle it as mere campaign fodder. But the candidate and the editor had anticipated such charges, the former declaring that he had simply chosen what seemed to him the best method of presenting an important subject to the public, and the latter asserting that his editorials had uniformly appealed to the people of both parties to examine the question dispassionately and then decide for themselves. It was shrewd campaigning, and it caught the interest of the public: at Asheville, the *Standard* reported, the candidates met July 4, in a discussion that lasted about seven hours before a crowd of between fifteen hundred and two thousand.[51]

Concomitant with free suffrage, Reid and Holden advocated an improved public school system, with every boy and girl assured an education; the editor, remembering his own youth, could take up the cudgels for this cause as earnestly as for the change in suffrage, even if it was not as dramatic an issue. He continued his warm espousal despite the growl of the *Register* that the school measure came with "very bad grace" from the Democratic Party, with its record of opposing such projects. "But the question," Gales said, "is not as to the rights of the 'boys and girls,' for all have a right to an education, if they can get it—but whether the people will consent to be taxed for this purpose."[52] This was one of the last editorials that Weston Gales wrote; he died unexpectedly on a visit to Petersburg, Virginia, and the *Register* passed into the hands of the third generation, Seaton Gales, who had been graduated from the University of North Carolina only that spring.

As the end of the campaign approached, it became apparent

that the Democratic issue had made a strong impact on the public. Just before election day Holden thought Reid really had won and wrote to the candidate: "Many Whigs here gave up. You never saw such long faces and heard such groanings! Free suffrage—beg your pardon—*equal* suffrage is a humbug—is it?"[53] But the victory was a moral, not an actual one. The Whigs managed to poll about their usual vote, getting only nine hundred fifty less than in 1846. The Democrats gained 6,056, not quite enough to wipe out the Whig majority of 7,859 of two years before, though it was whittled down to a scant 854. "Eight or ten counties in the centre might have elected you . . . by polling their full strength," Holden later wrote Reid.[54]

Furthermore, the Democrats succeeded in erasing the majorities of the Whigs in both houses of the General Assembly, though here, too, they did not quite capture the election themselves. The new Senate was to be composed of twenty-five Democrats and twenty-five Whigs, and the House of sixty Democrats and sixty Whigs. The Senate was organized later with Calvin Graves, Democrat, as speaker, and the House with Robert B. Gilliam, Whig, as speaker.

It was a time for rejoicing for the Democrats and of mortification for the Whigs. Though they had not quite succeeded this time, the former could look forward to 1850, when under the guidance of their two young progessive leaders, Reid and Holden, they might convince the public completely that they had ceased to be the reactionary party. The attitude of many Whigs, on the other hand, was expressed by the *Register*: "The result of the Election . . . gives cause for bitter and serious reflection. That it is humiliating and mortifying is beyond all question, a melancholy fact; and when the causes and effects which have brought it about are examined into, it is doubly so. We are vanquished, virtually if not really!"[55] The next week, however, young Gales recovered his poise and joined with Lemay and Charles C. Raboteau, editor of the Whig *Raleigh Times*, in ascribing the result to the apathy of the Whigs, who, the editors said, were so confident of their strength that they did not bother to go to the polls and vote against Reid. But these statements probably were for public consumption. The Whig vote was about what it had been for six years; the new votes were coming to the Democrats.

Although later, in the presidential election, the Whigs carried the state for Zachary Taylor with a majority of 8,154 votes, even this portended good for the Democrats. Many persons, the *Standard* said, voted for Taylor because he was a Southerner and it was thought that his views on slavery were safer than those of his opponent, Lewis Cass, a native of New England.[56] But this was a matter of men, not parties, for the general Democratic position on the slavery question both in the state and the nation—basically a position supporting state's rights—was more in accord with that of the North Carolina public than was the Whig stand. As the national crisis on this issue developed, the Democrats would be the ones to profit.

With their stand on slavery, with an issue like free suffrage to espouse, with their increasingly progressive attitude toward internal improvements, with the new voters joining their party, and with Reid and Holden at the helm, the Democrats, after years of eddying about futilely, were ready to surge forward with a rush that would engulf the Whig party. Thirty-five years later Holden made the quiet boast, "But for David S. Reid and myself, there would have been no triumphant Democratic party in North Carolina."[57] There is much truth in the statement. Hale, the Fayetteville editor, did not hesitate to admit, much later, in speaking of Holden: "A few years ago he had become unquestionably the most influential man in the State. His central position, and the skill with which he managed his Press, combined with an unwearied assiduity in intrigue, enabled him to mold public opinion so far as to reduce the Whig party to a minority and to elevate the Democratic Party to a majority."[58]

FIVE

THE MAJORITY for Manly of only 854 was as significant for Holden personally as for the Democratic Party, and he realized much more fully than the organization the meaning in the figures. More for him than for the party, for reasons to be considered later, it brought self-confidence, but for both it promised future fulfillments. After the elections of 1848, a new tone of assurance entered the *Standard*'s columns. For much of five years the editorials had spoken often with the positiveness of brash youth moved by optimistic impulse; now a note of knowledge of power based upon demonstrated capabilities was to be caught. He had no need to flail about, printing the cutting but imaginary "mysteries of Coondom"; he could bide his time, holding back until the proper moment information his opponents did not know he possessed. And so in the next two years, until the election of 1850, there were no cries of "woe unto the Whiggery," no boasts of "speading ourself" in campaigns. There was relative silence, slightly ominous, on state politics as Holden waited the start of the actual contest.

Financially, too, he could be proud. By 1850, he says in the *Memoirs*, he had paid off the debt of $2,000 incurred in buying the *Standard*, had laid out $1,350 for a house and lot, held on deposit in the Cape Fear Bank $5,000 to build his larger residence at Hargett and McDowell Streets, and had bought the new equipment for his paper.[1] There is no evidence to indicate that any of these items were exaggerated. With the prospect of Democratic success, there was hope that his earnings would further improve, because he probably would be given the public printing contract.

By the first of 1850 the *Standard* had joined the *Fayetteville Observer* in refusing patent medicine advertising. Holden expressed the opinion that these "nostrums" ought not to be foisted upon the public by the newspapers.[2] The result was that his advertising patronage was reduced to seven columns, whereas a year earlier, when patent remedy advertisements were accepted, it had averaged ten columns and sometimes more. Thus, if such advertising was paid for at the *Standard*'s regular rate, it cost Holden $30 to $40 an issue to make this decision. Yet he was laying plans to publish a semiweekly issue, in addition to the weekly paper; the added printing was begun November 6, 1850.

Frank I. Wilson of the *Mountain Banner* at Rutherfordton, who knew Holden well from their joint coverage of the legislature, gave a word picture of what the Raleigh editor looked like about this time. Holden, he said, "is not so ugly as some have pretended. Indeed, he looks well enough when you 'get used to him' or just after a Democratic victory. He is an able and a ready writer, a correct reasoner, and a high minded, honorable man, possessed of indomitable energy, unwearied industry, and imperturbable equanimity. He has worked his way from poverty and obscurity to comparative wealth and distinction. In stature he is rather under medium size, but with a good figure."[3]

Though the position of the *Standard* was secure, Holden, as the editor of the leading Democratic paper, faced a somewhat awkward situation in the party, and it kept the Democrats from feeling the self-assurance that the previous election might have inspired. Much of the predicament stemmed from the division of Democratic opinion on the question of internal improvements, until now the exclusive property of the Whigs. As the legislature of 1848–49 met, Holden and some other party leaders began coming out more openly for public works.

Even before Holden could analyze the results of the presidential election, the *Standard,* which for years had carried editorials censuring the Whigs for extravagance in voting state aid to various improvements, surprised readers with an editorial appealing to the party to forget past prejudices and to make North Carolina "what she ought to be, and what she is capable of being rendered, by the joint efforts and united energies of all her sons" if "we all wake up to the importance of doing something for North Carolina in the way of internal improvements."[4]

This editorial awakened resentment that did not die down for several years. In the next few months, a number of readers of the *Standard* canceled their subscription, and Holden grieved that "friends who were once cordial, and who stood by us when we first took charge of the paper and in the midst of our heaviest difficulties, have become estranged."[5] He argued that the party was united on all national questions, and he urged it not to divide because of differing views on state affairs. The federal government, he said, had no power to "construct roads through the states, or to open canals," and if those things were to be done in North Carolina, the state would have to take the lead.[6]

This was, in fact, an attempt by Holden to jockey the Democratic Party in a direction he thought it should go. As a young editor, he had accepted the party as he found it and had helped fight its battles on principles set forth by older members. Now that he was more mature and was a political power, he felt compelled to give the party a sounder basis, on the premise that some of the old tenets were simply wrong. In insisting that he himself had not changed, he was probably speaking truly. Quite probably he had had no deep convictions on the issue before, and his criticism of Whig extravagance was based on evidence that the Whig system had wasted money and had not provided improvements commensurate with the costs.

Holden was joined in his position by at least eight of the eleven

Democratic papers in the state and, naturally, by most of the Whig journals. A sufficient number of Democratic members of the legislature also agreed, and with their help financial aid was voted in that session for, among others, the following improvements: a railroad from Goldsboro via Raleigh and Salisbury to Charlotte, a line extending 200 miles; a plank road from Fayetteville to Salisbury and a turnpike southward toward Georgia; repair of the Raleigh and Gaston Railroad; improvements on the Cape Fear and Deep rivers above Fayetteville, as well as projects on the Neuse and Tar rivers; and the construction of a hospital for the insane. While Holden would have been the last to take credit for this flurry of activity, his support eased its progress.

At this time, too, Holden entered one of the more consequential phases of his career as an editor. He began to speak with a tone of authority on national questions that were coming to the fore, particularly on Southern and state's rights. In the preceding five years the *Standard* had seldom printed editorials on national affairs, and when it did, they rarely seemed to carry deep conviction. But the tide of affairs in the life of the nation was changing, and in 1849 and 1850 the slavery question, the right of secession, and Southern attempts to achieve a united front on those issues claimed many plainspoken columns in Holden's newspaper.

In his introductory message to the readers of the *Standard*, Holden said that he had joined the Democrats because he thought that "whilst they yield to the Federal Government the exercise of its acknowledged and undoubted Constitutional powers, they at the same time guard with peculiar vigilance the freedom, sovereignty and independence of the respective States."[7] Throughout his years in the editorship of the *Standard,* Holden clung to this view of state's rights, and it helps account for such widely disparate situations as his position on Southern rights in

1849 and 1850 and his hostility to the Confederate government a dozen years later.

His position, he said, was that Congress "has no jurisdiction whatever over the question of Slavery either in the District of Columbia, the Territories, or the States; and all we ask of that body . . . is to let the question alone. Though Congress, by the Constitution, is empowered to exercise exclusive legislation in all cases whatsoever over the District of Columbia, yet this power must be put forth for the purpose of regulating, preserving, and protecting, and not to impair or destroy existing rights."[8]

Holden feared, however, that the Wilmot Proviso, which would have banned slavery in the lands acquired from Mexico, would pass both houses of Congress (it never did) and be signed by President Taylor. In that event, he reasoned that the next step would be a prohibition against slavery in the District of Columbia, fomenting agitation in the North against the institution everywhere. He felt deeply that a Southern convention that would show the unity of the slave states was desirable, and he called on Governor Manly to convene a special session of the legislature to appoint delegates to such a convention, proposed for Nashville. In pressing his case he wrote editorially: "All they [the Northerners] have to do is to repeal their laws protecting our slaves when they escape to their soil, to cease the agitation of this question in Congress, and to let us alone. . . . *They* are the aggressors, not we."[9]

For several years Democratic and Whig opinion on the slavery question, at least in the press, had been converging in North Carolina. Holden and Lemay at the *Star*, normally archenemies, were united in their concern about activities in Washington, and both were strong advocates of the Nashville convention—although Lemay admitted that he might be at odds with a majority in the Whig Party.[10] Holden had no such reservations, although Democratic leaders, including David S. Reid, who again was to be the party's nominee for governor, opposed the movement. Holden was somewhat less dogmatic in private views expressed to Reid when the latter suggested that his position might make him an unsuitable nominee. Holden said that made little difference, that he himself had "but yielded to the wish of the majority"[11]—perhaps following his theory of an editor's duty, but perhaps also feeling that Democratic chances in the election depended upon Reid's candidacy.

Publicly, however, he honed the edge of the Southern axe, and he spoke for North Carolina in a manner that was to become more and more familiar:

North Carolina will never consent to remain in the Union an inferior or degraded State. She will have *equality* as a sovereign in the Union, or independence out of it. She will yield up everything but her honor and her vital interests to preserve the Union; but these she will maintain "at all hazards and to the last extremity." In this contest, forced upon her against her will by ambitious and wicked men, she will neither stand neutral, nor with the North, [but] by her Southern sister.[12]

With the debate over Henry Clay's Compromise of 1850, in which he was supported in varying degrees by both Daniel Webster and John C. Calhoun, Holden sensed that the mood of North Carolinians was against direct confrontation and in favor of a kind of accommodation, even one as limited as that which Clay proposed. So he joined with several other Democratic papers in reluctant retreat. Their acquiescence was summed up by the *Wilmington Journal*, which said, "Perhaps this compromise is not all that Southern men could desire. In some respects it is not but we believe the question is now narrowed down to this one—compromise or disunion."[13]

To add to the political stir in the state in the spring and summer of 1850, came the election of governor. Manly, who had not proved to be a popular executive, again was to be the Whig candidate, despite declarations in outlying Whig papers that his selection would be disastrous to the party. By the first of June the Democrats had made no move, although nominating conventions customarily were held months earlier. While rumors of a political deal with the Whigs circulated in the hinterlands, party leaders were stalled in a convention call because of factional strife over the Nashville assembly and the degree to which the Democrats would support internal improvements.

Meeting at night, the state central committee selected Reid for governor,[14] agreeing with the consensus of the county conventions already held. Although he had earlier told Holden he would run if he were not required to sanction the Nashville meeting or an act of the legislature chartering the North Carolina Railroad, Reid declined to accept the nomination. In a public letter to Holden he cited two reasons for his action: he believed his nomination was repugnant to a portion of the party, and he thought the shortness of time before the election would not permit him to mount an effective campaign.[15]

Holden withheld Reid's letter from publication and undertook, as in 1848, to induce the reluctant candidate to change his mind. The editor wrote Reid a long letter waving his objections aside and assuring him that *"you are unquestionably the first choice of the party."*[16] Although Holden outlined clear strategy, coupled with the conviction that Manly was a dead duck, Reid was unmoved, and on June 12, 1850, the day before the state convention was to be held in Raleigh, Holden reluctantly printed Reid's letter refusing the nomination. Notwithstanding, the convention called on Reid to be their standard-bearer again, and under such pressure he relented and undertook a zealous, if foreshortened, campaign, again making free suffrage the central issue. In attempting to counter that proposal Manly got himself all tangled up in the details of the suffrage formula then existing and found himself on the defensive on almost every relevant issue.

As election day approached, expectations of a Democratic victory grew. Holden made a final appeal to those "counties in the centre" that he had blamed for the earlier defeat, apparently with some result. Manly received approximately the same vote that had elected him in 1848. Reid, however, gained more than 3,000, getting 44,844, the largest vote yet given a candidate for governor in North Carolina, to 42,071 for Manly. The Democrats also won a majority of four in the Senate and of ten in the House. Under its two young leaders, one the attractive front man and the other the eloquent propagandist, the rejuvenated Democratic Party, despite internal differences, was attracting into its ranks most of the new and unaligned voters, while the Whig Party was struggling to maintain its traditional strength.

And, for the purposes of this narrative and as a footnote to history, the result was a singular achievement: the lad of "humble" origins in Hillsborough had vaulted his own man into the state's highest office. That fact had not entirely escaped notice. "Poor Manly is beaten," one Whig wrote to a friend. "Poor Fellow, he will take it I fear with but little fortitude. . . . And what a Governor we shall have in Reid! He will give Holden the reins of the State." [17]

Naturally, Holden was jubilant. "We have the high and rare gratification of announcing to our readers," he began his election account, "and to Democracy everywhere, that we have a DEMOCRATIC GOVERNOR and a DEMOCRATIC LEGISLATURE; and that North Carolina is at last completely and gloriously redeemed." Furthermore, as he went on to say, the victory had been won "under such circumstances and upon such issues as to render it certain that our success is permanent." [18] If in this latter statement he was simply expressing a wish, it turned out to be prophetic. The Whig Party was kept alive in North Carolina until the end of the Civil War, but its day of dominance had ended.

Reid did not, in fact, "give Holden the reins of the State," although he was sometimes accused of doing so and did, indeed, rely upon the editor for counsel. Holden had a duty of more consequence to him. Now that the Democratic Party was in the ascendancy, on principles he had been instrumental in formulating, he was to become its drillmaster, the top sergeant who, possessing a more commanding personality than the commissioned officers, virtually runs the company. As the next few years went by, the drillmaster was to become stricter and stricter in making his growing number of soldiers march to the tunes of accepted Democratic principles, reprimanding with more or less severity, or even jerking out of line, those who got out of step. Antagonisms resulted at times, of course, but Holden, insisting upon the superiority of principles to men, willing to sacrifice even warm personal friendship if it conflicted with the larger duty, took as little notice of these animosities as was possible. The great mass of the party appeared to realize that it needed just such a dominating leader to make it the victory-confident organization it had become and to hold it together.

Holden himself explained his conviction that this obligation of policing and regulating the party devolved upon him as editor of its chief paper. He wrote in reply to one of the numerous charges of dictatorialness that cropped up with growing regularity as the Democrats routed first the Whig Party and then its successor, the Know-Nothing organization: "The charge of dictation on the part of the *Standard* we totally disregard, for we know it to be unfounded. But we do profess to know what are Democratic principles, as laid down by our State and national conventions, and in applying these principles we profess to know who are Democrats and who are not."[19]

Some of Holden's party-drilling was to be observed in the winter of 1850–51 as the state resumed the discussion of Southern rights and the prerogative of secession. Both the *Standard* and the *Star* appealed to the South to organize for the crisis which appeared imminent, but Lemay emphasized the development of manufacturers and resources to prepare for any eventuality,[20] while Holden urged political action to forestall the contingency by convincing the North that a united South would demand that "agitation of the slavery question must cease in Congress, and that the Fugitive Slave Law, as it stands, must be enforced to the letter."[21]

Holden's position on secession was somewhat singular and anomalous. It may be regarded as a question, despite his "fire-eating" in the next ten years and despite the general opinion of him, whether he actually looked on secession as a practical political step. It is true that his expressed opinion won for him the title of "high priest of secession"[22] from one contemporary, and another called him the man who did "more than any other citizen of North Carolina to teach secession."[23] But as one examines his whole career as editor, reviewing the many editorials on secession, one is struck by the fact that he was considering secession more from an academic viewpoint, as the abstract right of a state and as a threat, except in a last desperate resort, rather than as a feasible and advisable political move to deal with fancied injustices. "We never maintained the doctrine of secession as practiced by the cotton States,"[24] he said later. In spite of all that occurred to aggrieve the South before 1860, Holden saw no situation demanding this precipitate step, seeing instead that there might theoretically be circumstances in the future that would call for such action; but whenever North Carolina or another state really approached the brink of secession, he drew back and cautioned deliberation.

Why, then, could his course be described later as having "educated the people in the doctrine of secession?"[25]

For one thing, the question of the right of secession had entered politics in the state as well as in the nation, the Democrats generally affirming and many of the Whigs denying the right. As a controversial topic involving the positions of the two parties, the question drew from the papers sweeping and defiant statements. Holden was vigorous in the expression of his views. He was "a Democratic Republican of the school of '98 and '99," supporting "the freedom, sovereignty, and independence of the respective States" and regarding the Union as "a confederacy, compact, neither a consolidation, nor a centralization."[26] He was an admirer of Calhoun. He was a member of the Democratic Party, which assumed a militant attitude on the protection of Southern rights and, in North Carolina, made political capital out of the slavery question. He was the editor of a leading party paper, from which much was expected. He impatiently told the Whigs and the North: "It is sufficient for us to say, that we hold to the right of secession as an original, pre-existing, reserved sovereign right; that whenever the Constitution is palpably violated by Congress . . . the Union is dissolved."[27]

For another thing, Holden was much concerned over the danger to slavery from the aggressions of the apparently growing number of Abolitionists in the North, and he believed that if the institution was to be preserved, the time had come for the South to speak out boldly. And he attempted that, writing, "The South has been driven back, inch by inch, on this question until she now stands with her back to the wall. . . . *But she will acquiesce and retreat no longer.* . . . What she has to say to the free States is this: let this question of Slavery alone."[28] Holden was joined in this ultimatum by Lemay, who also thought that the South had gone far enough in compromising and now ought to resist the "wanton and unjustifiable aggressions of Northern fanatics."[29]

The threat of secession, then, was to be used to unite the South so that she would speak with one voice, thereby forcing the North to respect the rights of the slave states. As long as the South vacillated or remained on the defensive, Holden believed, her political dues would be whittled away until what was left would be a union not recognizable as that of Washington and Jefferson.

Paradoxically, Holden felt deeply that a constitutional union, as he conceived it, should be preserved. Many times he assured editors who criticized his printed convictions that his stand made him a better friend of the union than they were, and he truly believed it. "In our humble judgement, that man who stands up most unflinchingly for the reserved rights of the States, is the best Union man, while he who is eternally crying Union! Union! is most to be dreaded as the advocate of consolidation, and of Constitutional liberty."[30] By taking liberties in their view of the Constitution, his opponents, he argued, were "the Disunionists, for instead of standing up for the Constitution on which the Union is based, *they tolerate encroachments upon it, apologize for wrong, and invite by their language and their action the repetition of the very aggressions which must in the end result in its destruction.*"[31]

The discussion of slavery, secession, and Southern rights, in an outburst of motions and resolutions, claimed a lion's share of the attention of the legislature which met in November, 1850. Holden early reported that, after talking with "many members of both parties on this vital question," he could say that "North Carolina will *stand and act*, if act finally she must. The mind of her people, judging from the tone of her Representatives, is made up, she will recede no farther."[32] However, the legislature took little definitive action on any of these issues, there being a general conviction that the timing was inexpedient.

There was movement, however, on free suffrage, and the legislature approved a constitutional amendment to implement it. Because of technical procedural requirements, however, it was not until 1857 that free suffrage actually was granted in North Carolina.

While the legislature was in session, Holden again was elected a city commissioner from Raleigh's western ward. "We were not a candidate for this post," he said, "and did not desire it. But as we have made it a rule never to seek office nor decline it, whether large or small; and as our fellow-citizens have thought proper to elect us, we shall serve them cheerfully and to the best of our judgement."[33]

Throughout 1851 the secession issue continued to absorb North Carolina editors, particularly as they viewed events to the south, but in the outpourings of the press there was considerably more heat than light. Holden, often on the defensive, took comfort in the positions already ascribed to him, finding little else to write about because of the complete unanimity in the Democratic Party over the gubernatorial nominee for 1852. At the state convention in Raleigh on May 13, Governor Reid was renominated by acclamation. "When the question was put to a vote," Holden reported, "it was received with a perfect hurricane of enthusiasm."[34] He did not speak of his own personal gratification, which must have been considerable, for Reid, it will be remembered, was *his* man.

In April the Whig convention had nominated John Kerr for governor, and he had gone to the stump without waiting for the formal designation of Governor Reid as his opponent. Kerr was popular and had an entertaining stage presence, but he was handicapped by the presidential candidacy of Winfield Scott, no hero in the South. Although no issues were introduced, the campaign was intense, and Holden worked so hard in behalf of Reid that he found himself "worn down and exhausted,"[35] partially because he was trying to counter with the *Standard* a number of Whig newspapers. (The illness and death of his wife also undoubtedly contributed to his exhaustion.)

Once more, however, Holden on August 11, 1852, had "the high gratification" of announcing to his readers "that Democracy is again triumphant at the polls in North Carolina." Reid increased his 1850 vote by more than 3,000, for a total of 48,484, while Kerr, with 42,993, did little better than Manly. In the elections for the General Assembly, however, the Democrats fared less well, winning control of the Senate twenty-eight to twenty-two, but yielding supremacy in the House to the Whigs, sixty-two to fifty-eight.

A stroke of more national significance was achieved in the

presidential campaign. No Democratic candidate had won the North Carolina electoral vote since 1836, but in 1852, in light November balloting, Franklin Pierce, running far behind Governor Reid in what was otherwise a national landslide, carried the state for the Democrats by 686 votes.

With losses at both the key state and federal levels, the Whigs of North Carolina found themselves in considerable disarray. As a party they faced demoralization, and one staunch Whig privately admitted that "we need help or our state is gone."[36] Their problem was that the Democrats had the issues which were most popular at the polls: they were recognized as the sponsors of free suffrage; they had the more satisfactory stand on slavery and Southern rights; they had even taken the internal improvements issue away from the Whigs; and, in general, they seemed to be more progressive and virile. Holden, even if more than a little biased, wrote with considerable insight in 1853 when he said that the Whig Party, "as it gave up its doctrines, one by one, lost public respect and went down in public confidence; and now, the announcement of a *Whig* issue or a *Whig* principle, is a subject of amusement or of wonder."[37]

At about the time that he wrote those lines, Lemay, who had edited the *Star* for eighteen years, a period that covered the golden age for the Whigs, was arranging to sell his paper, and at the age of thirty-five, Holden became the dean of political editors in Raleigh. W. C. Doub, who bought the *Star*, edited it for about two years, and then, as Holden said later, it "ceased to exist."[38]

In some intraparty wrangling at this stage, the cry was raised once more that Holden had set himself up as a party dictator. In a letter to the *Warrenton News* an angry Democrat, calling the Raleigh editor a "renegade Whig," protested: "Who, I would ask, conferred upon W. W. Holden the power and authority to pull down one man and set up another? Certainly, not the intelligent Democracy of the District; then, so far as you are concerned, he has not the power, or the authority to do either;

will any be so servile as to obey his insulting mandate? Surely not. The man who does so, has never breathed the pure atmosphere of true and genuine independence and is still in political slavery."[39]

Holden answered that "it is a favorite resort with certain persons to cry out 'dictation' whenever their peculiar notions are exposed, or assailed."[40] He said blandly that he knew of no "Democratic clique" in Raleigh or anywhere else, and he was undismayed when party malcontents launched a boycott against him in midsummer, which resulted in the loss of forty-two subscribers. During the same period, he crowed, he had added forty-six new subscribers to his list and "the threat to break us down has expanded itself in thin air."[41] Abraham W. Venable, a congressional candidate whom Holden had offended, went so far as to set up a rival Democratic paper in Raleigh, the *North Carolina Statesman*. First appearing on January 7, 1854, it folded after three weeks.

Meanwhile, the question of the Democrats' nominee for governor had arisen, and the Whigs had the consolation of knowing that they would not again have to face Reid, who had twice outrun them. In the *Standard*, Holden listed nearly a dozen Democrats he thought could win, but that was probably subterfuge. He had already been in touch with Thomas Bragg of Northampton County, and Bragg had said that he would accept the nomination if there was no serious opposition. Holden denied that Bragg's later selection by the state convention was the result of "cut and dried arrangements,"[42] but several years later he did quote with evident agreement an assertion in the *Goldsborough Tribune* that said: "We feel . . . warranted in saying that Mr. Holden did more to secure the nomination of Gov. Bragg than any other ten men combined in the State."[43]

At the convention on April 19, 1854, at which Bragg's nomination was unanimously accepted, Holden was struck by the large number of young men present as delegates. A Wilmington associate, David Fulton, said the fact that so many young men of education and intelligence were entering the Democratic Party, rather than, as formerly, the Whig organization, was worrying Whig leaders and newspaper editors. The University of North Carolina, Fulton said, once had been "a perfect nest, almost, we might say, a school of Whiggery, turning out few young men that were not imbued with a most bitter prejudice against the Democratic Party."[44]

The Whigs, meeting in convention before the Democrats, had nominated as their candidate Alfred Dockery, a former Congressman who the *Standard* said had been ready to vote men and money to the president to carry fire and sword against secessionist talk in South Carolina. The campaign developed into a rather reckless debate over which were most staunchly in favor of internal improvements, the Whigs or the Democrats; and Bragg, who as a member of the General Assembly did not have a shining record on public works aid, barely squeaked through. He received 48,705 to 46,620 for Dockery, a margin of only 2,085. To the Democrats the legislative results were more satisfactory; they won a majority of 12 seats in the Senate and of 10 in the House.

Just after the election Holden, in answering a letter, fired the first gun in a new political war. The letter was curious. It said, in part, "Since the excitement of the late elections has subsided, other subjects are agitating the public mind in this section. It is said that the great question which is to divide the country in the future will be Protestantism and Roman Catholicism: and that the Democrats are coalescing with the Catholics. You, Mr. Editor, are represented as having Catholic influence in the *Standard* office; indeed, it is charged by some that you are one yourself."[45]

Holden replied shortly that he did employ a clerk who was an Irishman and a Catholic. "We employed him because he suited us, and we shall retain him just as long as we may choose to do so. We did not stop to inquire whether he believed as we do in religious matters."[46]

That slight exchange was Holden's first encounter with Know Nothingism, the nativist-political movement sweeping down from the North. Some of its members were bound by secret orders to say nothing of internal principles and organization, thus giving rise to the "Know Nothing" appellation. For Holden it was a movement that was to arouse more impatience and more contempt than anything he had dealt with before. The first collision was not even a skirmish; in brushing aside a barely seen annoyance, Holden did not recognize it as a foe. It was not for several months, when Know Nothingism began to be recognized as the straw for which a large portion of the Whig Party in the state and some Democrats were grasping, that Holden, in common with North Carolina as a whole, caught the significance of early whispers and rumors.

A few months later, Holden gave his version of the movement's progress: "When Know Nothingism made its first appearance in the South, at least when it first began to be talked about, it was regarded as a sort of myth, a joke, a hoax, or a harmless order of fantastics, or something of that kind. Curiosity was excited, the scheme was deeply laid, and not being open to opposition it sprang up rapidly. It arrived, too, just at a time when the Whig Party was gasping its last breath over the defeat of its last principle; and the transmigration of its soul into the body of Know Nothingism was easy and natural, as soon as it felt the attraction of politics therein, and such politics as were hostile to the Democratic administration. Thus at one gulp down went the Whig party, while curiosity and false pretenses swallowed even some good Democrats and a large number of bad ones. Unscrupulous Whig leaders seized upon it as their last chance for riding into power—the Whig press wheeled into rank."[47]

Holden argued, in a strain that has since been echoed several times, that the Know Nothing order not only had no place in, but actually threatened to undermine, the American scheme of life. As one reads some of these arguments in the *Standard* and other papers, one can appreciate the comments of another Raleigh editor at that time, R. H. Whitaker, who described editors as being composed of "self-importance, a high order of patriotism, and a sentimentality of look."

Certainly sterling patriotism glowed through Holden's editorials as he took Know Nothingism, which had appropriated unto itself the designation of the American Party, to task.

Never before has there existed in this country a party so thoroughly anti-republican and anti-American, and it is no more entitled to the name of "American," than the devil is to the title of *saint*, merely because he sometimes assumes the garb of "an angel of light."

The American character is bold and open. The Know Nothing character skulks in secret. Americanism seeks the light and courts investigation. Know Nothingism seeks darkness and shuns investigation. Americanism opens its arms to the oppressed of all nations and says: "Come to this refuge and enjoy civil and religious liberty, worship God as your conscience dictates, and your religious beliefs shall not be a test of your fitness or unfitness for the rights and privileges of citizenship." Know Nothingism assumes a threatening attitude and says to the downtrodden of other lands: "Stay where you are; fester and rot in the chains that tyrants have thrown around you; we have liberty here, but you shall not share it with us." To both foreigners and natives it says: "Worship God in a particular way, whether your conscience approves it or not, or you are unfit for all the privileges of citizenship. Your religious opinions shall be the test of your fitness for office."

The American character emblazons its principles and unfurls its flag to the world. The Know Nothing character hides its principles in a dark lantern under a culvert. Americanism sets its light upon a hill and glories in its resplendent beams. Know Nothingism puts its light under a bushel, and trembles and flees at the approach of light—Americanism is day; Know Nothingism is night.[48]

It does not matter here how correct or incorrect Holden may have been in saying that Know Nothingism was un-American; there is no doubt that the movement was un-Carolinian. The state had few foreigners and few Catholics, and so far as newspaper records reveal, it had not occurred before to the native-born to feel any prejudice against these. The 1850 census figures show only 2,565 foreign-born out of a total white population of 553,028, of whom 529,483 had been born within the state. As for Catholics: there were only four Roman Catholic churches in the state, with a total accommodation of one thousand four hundred. The majority of North Carolinians could be educated at most to only a synthetic resentment against foreigners and Catholics, whose combined vote, even if cast, did not figure in election results. At best they could not muster one thousand votes.

Nor could the North Carolina character, largely of Anglo-Saxon ancestry, nurtured in the political ideals of Jefferson and developed close to the soil, appreciate readily the secret and oath-bound organizations. By stressing, as the *Standard* did, the "dark lantern" tactics and the midnight councils of the various orders, the Democrats saw to it that virtually the only prejudice aroused by the movement worked against it.

Holden left an impression that was not altogether correct when he wrote that "the Whig press wheeled into rank" in support of the Know Nothings. The *Fayetteville Observer*, one of the most influential Whig organs, never did. Hale, its editor, was too good a Whig and had too much intelligence ever to have anything to do with the movement. During all the Know Nothing excitement, Hale pursued without deviation what he called "our straight-forward Whig course."[49] The *Greensborough Patriot*, on the other hand, was guilty as charged. Published in the home of the Know Nothing candidate for governor in 1856, it defended proselytes of the order by saying that it believed the new party embodied "more of nationality, of conservatism; and less of sectionalism, than is to be found in either of the other existing political parties."[50] The *Patriot* published the Know Nothing platform, leaving "with our intelligent patrons . . . to decide how far the interests of the nation would be advanced or retarded by the prevalence of those principles."[51]

In May, 1855, a year also marked by Holden's marriage to Louisa V. Harrison of Raleigh, he was shaken to read in the Raleigh *Star* that his old Democratic friend and sponsor, James B. Shepard, would run as the American Party candidate for Congress from the Fourth District. He sought out Shepard and learned that his one-time sponsor was, indeed, to represent "the new party or cabal of proscription, intolerance and vengeance."[52]

Holden held strict party loyalty to be sacred, and editorially he said to Shepard: "This press knows no man when its principles are at stake."[53]

While the task of opposing his longtime confidante must have been disagreeable to Holden, he did not shirk it, mounting his assault with such vigor that the *Register* accused him of "the crime of ingratitude."[54] Shepard took much the same tack, asking in his public speeches, "Who made the Editor of the *Standard*?"[55]

Holden professed hurt, saying that Shepard knowingly was doing him "gross and inexcusable injustice," but adding this barb: "We may state that *we* tried for a number of years to *make* Mr. Shepard, but failed in the effort, on account of his lack of industry and common sense."[56] Whatever his motives, Shepard had jumped in the wrong direction by associating with the Know Nothings. Opposed by L. O'B. Branch, he lost to the Democratic candidate by 2,591 votes. Statewide, the Democrats won five congressional seats and the Know Nothings three.

The gubernatorial race was a runaway. In April, 1856, the Know Nothings held a convention in Greensboro and nominated John A. Gilmer of that city as their candidate for the state's highest office. In the same month the Democratic state convention, meeting in Raleigh, renominated Governor Bragg, whose

conservatism and quiet distinction fitted admirably into the turmoil, both state and national, in 1856. While the two candidates
in their joint debates toyed with the "squatter sovereignty" provisions of the Kansas-Nebraska Act (legislation that hastened
the formation of the Republican Party), the chief issue was
Know Nothing principles. North Carolina voters showed at the
polls that they had little sympathy for them, reelecting Bragg
by the largest margin received to that date by a North Carolina
governor. Bragg polled 57,598 votes to 44,970 for Gilmer, and
the Democrats won a majority of forty seats in the House and
sixteen in the Senate.

In the meantime, while active in the state campaign and the
national effort to elect James Buchanan, Holden had introduced
a revolution in newspaper sales. He broke journalistic precedent
in North Carolina by announcing that the *Standard* would adopt
the cash system for subscriptions, because "the credit system is
fraught with more evils than always appear on the surface of
society."[57] Although other papers predicted that the *Standard*
was committing suicide, Holden stuck to his guns, and within
a few years he was able to say that his subscription list was "larger
than it ever was under the credit system."[58]

At the end of 1857 Holden could look about him and see the
Democratic Party supreme in North Carolina, even if threatened
with some discord and the insoluble slavery question nationally.
Holden could say contemptuously of adversaries at home, "We
have nothing to fear from our piebald and unorganized opponents."[59] The editor could feel a proper pride in his own part
in bringing such conditions about, particularly as he saw the
once-haughty *Register* grovel in print: "As a party, those with
whom we have acted, and now act, are powerless. We are not
in the field even; and the Democracy need entertain no fear now
of doing what they know to be right."[60] The *Carolina Watchman* copied these plaintive lines, whereupon the *Greensborough
Patriot* flared up to demand who clothed these papers with the

power to declare the American Whigs helpless.[61] But it was largely true.

There were two hazards the Democrats might face. Opposition was sure to spring to life under some new name to challenge Democratic supremacy with some new issue, although Holden could say, "We have beaten them when they were organized and strong, and when they had leaders worthy of the name; and surely we can do it now."[82] The more dangerous possibility was that the Democratic Party's "very strength may produce weakness. It may neglect its organization, and thus encourage divisions and discord; and the aspirations, the ambitions, the selfishness of its leading men may obstruct and cloud its principles, and ultimately break it down."[63] That was Holden's warning, perhaps to new converts from the Whig ranks as well as to Democrats who might be inclined to lose their balance in the party's time of prosperity. The party must keep itself purged, always remembering that men were subordinate to principles. It was a pertinent warning.

That year probably brought the crest of Holden's power as a political journalist. For several years his sway had been undisputed, although now some disturbing signs were on the horizon. The *Register* painted a picture of Holden sitting in "the Vatican on Hargett Street,"[64] exercising "papal powers,"[65] as he strove to keep the party cleansed, intact, and mobile.

SIX

Early in 1856 Holden wrote: "We do not want office. . . . All we desire is, to labor here in our humble way, at the head of this press, for the advancement of Democratic principles and for the preservation of the Constitution in its purity."[1] A year and a half later, the *Democratic Pioneer* at Elizabeth City carried a communication from a Raleigh correspondent proposing the name of Holden as the next Democratic nominee for governor.[2] Sometime in the interim Holden is supposed to have become tired of being the Warwick-style kingmaker of North Carolina and to have become ambitious for high public office for himself, with a more tangible reward than praise for his labors.

The conception of Holden's life that has grown up is that it was a tragedy in the Shakespearean meaning of the word: he was a protagonist of unusual proportions; he came into conflict with powerful internal and external forces, and his sensitive temperament crumbled under the strain; he had one "vicious mole of nature," the burning desire to make himself ruler of his fellows; and it wrought his downfall—a fall, if one cares to carry the idea further, arousing pity and terror by its completeness and dimensions, and effecting a certain catharsis of those emotions.

How much truth there is in this conception—what occurred between 1856 and 1858—why an ambition apparently ripened to hold exalted office—whether, indeed, the desire had been latent all along and he was biding his time to give it expression—how much he himself had to do with instigating his candidacy and how much he was pushed into it by friends—can be in large part only matters of surmise.

There is little reason, however, to doubt his sincerity when he said he did not want office. No hint is to be found in his own paper that his labors had been directed toward important positions for himself; the inference that such was true does not take into account the surprise of his contemporaries when it became known that he was a candidate—and training had given them well-developed instincts in such matters. In view of his later career, the absence of such hints in his and other newspapers is striking. He had held two major political positions: one term in the legislature, voluntarily declining a second term he presumably might have had; and the post of public printer, to which he considered himself entitled as owner of the only Democratic press in the capital. Besides this latter place, he held in 1858 four semi-public positions: warden of the poor in Wake County; director of the state institution for the deaf, dumb, and blind; director of the insane asylum; and member of the literary board, which handled public school funds.

Possibly he was pushed into the candidacy, however far he needed to be pushed, by friends who kept reminding him of the great debt of gratitude that the party owed him; the state was told often enough in the next few months that the party was under incalculable obligations to him, and that he had made politicians who otherwise might have remained unknown. Probably it was pointed out that the West had had a governor in Reid, the East one in Bragg, and now the office was due the center of the state, which had no more outstanding and available candidate than he.

Possibly, too, on the other hand, his fighting blood was aroused by learning that a portion of the party, the "aristocrats" for whom he had so often expressed disdain, was hostile to the pros-

Thomas Bragg, governor of North Carolina 1855–1859

pect of seeing in the Governor's Mansion a man who had worked his way up from obscurity. Soon after the *Democratic Pioneer* had carried the first proposal of the editor's name, the same Raleigh correspondent reported the "cod-fish aristocracy, of both parties, turning up their nasal organs at the idea of a poor man's aspiring to anything above the club axe, hand-saw or jack plane."[3] This must have been extremely irritating as well as painful to Holden.

Whitaker, the Raleigh editor, wrote, some years later, that Holden and some of the other Democratic leaders in the capital quarrelled in 1857, but that he never could learn the cause.[4] Developments would indicate that such a quarrel did occur, and that one of those arrayed against Holden was Governor Bragg—whose selection for and election to the governorship was in large part Holden's handiwork. But whether the rupture—which is a fact—preceded Holden's mention as a candidate, or was the result of it, or led to it, cannot be determined. Holden, true to his policy of not parading his private affairs in his paper, made no mention of it.

Whatever may have been Holden's attitude before 1857 toward seeking public office, whatever may have motivated his decision then, he committed what seems to have been the great mistake of his life in accepting at the same time the overtures of friends and the antipathy of the "aristocrats." The decision to run was the turning point in his career. An active campaign soon was started, and certain editors began to trace a series of moves whereby they saw him trying to ensure the nomination for himself, as often as not, perhaps, reading into actions motives that were not there.

The communication to the *Pioneer*, with apparently the first newspaper proposal that he should run, was signed by "Hamet," who probably was one of Holden's friends among the two or three hundred Democratic voters in the capital. The missive was effusive in its praise:

82

In W. W. Holden we have the statesman and the scholar. He is thoroughly acquainted with the affairs of the State—he has done much for the Democratic party—he is of the original advocates, along with Gov. Reid, of Free Suffrage—he stood up and battled for the cause which you and I advocated, fifteen years ago when his party was 8,000 in minority, and his watch word ever has been, "Never give up the ship." If the Democracy of North Carolina have cause to thank any man for valuable service rendered, that man is W. W. Holden, who has worked his way from an apprentice in a printing office, to the proud position he now occupies. He is of the people—he is one of the people—he is for the people.[5]

The *Register* immediately noticed this mention of "our neighbor" of the *Standard* and printed facetious remarks in which John W. Syme, who had bought the paper from Seaton Gales in 1856, promised his support if Holden would make him private secretary.[6] This editorial of the *Register*, incidentally, struck the keynote for much of the ensuing preconvention comment in the Whig journals. Nearly all their remarks were pitched in a half-humorous, half-ironic key, as though the idea of one of their own craft, especially their powerful adversary who was not in the good graces of the "aristocracy," running for governor struck them as containing much of the comic and not a little of the sardonically tragic. These Whig-American editors, with no candidate of their own to choose from, took a lively interest in the Democratic family affair, and in many respects—if one overlooks the tone of some of the articles—the preconvention happenings may be followed much better in their papers than in the Democratic journals. These accepted the situation in all earnestness, or deliberately said nothing about it. The Whig editors notably sympathized with Holden partly, perhaps, because of a whispering campaign that was begun against him.

About the time "Hamet's" communication appeared, editors received from the *Standard* office printed copies of a speech Holden had made on July 1, 1857, before the State Educational Association in Warrenton. Holden also was scheduled to make the principal address to the Duplin County Agricultural Society at its meeting on November 7. These speeches, as well as a Fourth of July oration in Raleigh the year before, whether planned for the purpose or not, helped bring the *Standard* editor personally before the public. He had given up speaking, except at party gatherings, since becoming editor, and one of the objections reported to his nomination was the fear that he might not be able to meet an opposing candidate effectively on the stump.

The *Greensborough Patriot* was another Whig-American journal that followed the Democratic nomination contest attentively. In October it listed Holden as a leading candidate for the nod, and a few weeks later it reported that the "aristocrats" were trying to derail Holden and that they were grooming Judge S. J. Person for the party's blessing. "The aristocratic portion of the party will have to try again before they get clear of Mr. Holden," the *Patriot* said. "Judge Person is rather young and he is already very comfortably provided for. Holden is a self-made man, he has long permitted himself to be snubbed by the Democratic aristocracy. . . . The aristocracy can't beat him with one of their own class, and if they succeed at all, they will have to take a man who is a little high up and at the same time low down, forming as it were a link between the aristocracy and the common people."[7]

The following week the *Patriot* reported increased "commotion in the Democratic hive" in a frantic search to head off Holden. W. W. Avery, the report continued, was unpopular in the east because of certain of his internal improvement projects, Judge John W. Ellis was said to be unpopular in the mountains "and not particularly popular anywhere," and Judge Person and D. W. Courts, state treasurer, had made themselves unavailable.[8] Yet the politicians were resolved to forestall Holden, and it soon became apparent that Judge Ellis was to be anointed.

The Democratic State Committee, of which Holden was chairman, met in Raleigh on January 8, to plan the convention. It set April 14 as the date and did an unprecedented thing in selecting Charlotte as the place; conventions hitherto had been held in Raleigh. Holden explained that Charlotte was chosen both because that town had sent an urgent invitation and because the committee felt the meeting was due the "gallant Democracy of the West."[9] J. B. Godwin, editor of the *Democratic Pioneer*, which soon was to declare for Ellis, promptly pronounced the selection of Charlotte as a plot to keep eastern delegates away from the convention, since it was too far and would be too expensive for counties along the coast to send representatives. He protested what he saw as "wire-pulling."[10]

Just how much political strategy was intended in the action is not clear; such as there was worked both ways, and the selection of Charlotte seems to have been agreeable to both Holden and Ellis. The sportsmanship exhibited publicly by both candidates throughout the contest for the nomination seems to discountenance any suspicion of plotting in this matter. Ellis, because of his judicial position, could do no campaigning, and at no time did Holden use the columns of the *Standard* to his own advantage. One would not know, from reading his editorials, that he was running. His publicity was handled entirely by journalistic friends, just as was the publicity for Ellis and several other minor aspirants. It would be difficult to find a preconvention fight, at least one so closely contested, that was more dignified as far as the candidates were concerned.

Meanwhile the *Register* had been busy seeing to it that the Democrats were to be offered some sort of opposition. Since there was no organized Whig or American party, Syme, the editor, proposed that the members of those defunct organizations unite in supporting a Democrat who would favor the distribution of the proceeds of public lands.[11] If Holden should be the Democratic candidate, the issue would be clearly drawn, for he strongly opposed distribution and had avowed his intention to read out of the party any Democrat who declared for the scheme. Walter F. Leak, a perennial also-ran, hastened to announce himself for governor on the distribution issue; possibly he looked forward to reaping satisfaction from a canvass with Holden, who had never been a Leak admirer. Duncan K. McRae of Raleigh, who had been president of the Democratic State Convention in 1852, also entered the field, making his first speech in Wilmington on January 28. At that juncture Leak withdrew, and the party-line Democratic presses centered their fire on McRae.

Holden was formally recommended to the party by a meeting of Wake County Democrats in Raleigh on February 15; he was not present. A. M. Lewis made a talk in which he praised Holden as one who stood "high as a gentleman and among the first as an editor, and who has stamped his energy and spirit upon the masses of the Democracy of the State. There could be no doubt that the State owes Mr. Holden" the nomination; there was "no knowing what the political condition of the State would have been had he not wielded his great power in our behalf. But he believed the nomination could not exalt that gentleman—could be hardly a feather in his cap—but if he wanted the office, he was entitled to it, and in God's name let him have it." [12]

The *Standard* printed the proceedings of the Wake meeting in the same way it published reports of other county conventions, whether they were in favor of Holden, Ellis, or others. A total of about seventy county-meeting proceedings was printed in the *Standard*; of these, twelve expressed a preference for Holden, seventeen opted for Ellis; there was scattered sentiment for lesser figures, and some merely pledged their support to the eventual nominee.

The usual interest taken by the public in the contest, as indicated by the number of county conclaves, was more than matched in the newspapers. The *Wilmington Journal* vainly tried to head off party bitterness by urging Democratic papers to print no endorsement until after the convention.[13] A number of editors agreed, but others had already jumped into the fight, and some heated quarrels developed, especially in the east, where the Holden advocates seemed to be abnormally sensitive, probably because they were in territory generally regarded as favoring Ellis.

The *Goldsborough Tribune* and the *Fayetteville Observer* pointed out that the lawyers of the state, as well as the "aristocrats," were against Holden. The *Tribune* thought one reason for this was that the nomination of Ellis would create a vacancy on the bench that each lawyer hoped to fill.[14] (Incidentally, fantastic as this reasoning may seem, records show that a large number of applications for appointment to the judgeship held by Ellis were made to Governor Bragg in the first six months of 1858.)[15] The *Observer* dwelt upon the irony and injustice in the situation, Editor Hale saying the lawyers believed Holden to be

very well where he is, does well enough for an editor, but is not the man to be honored with the Governor's place; may be paid for his services with a long list of subscribers, but must know his place. ... Without him these Democratic lawyers would never have been Judges, Governors, Congressmen, Legislators, scarcely heard of. But the work is done. And when he or his friends for him ask a participation in the honors of the victory, it is only natural . . . that his creatures should "take down his load, and turn him, like to the empty ass, to shake his ears, and graze in commons." How dare an editor of a newspaper, a *printer*, a man who has worked with his hands, aspire to reward from the Democratic party?[16]

Written by a journeyman editor, those lines might merely have reflected a kind of journalistic bitterness, but coming from Hale, who, although a Whig, was one of the most respected commentators in the state, they bespeak the quality of antebellum politics in North Carolina.

On the day of the Charlotte meeting, Syme reported that "as

the time for holding the Convention drew nearer and nearer, the excitement between the respective friends of Holden and Ellis has risen higher and higher."[17] Both candidates looked to the many uninstructed delegations, since fewer than half had expressed a preference. Whig editors could see that opposition to Holden had gained much strength. In fact, two months earlier the *Greensborough Patriot* had said that Holden's chance for the nomination "has been whittled down to a very small point," although for a time it had appeared that "Mr. Holden would be too hard for the Raleigh and Eastern aristocracy."[18] Nevertheless, Holden's friends were confident that the masses of the people were for him and that this would be reflected at the convention; it seemed to be understood that ten delegations then pledged to W. W. Avery would swing to Holden, as they subsequently did.

A number of fanciful stories and legends about the Democratic convention of 1858 have sprung up; it has been written about many times—yet the real narrative of what happened never has been told and possibly never will be. That is true because those who reported it for the papers were careful to write only about the actions of *public* meetings;[19] if they knew anything that occurred offstage, behind the scenes, they kept it to themselves, and the principals left no written accounts of the transactions and exchanges that took place off the record.

The convention was something of a topsy-turvy affair, with a personnel that must have looked strange to Democratic veterans. C. M. Avery, a former Burke County Whig, was chosen president on the recommendation of a nominating committee headed by Henry K. Burgwyn, also a former Whig. John Kerr, who had been defeated as the Whig candidate for governor in 1852, wrote the platform, and James W. Osborne, who had been defeated as the Whig congressional candidate in the Seventh District in 1853, seconded the resolutions presented by Kerr. The *Register* observed that there were so many renegade Whigs present that they made a list "formidable enough to elbow out the old sinners, and make them look like so many poor boys at a frolic given by the upper crust."[20] Holden, after doing so much to destroy the old Whig organization by taking up the cudgels against many of these men now prominent in his own convention, must have had doubts about receiving any favors at their hands.

The first clash between the keyed-up factions occurred almost as soon as the convention was called to order. W. J. Houston, one of the Holden leaders, moved that the delegates from each county should cast the same number of votes that the county had given Bragg in the gubernatorial race of 1856. A. M. Nesbitt of Rowan, Ellis's county, offered an amendment that a majority of the popular vote should nominate. A. M. Lewis, a Holden advocate from Wake, begged Nesbitt not to throw a firebrand into the Convention at such an early stage, and after M. A. Bledsoe, also of Wake, added his plea that the amendment be withdrawn, Nesbitt acceded. The original motion then passed, and the fight was postponed but not averted.[21]

Following this first skirmish, won by Holden, came an argument regarding the proxy of Rutherford County, representing 1,070 votes. A young delegate claimed the right to cast the county's vote (and there is some reason to believe he would have lined up with Holden), but W. J. Hoke of Lincoln, an Ellis county, moved that his name be struck from the roll because he was underage and because his name was not on the printed list of delegates. W. J. Yates (who said later, in his *Western Democrat*, that he personally had been for Holden,[22] although his Mecklenburg delegation voted for Ellis) reported as convention secretary that he had a letter from Rutherford County instructing him to give the county's proxy to New Hanover, which meant that Rutherford's vote would go to Ellis. This provoked Jacob Mordecai of Wake to declare that he was in favor of the delegate before any proxy, and in answer to Hoke's objection that the delegate was not twenty-one, Mordecai drew attention to "the renegade Whigs and Know Nothing Democrats, with the egg shell scarcely off their heads, who were not only delegates but active wireworkers in the Convention."[23] The question was referred to the credentials committee, which reported in favor of the New Hanover delegation.

Of the other proxies, six, representing the 3,023 votes of Caldwell, Henderson, McDowell, Polk, Yadkin, and Madison counties, were controlled by J. A. Dickson of Burke County; W. M. Hardy of Buncombe held the 999 proxy ballots for Cherokee and Macon; and W. H. Thomas held the proxy of Haywood, 537 votes. All of these proxies were cast for Holden. For Ellis, J. C. Badham cast the ballots of Pasquotank and Washington, 591 votes; and the New Hanover delegation cast the 1,070 votes from Rutherford.

Battle lines were drawn more closely when the delegates reconvened the following morning, anticipating a heated contest over the two-thirds rule. During the night the delegations apparently had been canvassed, and it had been learned that Ellis had a certain majority. A member of the New Hanover delegation immediately left for home and wired the *Wilmington Journal* from Goldsboro, "Ellis has a clear popular majority of three thousand," although the balloting for the nomination had not taken place.[24]

When the session was called to order, Houston, the Holden backer who had led the opening skirmish, at once moved the adoption of the two-thirds rule to govern the nomination. Badham offered a substitute motion that the nomination be decided by a majority vote. A long and animated discussion followed, Holden men for the most part favoring the original motion, and Ellis men arguing for the substitute, although there were some in both factions who thought the adoption of the two-thirds rule would work against both candidates, opening up the possibility of giving the victory to a compromise entrant.

Houston led the Holden forces, contending each point. Dr. W. J. Blow of Pitt County, an Ellis man, said he thought the rule would be an innovation. Houston replied that it had been used to nominate Bragg, but that he assumed that was before Dr. Blow stopped being a Whig. Another Ellis man, W. McL. McKay of Cumberland, thought it would be better to offend one side rather than both by letting a third man in, and Houston vigorously denied that the purpose of the two-thirds rule was to introduce another candidate. Other Holden men contended that the convention had no right to force a candidate on the party by a bare majority and that the adoption of the two-thirds rule had many precedents in Democratic history.

The Ellis men, confident of their strength, finally terminated the debate with demands for the question, which was to lay the substitute on the table with the understanding, under the procedures in force, that this action would kill the original motion. On the vote that followed, 38 counties, representing 26,766 votes, favored the motion to table, and 30 counties, with 24,276, opposed it.

After the decision on the two-thirds rule, the vote on the nominations was easy to foretell. Nevertheless, the Holden men acted as though they were still confident of winning. Capt. John Walker of Mecklenburg, who had served as temporary convention president until the election of C. M. Avery, presented a letter containing W. W. Avery's withdrawal and then nominated Holden. His speech reviewed the editor's achievements for the party, pointing out how he revived the organization at a time when it was most discouraged, when "the darkness of night was upon our cause"; how in the past fifteen years, "by his masterful planning and indefatigable exertions, by day and by midnight lamp, he has hoisted many a candidate from the dirt."

"I don't speak of the services of Mr. Holden from hearsay, Mr. President," Walker continued, according to the report in the *Fayetteville Observer*,

I speak what I *know* and have *seen*. I have witnessed his labors with his types and his editorials; and I *know* how many have become distinguished by his aid, who are now proudly waving their plumes. (Cheers.) Think, sir, of the victories he has caused us to win—of the majorities he has helped us to swell—of how many, but for him, would never have waved a plume! (Continued cheering.) And now, when we have an opportunity of putting a *feather* in *his* cap—shall we stand back in a spirit of base ingratitude? (Cheers.) To the Democracy I say, hold him to your hearts—keep him there still. By his talents and industry we shall yet pour many volleys of light and truth into the ranks of the enemy. Honor to him!—do not cast him from you! He has done more for the elevation of the Democratic Party of the State, *than any other five men in it.*[25]

How influential such an appeal could be, reminding some of the delegates of what Holden had done to destroy their former party, may be regarded as problematical. Certainly the cheering was not unanimous, and by this time it was quite evident that nothing Captain Walker or any other Holden supporter could say would change the course of events.

Ellis was nominated by William Lander of Lincoln County in a much briefer speech. As the *Standard* reported it: "Mr. L. would attempt no eulogy—Judge Ellis needed none. His Democracy was well-known from his infancy—(loud cheering)—none was better known in the State. (Continued cheering, during which Mr. L. resumed his seat.)"[26]

A ballot was taken on these two names, with Ellis receiving 25,051 votes from 40 counties and Holden getting 21,594 from 27. The votes in the Greene, Onslow, and Yadkin delegations were tied. Green and Onslow diverted their ballots to favorite-son types, and Yadkin at first did not vote. After the roll call, however, Yadkin received permission to record her vote for Ellis, and he was thereupon declared the nominee with a majority of 2,254 of all the ballots cast.

Holden men hastened to show a spirit of magnanimity and

John W. Ellis, governor of North Carolina 1859–1861

devotion to the party. M. A. Bledsoe claimed the privilege of moving that the nomination be made unanimous. Dickson, who had cast more votes against Ellis than any other delegate, pledged the mountain district to deliver as great a majority as was ever given a Democratic candidate.

That some things not told in this account occurred at the convention was more than hinted at by various papers, but none of them said specifically what happened. One persistent story, surviving today, tells of a Western delegate rushing to the convention with a pocketful of proxy votes that he cast to defeat Holden. The vote on the two-thirds rule gave rise to a version of this story that Dr. J. G. deRoulhac Hamilton told in an article in the *Charlotte Observer*, May 3, 1908, calling it a "well authenticated tradition." This was that the delegates had polled themselves on their stand on this question and "it became evident that all depended upon the way 'Dick' Reeves of Surry County cast the proxies that he held. Reeves was detained by high water and had to swim several streams before he finally reached Charlotte. There was intense excitement while his coming was awaited." Then Reeves voted for tabling the motion, according to the story, and Holden never forgave him, believing that this vote defeated him.

The grounds for this story are not evident in the actual convention proceedings. R. E. Reeves and J. E. Reeves, the two delegates from Surry, voted against tabling and supported Holden in the nominating ballot. R. E. Reeves, at least, must have reached the convention early, without swimming, for he was called upon for a speech at the evening session of the first day, whereas the contest over the two-thirds rule did not come until the second day. Nor is Reeves listed as voting any proxies.

Samuel A'Court Ashe, in his *History of North Carolina*, gives a less specific version of apparently the same story: "One delegate from beyond the mountains brought down in his pocket many proxies, and it was his vote that nominated Ellis."[27] Whitaker, the Raleigh editor who was present at the convention and should have remembered more clearly, wrote fifty years later that a western delegation cast the proxy votes of nineteen counties to defeat Holden.[28]

Probably this curious story of western proxies grew out of the competition for Rutherford's votes and became altered and misrepresented with various retellings. It is a fact, however, that Rutherford's votes given to Holden on any ballot would not have changed the results, though they would have made a difference of 350 in the two-thirds rule contest and a difference of only 1,316 in the nomination vote.

Something, however, must have occurred, at or in connection with the convention, which was not told by the reporters. Holden's supporters left Charlotte not only disappointed, but angry. At a meeting in Raleigh the next night, Houston said that "Mr. Holden's friends had not a fair fight there. There is no doubt but that a squabble had been allayed by them, but . . . [addressing Holden, who presided] it was by laying you, sir, in the shade."[29] W. A. Allen, also of Duplin, spoke of "threatened difficulties at the Convention, and was free to confess that he had consented to a course which preserved the harmony of the party, but which had also sacrificed his friend."[30]

Two years later Holden, after a quarrel with Ellis, said the latter had obtained the nomination "by resort to means which would be considered unfair even by New York politicians."[31] What these "means" were he did not explain. It would appear that they could not have concerned proxies, despite the interesting stories. Three other, more plausible possibilities suggest themselves from allusions in the newspapers.

The first of these possibilities, as stated by Syme in the *Register*, was that Holden was defeated "by primary meetings, packed by Lawyers and Renegade Whigs, who turned up their aristocratic noses at the idea of making a Governor of one who owed his claims to his own talents, exertions and services. These packed meetings packed the Convention."[32] The proceedings were almost preordained by the time the delegates met in Charlotte, and there is no doubt that the hall itself was packed with Ellis men. Of the 477 delegates, 335 represented counties that had voted for Ellis, while there were only 131 delegates from Holden counties. Syme also pointed out that Holden at times had antagonized lawyers by his attitude toward the profession, which he had given up to become an editor, and he asked Holden if there was not a "small modicum of *retributive justice*" in the lawyers' position toward him.

Did he not know that lawyers get up nearly all the primary meetings, draw their resolutions, and advocate them on the stump more than all other classes together? ... We have heard a distinguished Democratic lawyer ... say, that Mr. Holden had strangely miscalculated their power, and shown less discretion on that score than any other; and that he would find it to be so at the Charlotte Convention.[33]

Possibly another "means" used was pressure upon uninstructed delegations, during the first-night canvass, to support Ellis and to agree to vote the next day against both the two-thirds rule and Holden. The *Greensborough Patriot* wrote that "by a coalition of the renegades and the aristocracy, Mr. Holden was tricked and caucused out of the nomination."[34]

A third possibility is that the "means" was the refusal of the Ellis men, once they saw that they had a majority of the votes, to adopt the two-thirds rule, despite precedent for it. This was suggested by both the *Register* and the *Fayetteville Observer*, although the *Western Democrat* said that "if the two-thirds rule had been adopted we have no doubt the same gentlemen would have received the nomination that did receive it."[35] But Holden floor managers evidently thought otherwise and were convinced that adoption of the rule would have given their candidate a chance.

Any "means" such as these, which no doubt were used, must

have made Holden all the angrier, because, at the time, a majority of Democratic voters apparently were for him; in a primary, he probably would have won. The *Patriot* said that "two-thirds of the masses of the party" were for Holden,[36] and Syme repeatedly had said that the "unwashed multitude," representing a "large majority" of the Democratic Party, wanted Holden.[37] In this situation (and he indicated that he thought it existed), Holden surely must have felt that not only he, but also the common people, for whom he often expressed admiration and solicitude, had been tricked by a handful of politicians.

In view of this testimony that the larger portion of the Democratic masses favored him and in view of his long party service and leadership, the question arises not only as to *how*, but *why* Holden was denied the nomination. One element was the animosity of former Whigs. Houston told the Wake Democrats that the most evident opposition to Holden came from "recent converts to Democracy—an opposition which resulted in 'snowing under' the Champion of Democracy in North Carolina."[38] It was a plausible assumption; former Whigs could hardly be expected to show enthusiasm for the man who had broken their party. The *Wilmington Journal* denied this and thought a glance over the vote would show that counties which until recently had been Whig were about equally divided between the two candidates,[39] an argument that might not mean much if the conventions in these counties were packed by the turncoats and the "aristocrats."

Another consideration was the general prejudice that seems to exist, especially among politicians, against an editor's seeking office. "The history of his life," Josephus Daniels wrote in an obituary on Holden, "is in many ways the history of every editor who has made his paper second to his political ambitions."[40] This may not be hard to see today, but in 1858 the circumstance was not so evident. No editor in North Carolina had sought high office; the outstanding national example of Horace Greeley came a decade later. Holden in 1858 did not actually make his paper subordinate to his political ambition, except as he sought indirectly to use the reputation and influence he had gained as an editor as stepping-stones to office. This destroyed the picture that he had helped draw of himself, and that politicians had come to have of editors, as self-sacrificing party wheelhorses. As an editor, Holden supposedly had been performing disinterested labors for the party, looking selflessly after the general welfare. As a candidate, he appeared to be self-serving, working for himself rather than for the party. Politicians who had used him, according to the *Register*, "as the ladder up which Democratic aspirants climb,"[41] and who had rejoiced for themselves that he exerted so much influence with people, were fearful of permitting him to combine the power of the pen with the power of office.

Finally, in this complicated equation, there was an overriding factor with a purely social basis. Too much was said both before and after the convention to ignore this point, and there is an ineradicable suspicion that it was much bruited in the back rooms in Charlotte. To specify, it might be pertinent at this juncture to cite comments made by Duncan McRae in Raleigh several years later, when Holden was again running for governor. McRae purported to be speaking of Andrew Johnson, born out of wedlock, but for *Johnson* his audience could easily substitute *Holden*.

Andrew Johnson was born and reared in this city—or rather its obscure suburbs—and some of our inhabitants remember him as a low-down blackguard, without character, save for viciousness and depravity. His antecedents, were also of the vilest and most degraded caste. . . . In examining the claims of any man to confidence and station, we cannot overlook *pedigree*. . . . We have seen many instances of what is called men rising by their own talents, or virtues, or merits, to places supposed to be above their plane of birth; but it will generally be found in these cases, that the men really had the benefits of pedigree, although obscure and dimmed; and they certainly had good mothers, and otherwise inherited good blood.[42]

By his middle name, William Woods Holden, son of the unwed and unpedigreed Priscilla Woods, conceded his illegitimacy. And the aristocrats of North Carolina, both Whig and Democratic, were determined that the blot on the Hillsborough escutcheon should not befoul the patrician air of the Governor's Mansion in Raleigh. That, it would seem in Holden's case, was the ultimate stroke.

Anyone expecting Holden to show outward bitterness watched in vain; he did not give opponents such satisfaction. Knowing that the next issue of the *Standard* would be perused with particular interest and curiosity, he wrote for the paper an editorial and a personal statement to the Democratic Party. Both praised the nominee and appealed to Democrats to forget the passions of the convention and to "spring with alacrity" to the support of Ellis. "John W. Ellis is a tried Democrat, an able statesman, and deserving man,"[43] he wrote.

Yet the blow hurt. At the Wake County ratification meeting the night following the convention, Holden made a speech praising the platform and the nominee and added a few thoughts about his own feelings: "Next . . . to the loss of the hope of heaven and the beatitudes of the eternal hereafter, next to the loss of 'wife, children and friends,' is that feeling of desolation and loneliness which comes over the bosom of the faithful public servant, when he thinks he has reason to conclude that the people have abandoned him without cause." He went on: "But . . . the people have not abandoned me . . . and so help me God, I will never abandon the people, nor their cause, nor the Democratic party in the country."[44]

His disappointment must have rankled all the more because the underlying reason was personal, not political. The man who had led the Democratic Party out of the doldrums, who had created opportunities for many politicians, who had fought to give the state free suffrage, a better school system, and more internal improvements was not considered good enough personally to be the governor of the state. This was the sort of thing that he might try to forgive at the time, but he would never forget it. The Whig *Carolina Watchman*, published in Ellis's hometown, said the nomination "may be regarded as unfortunate to the State, by the loss of a competent Judge; and to the party, by putting in motion first a feeling, then a prejudice, and then a ball, which, in the end, will probably crush more than aristocratic assumption."[45]

J. J. Bruner, the editor, proved himself something of a prophet.

The Charlotte convention marks the turning point in Holden's life. He determined to give Ellis cordial support, and he went through the motions insofar as they were needed. But the old exuberance, the dauntless optimism of the *Standard*, the expansive buoyancy born of confidence were to some extent gone. Holden had been made too acutely aware of the circumstances of his obscure birth and had been reminded too sharply that he was the craftsman among gentry for the memory of the experience to be effaced. And before time might have salved some of the hurt, he was dealt another crippling blow.

While the Democratic Party appeared calm as it faced Duncan McRae, the waters underneath were roiled with anger, at first more on the part of Holden's friends than of the editor. Wake County held the first meeting ratifying the nomination, but at the same time Houston promised that "the day is not far distant . . . when the old-time Democrats will proclaim a faithful servant's reward to the world."[46] Syme at once interpreted this to mean that Holden's friends were resolved to make him United States senator when the legislature voted in the fall.[47] This would shelve Bragg, who coveted the position.

Except for this one hint in the *Standard*'s account of the meeting, the party's papers kept its inner discord submerged during the ensuing gubernatorial campaign. Even Ellis papers were surprised, several being moved to comment on the restraint of the Holden camp. In the August election, as anticipated, Ellis came out on top, receiving a majority of 16,247 in a total vote of 96,177. In the General Assembly the Democrats won a majority of 14 in the Senate and 44 in the House.

With those formalities out of the way, however, the smoldering animosities kindled at Charlotte began to work into the open. The time had been reached, against which Holden and other editors had warned, when the party was threatened from within by the personal ambitions of some of its members. The imbroglio soon reached that point when, as Hale said, Holden, because of "unfriendly relations which exist between himself and the Governor, and other dignitaries"[48] felt it necessary to resign as a member of the literary board, on which he had served for seven years. At the same time rumors began to circulate about plans for the establishment of a new Democratic paper in Raleigh. Such a move could hurt Holden principally by denying him the public printing contract; otherwise he was too firmly entrenched to worry about it.

The flames were fanned in October with the publication in the *Warrenton News* of two articles criticizing the Bragg administration for giving state and federal appointments to recent converts from the Whig ranks. The editor of the *News* had been employed at one time as clerk in the *Standard* office, and the conclusion was drawn that he had been influenced to write the articles, even if Holden himself had not written them.

As this and other charges were bandied about, Holden seized upon them to make both a categorical denial of all accusations and a scathing personal statement. A portion of the latter was highly significant:

There are a few persons in North Carolina professing to be Democrats, who are really aristocrats, and who will never forgive me for consenting to the use of my name for Governor. Of course, these persons have their dependents who echo what they say. If I were to say, what I do not choose to say, that in no event would I accept a Senatorship, *they* would be gratified, and charges like these to which I am now replying would no longer be made. It was my lot to be born in humble circumstances, to an inheritance of ignorance and poverty, and to be brought up to a mechanical trade; and there are some who would "punish" me on account of my origin, and because I have had the energy and the ambition to struggle upwards in life, who, if they had been born in the condition in which I was, would have been there yet. Proud towards the proud, and humble among the humble, I have never cringed to a rich man because he was rich, nor slighted a poor man because he was poor. Nor have I played the demagogue, seeking to array one class of society against another. I have been the friend both as an Editor and as a man, of *all* interests and *all* classes in North Carolina, from the College in which those who have means are educated, to the common schools, where the "children of the people" are cared for and educated by the State. Unpretending as was my origin, I thank God that He has given me disposition to love my State, and my whole State with the affection of a son, and though others have served her with far more efficiency and ability than I have, yet none have laid upon her altar the offerings of a more loyal or patriotic heart.[49]

This statement, particularly the recrimination against "aristocrats," attracted general attention. Whig and Democratic editors looked at it entirely differently. In the *Wilmington Journal* James Fulton, speaking for the Democrats allied with the administration, regretted that "a gentleman of Mr. Holden's large experience and clear sense should have felt himself called upon to furnish his and our enemies with a text from which to read hypocritical homilies, and over which they shed crocodile tears,"[50] especially editor Fulton's archenemy on the Cape Fear, Fayetteville's Hale, and the opposition organ at the capital.

Whether the editorial comments were hypocritical or not, both Hale and Raleigh's Syme made them. It is doubtful that hypocrisy underlay Hale's, at any rate, for he was not given to double-talk. He called the statement of Holden "but the distant muttering of the storm," and went on: "It is hinted that there is a powerful combination of the *aristocratic Democrats* who are against Holden, and that we are on the eve of stirring events in the camp of the party. Holden was the ladder upon which most of them did their climbing. They fear he has elevated his own head too high, and are now endeavoring to kick him down."[51] In his next issue Hale indicated that his sympathy for Holden was sincere: "There is a class of people . . . for whom we have a thorough contempt. It is the class which is everlastingly pluming itself upon that sort of love (for the 'common people'), and yet in manners and habits is more aristocratic than a British Lord. The leading men of the Democratic Party are found in this class; and they are of that class who now turn up their aristocratic noses at W. W. Holden."[52]

Syme's remarks were more pungent and perhaps more revealing: "That these men will again and again thwart Mr. Holden's laudable ambition, we do not in the least doubt, and if he submits to it, he will show more of heavenly grace than we can lay claim to, for if we were in his place, and could wield the power he has, we would put our heel on the political necks of those 'aristocratic Democrats,' and grind them to powder."[53]

As the time approached for the legislature to meet, with two United States senators to elect, Holden moved to forestall party rupture by urging that all "unite in caucus, and adhere with an iron will to caucus action and party organization." He said the political opposition was hoping to exploit division within Democratic ranks and was already exulting at the prospect of disunited councils.[54]

The *Fayetteville Observer* thought at one time that Holden and former Governor Reid would receive the senatorial honors; but later, when the legislature met, it predicted that the reelection of Thomas L. Clingman was certain and that Bragg, with few friends in the State Senate, would form an alliance with

Clingman that would give him an advantage over all other candidates. Factional lines of "Holden and anti-Holden" were drawn, the *Observer* said, and "the parties are so evenly balanced that a Holden candidate for Clerk of the House [Col. J. W. Alspaugh of the *Winston Sentinel*] was beaten by only one vote in caucus."[55]

The *Greensborough Patriot* also reported that the "aristocracy, together with the Salisbury branch of the Raleigh Clique, are decidedly in the ascendant, and such old line plebeian Democrats as Gov. Reid, Messrs. Holden and Alspaugh, are doomed to walk the plank."[56] On the day the awaited caucus was held, the *Wilmington Journal* expressed regret that "the bitterness of feeling which unfortunately exists between certain persons and their friends, grows in intensity."[57]

Finally "the great agony" was over. The caucus decided to reelect Clingman and to give Bragg the junior senatorship. Bragg was chosen on the second ballot. A correspondent for the *Western Democrat* reported that on the first count Bragg polled fifty-five votes, with twenty-six each for Holden and Reid and four for minor candidates. The second time around Bragg climbed to an insurmountable sixty-two, and his nomination was made unanimous.

Holden accepted the result more calmly than other editors, especially those of Whig papers. He wrote a bland editorial praising both senators and urging that past rivalries be forgotten "in the name of the party which is so dear to us all."[58]

Other editors were less polite. Hale wrote:

And so Gov. Reid and W. W. Holden, who revolutionized the politics of the State and placed the Democrats in power, have been whistled down the wind, and a new convert, Mr. Clingman, and an old Democrat, Gov. Bragg, who only came to divide the spoils after the battle was over, have received the highest honors of the State! . . . So far as we concerned we are neither disappointed nor grieved at the election of Mr. Clingman. . . . But as to Gov. Bragg, we are disappointed. We regard him as inferior in all respects to Mr. Holden, and especially are we amazed that the party overlooked, in his favor, Mr. Holden's talents and services.[59]

The *Greensborough Patriot* saw in the election another angle, viewing the defeat of Holden especially as tightening the power of "a certain aristocratic clique among the democracy, who, like the Kings of Europe, have come to regard the honors and spoils of office as belonging to them by divine right." It continued:

The late Senatorial election was not a mere ordinary contest of political parties; it was more of a struggle between classes, and as such, it is regarded by the aristocrats as a great triumph, and as a great step towards making, in effect, the offices of honor and profit as hereditary in certain families. . . . And unless the people rise up in their majesty and overthrow this democracy which is fastening upon them, an aristocracy who will soon claim the divine right of Kings, we may soon bid adieu to all our liberties. It is well known that the people desired Mr. Holden for Governor, but the aristocracy said no. It is also well known that failing in getting their choice for governor, the people desired Mr. Holden for U. S. Senator, but again the aristocracy said no.[60]

The election, no matter how philosophically Holden might try to take it, naturally widened the gulf between him and the upper crust party leaders. His rejection had begun a quarrel which, though not always carried on as class warfare, was always with the same general class, and was to be unremitting until one or the other should be crushed. Holden himself grew noticeably more sensitive after 1858, more suspicious of and at odds with his known antagonists, more reliant on his good relationship with the common people. At the same time the number and malice of the attacks on him increased, so that, emboldened by their successes in Charlotte and Raleigh, his enemies were seen by even the conservative Hale as determined to utterly destroy him.

It should be noted here that Holden's contemporaries did not themselves, at least publicly, base their opposition to him on social grounds, except in 1858. Only one time, in all the years he was before the public, did a paper so much as refer to the circumstances of his birth, and that was a casual reference during the Civil War. It may be significant, however, that it was chiefly uninvolved Whig bystanders who voiced the charges of social discrimination. Before the Charlotte convention, caste prejudice had little occasion to show itself. Any dislike for Holden was unorganized and appeared to be based principally on fear or antipathy on the part of individuals; since he asked for no favors for himself, there was no cause for this fear to coalesce into group hatred.

Then, as Hale said, "Mr. Holden committed the unpardonable sin of aspiring to be Governor or Senator,"[61] and at once an irreparable schism was created. North Carolina politicians never forgave Holden for what they did to him in 1858; and although Holden, the Hillsborough outcast, suffered in silence at the time, a fury was born in him that was to effect the whole party and the entire state.

SEVEN

AFTER THE political disappointments of 1858 Holden immersed himself in the management of the *Standard*, as if that labor were the only kind he had ever aspired to. He was again elected public printer, winning over Syme; during the legislative session, he issued the paper thrice weekly; at the same time, the *Standard* again put on a "new dress." Wilmington's Fulton complimented it as looking "remarkably well; but in truth the *Standard* is always so well printed that even new type fails to make any great change in its appearance."[1]

This evidence of the *Standard*'s business success came in a year that brought financial difficulties to several of its contemporaries, including Loring's *Wilmington Commercial* and the *Salisbury Herald*, which was sold at public auction for $796, the highest bid.[2]

In Holden's editorship, however, there were minor lapses that suggest that his mind was not entirely on his work. In the fall of 1858 he printed the news of a wedding in Johnston County which had not, in fact, taken place.[3] A few months later, he published a news item received from a correspondent about the suicide of "Mr. Ringwood Linster, a respectable and influential citizen of Olin, Iredell County."[4] "Mr. Linster" turned out to be a dog. Today's corporate giants, caught in such a hoax, would merely print a buried correction and hope the matter would soon be forgotten. Holden, however, made an issue of it, saying that if he could learn the identity of the jokester he would "blazon his name to the public as the synonym of malice and meanness."[5] In no subsequent issue of the *Standard*, though, did the blazoning occur.

But these were minor diversions. Events of great scope were engulfing the nation, and North Carolina was to be caught up in the march toward war as the slavery and state's rights issues were vigorously debated in the press and in party councils. Nearer home there were important state questions, some related to the national furor and some not. And Holden was wary of a development that might concern him directly.

Raleigh correspondents, especially those of Whig papers, were busily reporting to their home offices rumors of the impending establishment in the state capital of a new Democratic newspaper. With the arrival in the city of B. M. DeWitt, formerly of the *Richmond Examiner*, there was speculation that he might be the editor-elect,[6] but these conjectures proved to be false.

Holden tangled with a competitive *Live Giraffe* in Raleigh, but it expired before a real newspaper war could get under way. With its bones, however, foes of Holden, including R. H. Whitaker and Edward Cantwell, proposed to start a new paper with sufficient backing to challenge the *Standard*'s leadership. Both before and after it was begun, Holden resisted the publication of the new journal because he believed its purpose was to broadcast the views of a small group of politicians. The development of plans for the paper brought forth a statement in the *Standard*, the latter part of which became famous: "It will not do to denounce the *Standard*, and endeavor to supplant it with some other paper designed to express the views and advance the interests of a certain few ... for the *Standard* speaks the sentiments, and has the confidence of the Democratic masses of the State, and *because* of this, it can kill and make alive."[7]

Except in his own case, that had been true for some years.

The starting of the *Democratic Press* was the first real invasion of Holden's journalistic domain since he had become editor, the first questioning of his right to speak for the Democrats, and he was probably more irritated by it than he would have cared to admit. He dubbed the paper the Firebrand and assailed it with a seriousness that seemed hardly warranted. The quarrel soon became an embarrassment to the party, and Holden was discreetly warned by good Democrats that the bickering was a political disservice. Notwithstanding, this lately sprung rival must have seemed to Holden a plot of the "aristocrats" against him, a challenge in his own field, and it was not to be tolerated.

As suggested, however, there were other matters to occupy the *Standard*'s attention in the first half of 1859. For one thing, the Know Nothing members of the legislature held a caucus on February 5 and decided to readopt the Whig name.[8] Under this label they were able in the August elections to capture four of the eight congressional districts, whereas two years before they had won only two.

Nor was the slavery question to be avoided in view of the "unsatisfactory"[9] turnabout of Stephen A. Douglas on squatter sovereignty (local determination of the status of slavery), the increased abolitionist agitation in the North, and the proposal from the cotton states to reopen the African slave trade, which had been illegal since 1808. On this last issue Holden thought the people of the South were "nearly unanimously opposed" to any such revival, not because they regarded it as sinful, but for the economic and political reasons that they already had enough slaves and that they believed any attempt to bring in more would produce dangerous agitation.[10] Holden looked for relative harmony at the Democratic National Convention in Charleston the next year, with little demand for the slave trade, and with the South insisting upon nothing more "on the subject of slavery in the Territories than the resolutions of the last Convention and an endorsement of the Dred Scott decision" (which held that Congress had no authority to prohibit slavery in the territories).[11]

Throughout the first nine months of 1859, despite the great national stirrings, there was "comparative quiet" in North Carolina regarding slavery until John Brown startled the country with his raid at Harpers Ferry.

In June President Buchanan visited the state to attend commencement at the University of North Carolina. Holden was a member of the welcoming committee to meet him at Weldon and to conduct him to Raleigh, where he spent the night. The *Standard* was copious in its coverage of the visit, which was an event in the life of the state. "It is not often we catch a live President in North Carolina," the paper said, "and when we do whose business is it but ours—we North-Carolinians? Our printers never saw one before—and we have not seen much of our printers since."[12]

In his address at Chapel Hill and in shorter talks at Weldon and Durham's Station, Buchanan made strong pleas for the preservation of the Union at almost any cost and pointed out the service that North Carolina might render toward that end. "As long as the people of North Carolina entertain the principles and the feelings for which they have been remarkable," the president said at Weldon, "as long as they entertain that love of country which has always distinguished them, as long as they entertain that conservative spirit which binds together the different States of the Union, so long will they be glorious and useful to their fellow citizens of other States."[13] Buchanan's appeals appeared to impress his audiences, and they may have had something to do with Holden's course in the following year. That, however, is only supposition.

North Carolina editors were mesmerized by what Holden called the "practical illustration of abolitionist doctrines"[14] in the John Brown raid, and they reprinted column after column about the affair from the papers of Washington and other cities. Whig and Democratic papers forgot party lines in the first volleys of protest, but many soon remembered them in attempts to analyze the circumstances attending the raid. The *Standard* pointed out with satisfaction that *"not a single* Democrat, in any quarter, has yet been implicated, in the slightest manner,"[15] but the *Greensborough Patriot* charged that Southern Democrats, and especially the *Standard* in North Carolina, were at least indirectly responsible because of their "insane and mischievous efforts . . . to make the impression that Southern Whigs and Southern oppositionists, are at heart Abolitionists, and ready to join in with the Northern fanatics and incendiaries."[16]

As the ramifications of the plot came to light, showing the support that had been given the raiders and the sympathy bestowed upon them in the North, the papers reflected the excitement and concern of the state over a possible recurrence of such an outbreak. The *Standard* thought that the privileges given slaves by owners might well be curtailed to forestall insurrection[17] and that the public ought to be especially vigilant in watching all strangers. Northerners were traveling through the South "professing to be engaged in business of various kinds, whom it would be well enough to *watch*. If they talk against slavery, or if they even apologize for [Senator William H.] Seward and his infamous doctrines, give them notice to leave, and *make* them leave. It was the Seward doctrine [of abolition] that led to the outrage of Harper's Ferry."[18] At the same time, Holden recorded an incident which showed that the state capital was setting a proper example for other communities. It concerned a New York man, "of the name of Sanburn, whose business appeared to be that of selling Caloric Engines. His conversation on the subject of slavery was not what it should have been; whereupon our Mayor had a talk with him, and advised him to leave. He did so on the next morning's train."[19]

The John Brown incident furnished the *Standard* with the opportunity to be the first North Carolina newspaper to carry a special report of a nonpolitical news story. Frank Wilson went to Virginia, at his own expense and by his own wish to witness the execution of the raiders on December 2 and rushed back to Raleigh to write a breathless account for the next issue of the paper. It contained more detail about his travels than about the news event, by today's standards an inadequate job of reporting. But as his last line he carried an apologia for not doing "full justice" to his excursion: "Take into consideration that I have slept only one night in six, then blame me if you can."[20]

The Harpers Ferry affair made the press of North Carolina almost a unit in demanding military preparation by the state for any emergency or crisis that might arise, such as another insurrection or the election of a "black," i.e. anti-Southern, Republican president of the Seward ilk. "Even if the black Republicans should be defeated in 1860," the *Standard* argued, "there is no certainty that they will not be [victorious] in 1864 or in 1868. . . . Let North Carolina be ready. Let her be put on a war footing at the next session of the Legislature."[21] Holden said that after the Harpers Ferry outrage and other aggressions, "the people of the South will not submit to black Republican rule," and he thought that "ninety-nine hundredths of those who read this article will agree with us."[22]

The *Wilmington Journal* and the *Register* wanted a well-planned volunteer system begun at once, with attention given to obtaining or manufacturing ammunition and arms for storage in large arsenals. These two papers joined the *Fayetteville Observer* in urging that the South begin striving at once for economic independence from the North, both to punish that section and to build up Southern manufactures. "This will be a constitutional war upon the North," the *Register* said, "this will be fighting the North within the Union, and by so fighting her, we shall damage her as effectually in a commercial point of view, as we could hurt her physically by using Sharpe's rifles against her."[23]

There was no doubt that North Carolina was stirred more deeply than at any time since the passage of the slavery compromise measures nearly a decade earlier. "The 'irrepressible conflict' [Seward's term] *has* come," the *Wilmington Journal* said.[24] One of the most disturbing factors in the situation was the apparent connection of the black Republicans with John Brown. The editors shuddered to think what would happen if these came into power in 1860, as it was believed they had a chance to do, and Holden was one of the leading shudderers.

"We call the attention of the North," he wrote belligerently,

to the fact that our young men are arming, and that our old men are prepared to aid them with means and advice, and, if necessary, with arms also in their hands "in the imminent deadly breach." The whole north could no more conquer North-Carolina than North-Carolina could conquer New York. We are determined to have and enjoy *all* our rights at all hazards, happen what may. Let Seward and his followers look to it. North-Carolinians will never be his slaves or the slaves of any other man. If he thinks he can subjugate us, let him try it if he should ever get the power.[25]

Three days later he spoke in absolute terms: "We will be ready, in the event of Seward's election, to dissolve every tie that binds North-Carolina to the Union."[26]

Early in March the State Democratic Convention met in Raleigh to plan the gubernatorial campaign. There was no doubt that Governor Ellis would be renominated unanimously, and the convention, lacking the prospect of a scrap like the one two years earlier, was a smaller one. Efforts apparently were made to heal some of the wounds of 1858 by electing former Governor Reid president, and Holden, W. W. Avery, and William S. Ashe were chosen the state's delegates-at-large to the Democratic National Convention scheduled for Charleston in April.

Much of the party platform was devoted to expressing the Democratic stand on slavery and state's rights, declaring that "while we make no threat, we solemnly declare that the people of this State will resist aggression upon their Constitutional rights whenever the emergency arises."[27] The John Brown raid was called the "legitimate result of the principles and teachings of the black Republican party," and it was asserted that "the triumph of that party would be followed by continued bloody raids of like character upon all the border Southern states." No preference was expressed as to a presidential candidate.

One thorny issue, on which Holden, over a period of many months, had uncharacteristically waffled, was a hotly debated proposal for the *ad valorem* taxation of all Negro slaves as personal property—strictly a revenue measure, but one touching peripherally on the propriety of slaveholding. Previously slaves under twelve and over fifty had been left off the tax books, and those untaxed were estimated to have an assessable value of $50 million. The Democrats, traditional defenders of slavery interests, declared the extension of *ad valorem* taxation "premature, impolitic, dangerous and unjust," but added that it was the duty of the legislature to impose equitable taxation within the limits of the constitution.[28]

It would be extremely interesting to know whether anything took place at this convention that caused Holden to change his point of view on the national situation and North Carolina's duty in it, or whether something happened in the succeeding two months to provide him new insight into the meaning of the drift of events. Whatever the case, by the spring of 1860 he had written his last militant defense of the prerogative of slaveholders, signalling a whole new line in his editorial expression and, no doubt, in his personal thinking. Now, while the war clouds, which he had foretold and had had some part in summoning, were gathering, he appeared to be more absorbed in *ad valorem* taxation and the state campaign than in the national crisis. The reason for this is not specifically evident in the files of the *Standard* and is left largely to conjecture in the private papers available for the period.

The Whigs had met in February and had nominated John Pool of Pasquotank County for governor on a platform advocating *ad valorem* taxation of all property, including slaves. Led by the *Greensborough Patriot*, the Whig press tried valiantly to make the taxation issue as popular in 1860 as free suffrage had been earlier for the Democrats. Holden, unable to denounce such taxation as enthusiastically as other Democratic editors, nevertheless pointed out that it would penalize the poor by taxing for the first time such property as horses, cows, pigs, and household goods.[29] He probably did not render aid to his party in 1860 as he had in previous years, but his arguments may have held in line many Democrats and independent voters who wavered on the issue and who normally looked to him for direction.

Holden interrupted his labors in April to attend the Democratic convention in Charleston, and it was there for the first time that he came into direct contact with "the doctrine of secession as practiced by the cotton states."[30] Although until that time he had given every indication of being a state's rights extremist, he says in his *Memoirs*, and only there, that he was "shocked and disturbed" at the extent of the determination to disrupt the Union. After he had heard the arguments of fanatic Southerners and had even heard cries of "Damn the star-spangled banner," he made up his mind that he "would stand by the American Union at all hazards, and to the last extremity."[31]

It was a resolve that was to play havoc with his life and with North Carolina politics.

The North Carolina delegation, made up largely of conservative men, apparently played an important part in attempting to maintain harmony at the convention, although one member, W. W. Avery, as chairman of the platform committee, submitted and defended the majority report of his group, which reflected the more radical proslavery sentiment. Bedford Brown and William S. Ashe both made forceful talks when the convention was considering a clause in a majority report that called for referring the question of slavery in the territories to the Supreme Court. When the minority report was adopted without this clause and the Alabama delegates withdrew, to be followed by other cotton states delegates, the North Carolina group sat firm.

Holden later told *Standard* readers:

If North-Carolina had gone out, or even wavered, the middle states of Virginia, Tennessee, Maryland, Kentucky, and Missouri would have followed her example, and only the non-slaveholding States would have remained. This would have rendered the Charleston Convention a sectional body, without authority over a national Convention to adjourn. The party would, therefore, have gone to pieces at Charleston, having no common basis on which to re-construct or re-unite its disjointed parts. By her firm stand, therefore on this occasion, North-Carolina saved the party, and, to that extent, contributed to save the Union.[32]

The Raleigh editor spoke twice in the convention, according to the *New York Times*, which gave long accounts of the sessions. Once, while the cotton states were withdrawing and there was apprehension that border states might follow, he arose to say that he "saw nothing that should warrant the Southern delegates in seceding. He was opposed to 'Squatter Sovereignty,' but was willing to take the Cincinnati platform with an endorsement of the Dred Scott decision. This was sufficient for him."[33] The second time he spoke was after the walkout, at the session of May 1. A vote by states was demanded on a motion to adjourn. The remnant Georgia delegation gave the full vote of the state; the vote was objected to, and the presiding officer ruled that the delegation could not cast the vote. Holden "appealed from the decision of the Chair, and contended that they were carrying out the instructions of the state, while the seceders and bolsters were not. They were sent here to vote and not to bolt. If the remainder of the delegation were not here, it was not the fault of those that remain."[34] The decision of the chair was sustained by a vote of 148 to 100, however, and the 9 remaining

Georgia delegates withdrew. The convention adjourned May 3, after fifty-seven ballots, without nominating a presidential candidate. It was scheduled to resume in Baltimore on June 18.

The course of the North Carolina delegation received general approval in Democratic papers and in the party. The one exception among the papers was the *Charlotte Bulletin*, which Holden described as being "in some respects an unreliable, guerrilla print."[35] It criticized the delegates for not going out with South Carolina. Soon after he returned, Holden attended a meeting of Wake County Democrats called to nominate candidates for the legislature and was asked to report on the convention and to give his view of the situation. He offered resolutions declaring the belief of the Democrats that Douglas was the strongest man in the party and the only one who could defeat the Republicans nationally. The resolutions, which pledged the support of the county to Douglas, were unanimously adopted. The *Standard* reported that "every allusion to the name and services of Judge Douglas was greeted with enthusiastic applause,"[36] although at Charleston Douglas had received only one vote from North Carolina in the entire fifty-seven ballots. The *Charlotte Bulletin* attacked the participants in this meeting as allies of Northern Democrats and opponents of Southern rights.[37] Holden denied this accusation stoutly, defending Wake Democrats as true friends of the South, but "they are neither submissionists nor disunionists. They will have confidence in the Northern Democracy, and they are not afraid to trust Judge Douglas."[38]

At this county meeting Holden defied his party by nominating M. A. Bledsoe, an "*ad valorem*" advocate, for reelection to the state Senate. Bledsoe was turned down 20 to 1, and George W. Thompson received the nomination. Bledsoe, however, immediately offered himself as an independent candidate, and in the election he beat the party regular by 146 votes. His victory was another political sin held against Holden, the charge being made that the *Standard* could have defeated Bledsoe if the editor had turned his hand to it.[39]

The state campaign was now in full swing, with Ellis and the Democrats doing rousing battle over *ad valorem* tax issue. Holden appealed to readers not to lose sight of larger, more important matters. The great issue, he said, was "not slavery in the territories—not squatter sovereignty—not *ad valorem* taxation, but whether the Union is to continue in peace and harmony, without convulsions and bloodshed, or whether it is to rock to its foundations and be broken up by abolition rule."[40]

Not yet, however, could Holden go all the way in preserving the Union. For one thing, he would not have the South submit to the inauguration of the "author of the doctrine of the 'irrepressible conflict,' "[41] although he believed that the platform adopted by the Republicans was surprisingly moderate, not differing materially "from those adopted ten or twelve years ago by the old Whig Party in the non-slaveholding states."[42] One result of the success of Abraham Lincoln, he thought, would be that the Supreme Court would be changed and its power used against the South; though

if the people of the South are true to themselves and their posterity, they will never be troubled by the decisions of black Republican judges. But if they submit to the inauguration and rule of black Republicans, they will bind themselves likewise to the decision of an abolition court. It will be too late to resist the court, after having submitted to the President."[43]

At the time he left for Baltimore for the resumption of the Democratic Convention, Holden believed that the necessity for drastic action might be averted, that the enemy could be met and conquered at the polls with the South supporting a candidate behind whom the entire party could unite to crush Lincoln. Above all, there must be no more bolts and deadlocks; "let the

Baltimore Convention . . . *proceed with a stern and unfaltering step to the work before it. Let it nominate at all hazards,* and then appeal to God and the country against extremists in the North and extremists in the South."[44]

The delegates at Baltimore, however, found the situation even more trackless than at Charleston, and this time fifteen of the North Carolina representatives joined the seceders, leaving only Holden, R. P. Dick, and J. W. B. Watson to speak for the state. When the ballot for the nomination was taken, only Dick voted for Douglas, Holden and Watson declining to act. Holden said his refusal to vote was out of respect for the opinions of the fifteen seceders and because of the pending elections at home. "If we had acted or voted at all," he said, "we certainly would have voted for Stephen A. Douglas. We are now free, however, to make our own choice, not considering ourself irrevocably bound by either convention."[45] (By "either" he referred to the independent action of Southern Democrats, who had convened in Baltimore June 28 and nominated John C. Breckinridge.)

Upon his return to Raleigh Holden attempted to follow a neutral and conciliatory course, but his peacemaking role got him into trouble. He announced that for the present he would indicate no choice between the two Democratic tickets but would support "the present Electors, leaving them to cast the vote of the State as the majority of the party may decide; or we will support either Breckinridge or Douglas, as a State Convention may determine; or we will leave the Electors free to cast the vote of the State in any way so as to defeat Lincoln."[46] While awaiting the party's pleasure, however, Holden noted that five influential newspapers already had declared for Breckinridge, while Douglas had won the support of only one.[47]

Seven of the seceding delegates at Baltimore joined Holden in a recommendation that the State Democratic Executive Committee call a convention as soon as possible to establish a definitive party position. But the Breckenridge papers would listen to no such proposal and assailed the *Standard* for making it. Holden replied that he began to understand

the nature of the combination that exists, but we defy the worst that selfishness and ambition can accomplish. We will appeal to the people if necessary, against secession and disunion. . . . The truth is, a great battle is to be fought in this State sooner or later; and between *Union* and *Disunion*. Our friends will know where to find us when that battle begins. We will stand or fall by the people—we will stand or fall by a Constitutional Union.[48]

The "combination" that Holden thought he understood was an increasing disposition on the part of a powerful Democratic faction to become ultra-Southern in its views, more sympathetic toward South Carolina secessionist views. Holden set out to fight this. "In a word," he said, "no reason exists why North-Carolina should contemplate at this time a dissolution of the Union." Secession, he warned prophetically, would bring "fraternal strife, civil and servile war, murder, arson, pillage, robbery, and fire and blood through long and cruel years. . . . It would bring debt, and misrule, and oppressive taxes, to be followed, perhaps by the military rule of titled tyrants."[49] He did not yet know it, but he had defined exactly the results of the Civil War.

Holden was not long in getting the awaited mandate as to which of the candidates to support. Along with the majority of Democratic papers, nearly all the delegates to the national convention were for Breckinridge, as well as all the electors except one, a large block of the Democratic State Central Committee, Governor Ellis, and every county which at that point had held a meeting. And so, in his issue of July 18, Holden printed the names of John C. Breckinridge and his running mate, Joseph Lane, in the customary place under the masthead, accompanied by this announcement: *The Democratic people, whose voice is above all committees, conventions, and caucuses, have commanded us to raise the names of Breckinridge and Lane, and we obey.* We go, in the last resort, with our State."[50]

Meanwhile the Whigs had been making surprising gains in the state campaign. John Pool was an adroit campaigner, *ad valorem* was proving a good party issue, and the Democrats were troubled by their divisions in both national and state affairs. In the August election Ellis beat Pool 59,463 to 53,123. The governor's majority had declined by almost 10,000 compared with that of two years before. In the legislature the Democrats lost thirty-four members of the House and two members of the Senate, cutting their majority on joint ballots to twenty-two. It had been fifty-six. The Whigs were jubilant, sensing victories for the future if the indicated tide continued to run, but neither time nor tide were to work in their favor.

The Democratic situation within the state was complicated by a visit Douglas made to Raleigh for a convention of his adherents. About one hundred representatives from thirty-three counties showed up, and Douglas made a strong plea for the Union, urging them to "fight against all disunionists. Beat them for the Legislature; beat them for Congress; beat them for Governor; and teach them to love the Union at the same time that they say the Lord's prayer."[51] He said that if he were elected, he would use force to preserve the government, if that were necessary.

Holden found Douglas's address "able and interesting,"[52] but he regretted the candidate's visit, feeling that except for it a compromise between Breckinridge and Douglas supporters might have been achieved. Until election day he continued to argue that every vote for Douglas would be a boost for Lincoln.

Holden and L. O'B. Branch were the speakers at a meeting of the Breckinridge-Lane club in Raleigh on October 10, and he quoted himself as saying that

we did not think the election of Lincoln would be good cause for dissolving the Union. We added, however, without expressing any

121

opinion as to the right of a State to secede, that some State or States south of us might secede; that while we would oppose such secession, we knew of no federal road through North-Carolina over which Lincoln could send troops for the purpose of subjugating sovereign Southern States; that Lincoln might blockade the ports, and send troops by sea to ravage Charleston, or Mobile, or other Southern cities; but that, though we believed the middle States, North-Carolina included, would not secede, yet volunteers would go from those States to the aid of their Southern brethren thus assailed; and that for every thousand men Lincoln might send for his work of subjugation, the middle States would send two thousand, as volunteers, to aid their Southern brethren and to arrest Lincoln in his work of blood.[53]

Holden had come far within the year. Inch by inch, as secession had become more imminent, he had receded from his ultra-Southern views, shrinking back as disunion grew closer. At the first of the year he had had a ready answer to the question: "What are we going to do about it if a black Republican is elected?" Even in the summer he had warned the South against submitting to the inauguration of Lincoln. But now secession was no longer a rhetorical question to be discussed in the abstract or to be used as a party weapon; it loomed as a probability as Lincoln's victory appeared more and more certain. And now Holden argued that this latter event would not be sufficient cause for immediate dissolution of the Union. "If so great a calamity as his election should befall the South," Holden wrote, "it will be the part of wisdom to wait and see what he will recommend in his Inaugural, and what he will attempt to do. If he should touch the South at all vitally, the South will be able to defend its interests and its honor against all odds."[54]

Even in announcing Lincoln's election Holden maintained his equanimity, editorially counseling, "Watch and wait." His motto became the slogan of those in North Carolina who did not want to see the state leave the Union.

While awaiting definite word on Lincoln's course, the *Stan-*

dard cautioned the people against panic, especially regarding slave property, and tried to forearm them against impulses to precipitate action by explaining the reasons for its "watch and wait" position. Holden reminded his readers that the federal constitution provided checks and balances in the government whereby any branch, if it fell into the hands of bad men, might be curbed by the others; Congress could check the president, and the Supreme Court could check them both. No matter what Lincoln might propose, he said "it will be the duty of the Southern people . . . to strengthen their defences *in* the Union."[55]

The election of Lincoln accomplished what Holden had been trying for two weeks to avoid, a definite break with the Democratic administration in North Carolina. While he continued to shout his slogan of "watch and wait" with all the lustiness of the *Standard*, the slaveholding interests, toward which the administration leaned, found growing sympathy with the cotton states in their determination to resist the black Republicans, and Holden's attitude was the last of cumulative factors in their case against him. They could look back at his passive support of some Democratic candidates, at his wavering on *ad valorem* taxation, at his vacillation between Douglas and Breckinridge, at the absence in the national campaign of fire-eating Southern statements, and finally, at his calculated restraint while the cotton states were preparing to secede.

When the legislature met, some of the Democratic leaders decided to drop Holden and get an editor with views more nearly in accord with their own. Holden apparently was given a last-minute opportunity to recant his Union stand,[56] and when he refused, a caucus of party members on the first night of the session chose John Spelman, a former *Standard* employee, the party's nominee for public printer, defeating Holden by five votes; the next day Spelman, who had left Holden to become editor of the *Salisbury Banner*, was elected by the legislature. A contemporary said that the *Standard*'s opponents "demanded the decapitation of Holden, because he was known to be for the Union."[57]

The defeat for public printer was a hard blow for Holden, but he saw in it something more than punishment of him. He thought it indicated "the courses which public events are taking in the momentous crisis. A bare majority of the party has solemnly declared, by this act of proscription towards us, that no man is to be recognized as a true Democrat or friend of his country, who is opposed to disunion at this time and for present causes. We are but the humble victims of this sweeping declaration. We denounce the disunionists, and we appeal to the people against them."[58]

This latter clause was to become familiar to *Standard* readers in the next several years. Having broken with the leaders, Holden fell back on his trust in the people, and he kept his reliance largely placed there during the remainder of his editorial career. There was irony in the situation now, for in appealing to the people against the disunionists Holden also was, in effect, returning to the Whig Party, which he had helped beat down, and leaving the Democratic Party, which he had been instrumental in building.

The breaking of strained relations between Holden and party leaders must have been something of a relief to both sides; they really had little in common, and now they could come out openly with their hostile views. Fulton, the Wilmington editor, probably expressed the opinion of the Democratic hierarchy in saying that, while the method of bringing about the rupture might "not be the most dignified in the world, it is certainly preferable that it should be done thus than not at all."[59] And Holden was left free to criticize as harshly as he pleased the program advocated by Governor Ellis and his supporters. He did this promptly in the issue in which he told about the election of Spelman as public printer.

There were portions of Governor Ellis's message, the *Standard* said, to which it strongly objected, believing that they tended toward disunion. These portions, Holden said, were the recommendations that a consultation with the other slaveholding states be held through commissioners appointed by the legislature, and that then a state convention be held to consider the report of the commissioners. "In other words," Holden said,

> steps are to be taken to dissolve the Union on account of the election of a President according to the Constitution, and the people are then to be called on, not to direct or control the consultation, *but merely to register and carry out the disunion schemes of the disunion leaders.* There it is, fellow-citizens, in plain English. *That* is the plan of your Governor. He desires to dissolve the Union, but he fears to trust the people with the question. . . . We denounce and defy the disunionists and we shall make war upon them until the people of this State, of all parties shall rise in their might and teach them, and teach all professionals and designing politicians that their property, their fortunes, their lives and the integrity of the federal Constitution *shall not* be subjected to the control of demagogues lusting for power and for new places in a Southern Union.[60]

Of course, Holden was not to go unchallenged. Immediately upon his election as state printer, Spelman, with the backing of Democratic leaders, bought the equipment of the *Democratic Press* in Raleigh and used it to begin publishing *The State Journal*, which would be the organ of the administration at the capital. It was the third time that Holden's position as party editor had been challenged; each succeeding time the challenge had been a little stronger, and each time his denunciation of the move had been caustic. He greeted *The State Journal*: "A pretty press truly, to speak for the people! The organ, or rather the slave of a clique!—The mouth-piece of scheming and rousing politicians!—the sewer into which all bad passions, and all hatreds against us are to be emptied, and that too, and that only, because we are true to the people and their rights."[61]

In his prophecy of the animus that would be displayed against him by the *State Journal*, he was correct. Even more than Syme's *Register*, the Spelman paper was to be given over principally to attacking Holden and taking the sting out of his editorials. Naturally, the *Standard* kept Spelman busy. Holden threw himself into the fight against disunion more impetuously and more uncompromisingly than he had entered any battle in the nearly two decades of his editorship. Veteran campaigner though he was, his other fights paled beside the one he now faced. He was warring, it seemed to him, not only to save his state from disunion, but his party from the disunionists, and himself from personal enemies who were bent on crushing him. If *Standard* readers thought they knew a vigorous Holden before, they must have been surprised at the fury of his energy now. Each issue of the paper fairly crackled with the volleys against his opponents.

The fight to keep North Carolina in the Union largely centered upon the *Standard*. The Union element appreciated having such an ally, with its location in the capital and with its power to combat the influence of Democratic leaders. "We verily believe," the *Greensborough Patriot* said, "that at this time, there is no man in North Carolina upon whom rests a greater responsibility than upon the editor of the *Standard*."[62]

Whatever influence Holden possessed had been growing during the year. In September he boasted that "since the first day of January last our increase has been equal to the total subscription list of perhaps any one of half the newspapers in the State,"[63] and in December that "our subscription list had never increased as it is increasing now, and the *Standard* establishment was never as prosperous as it is at this time."[64] This latter probably contained some exaggeration, for he had hardly obtained enough new subscribers to compensate for the $3,000 annual loss as public printer. The circulation of the *Standard* at this time was about twenty-five hundred for the weekly issue and four hundred for the semiweekly. At the price of $2 per year for the weekly and $4 for the semiweekly, the paper had a subscription income of $6,600; estimated advertising revenue was about $3,000. He paid ten cents a pound for paper, or about $1,400 a year. The wage for journeymen printers was $9 a week, and that of the office clerk about the same. Ink, a minor item in the budget, was twenty-five cents a pound. At the prevailing price of general commodities, Holden had an unusually good income. He calculated that a year's subscription to the weekly would buy two bushels of corn, or twenty pounds of bacon, or twenty dozen eggs, or ten pounds of butter, or a four-horse load of wood, or twenty yards of cloth.[65]

John Spelman of the new administration paper and James Fulton of the *Wilmington Chronicle* were the leading editors for the disunionist faction, and both attacked Holden's "Watch and Wait" slogan. They were "very good words," Fulton said, "but not quite all that the present contingency calls for."[66] Spelman demanded to know for what the state should watch and wait, and he rephrased some of Holden's earlier expressions. Watch and wait, he asked, "for the enemy to be upon us and begin to disarm us and to cast us to earth? To ascertain if arsenic which has been taken by mistake will produce death? To see if cold steel, well sharpened, will sever the jugular vein? *Must we watch and wait and become weaker, or act and gather strength by preparation* based on our own stern resolve?"[67]

On the night of November 30, 1860, Union men in Raleigh staged an impromptu rally in answer to speeches made by two South Carolinians who, passing through Raleigh to Washington, talked to a crowd in front of the Yarborough House, the hotel that served as Raleigh's social center. Union sympathizers lit a tar barrel in the courthouse yard across the street and began ringing the bell to attract a crowd. When one assembled, Everard Hall was chosen chairman of the meeting and Frank Wilson one of the vice-chairmen. Zebulon B. Vance, then a congressman from the extreme western district, was called upon and made a Union speech of two hours' length. At the end, a committee of seven, with Holden as chairman, was appointed to draw up resolutions for adoption at a meeting set for the following evening. At that meeting Holden made a talk and presented resolutions declaring that the mere election of a sectional president, achieved over disorganized parties, was not sufficient cause for dissolving the Union; that North Carolina was attached to the Union as long as the Constitution was respected and no longer; and that the militia system should be revised and equipment obtained.[68]

The *Standard* urged the people over the State to hold similar meetings and to "*speak* out against disunion." It continued this "appeal to the people against the disunionists and professional politicians" in almost every issue in the next few months, and Holden spoke at several of the rallies. "If we *must* dissolve the Union," he argued, "let us do it as one people and not by a bare majority. Let us wait until the people of the State are more united on the subject than they are now. Depend upon it, our people are not submissionists."[69]

Holden answered the *Goldsborough Rough Notes*, which had said that "nine tenths of the people are opposed to the present Union as it *now* exists," with the statement:

The very reverse is true. The people of this State are in favor of the Union as it now exists, and they will "grind into powder" those politicians who are for destroying it for existing causes. . . . "Watch and Wait"—that is our motto. Old Putnam watched and waited at Bunker Hill until he saw the whites of his enemies' eyes. If we "watch" we will be ready when the danger comes, if come it should; if we "wait" we will be able to unite and act as one man. But if we divide in a contest with our abolition enemies, *then farewell to slavery*.[70]

The *State Journal*, digging a decade into the *Standard*'s back files, attempted to weaken Holden's position by proving him to be inconsistent in his opposition to secession; that attack was joined by the *Warrenton News*, which charged that Holden's "views of Southern policy have undergone a remarkable change in a very short space of time."[71] Holden responded somewhat peevishly,

Now gentlemen, one and all, we point you to the record. Take the broad daylight, with the aid of the lamp of Diogenes, and examine it carefully. There it is, for eighteen years. There is no blot upon it even to the present hour. Watch us in the future, and see if we deviate from the old landmarks. What are they? Here they are: *a strict construction of the federal Constitution*, the reserved rights of the States; the greatest good of the greatest number.[72]

Despite his contentions, there can be no question that the *Standard*'s views had undergone a change during the year, in spirit if not in letter. However, when Holden's own party within the state shifted its ground, Holden's switch was magnified, making it appear greater by the contrast between using secession as a threat and demanding it as a present resort. When Holden insisted "it is our secessionist assailants who have changed,"[73] he was probably as correct as they were.

Soon after the legislature met in the fall of 1860, two reports on federal relations were laid before it. One implemented Governor Ellis's message proposing a conference with other Southern states to be followed by a state convention; the other opposed Ellis's moves as unnecessary and dangerous. When the assembly adjourned for a two-week vacation at Christmas, no action had been taken on either report, despite the imminence of the secession of South Carolina. This ignored the plea of the *Wilmington Journal* that North Carolina should join the Southern states "early enough to take a part in forming the rules of the new confederacy, not be forced to accept rules already formed by others."[74] The *Standard* argued that "it is neither the duty nor the destiny of North-Carolina to follow blindly South-Carolina and the 'Cotton States.' The idea that North-Carolina must go out of the Union because South-Carolina is going out, ignores

State will, State sovereignty, and State independence. It is not 'the Carolinas,' or 'Carolina,' but it is South-Carolina and North-Carolina."[75]

"Prepare, and then Watch and Wait," Holden urged once more, and this was the course that the state followed. Just before the legislature recessed for Christmas, the Senate passed a bill appropriating $300,000 to arm the troops of the state, and Governor Ellis was making every effort to obtain for the militia sufficient military equipment to prepare for any emergency. The position of Union men in North Carolina was weakened by the secession of South Carolina on December 20, which served to add tinder to the flames being diligently fanned, but Holden continued to fight disunion at every point. He asserted that many papers were printing rumors and false reports along with exaggerating news for the purpose of stampeding public opinion and bringing about hasty action just when the conservatives of the North needed time to do their part in saving the Union. "Beware of panics and false alarms," he told his readers. "Sift every rumor to the bottom." North Carolina "is too brave to *run out of the Union* under temporary panics, and she is too wise to commit herself to revolution for the purpose merely of imitating the examples of other States."[76]

Holden issued a *Standard* extra on January 2, 1861, when the *State Journal* of that day carried a telegraphic dispatch that Buchanan's cabinet had broken up in a quarrel, with some members resigning, and that the president was on his way north and federal troops on their way south. Holden telegraphed immediately to a "reliable friend" in Washington, receiving the reply, "No troops ordered South. No new ground for excitement known." The extra momentarily set the record straight, and Holden used ridicule and mockery to explode many of the rumors given currency.[77]

As other spurious accounts multiplied, some more inflammatory than others, Hale of Fayetteville exclaimed that there seemed to be an "organized band of conspirators from Washington City to Charleston, earnestly and unscrupulously engaged, by foul means, in fomenting ill blood and exciting rebellion by propagating false reports of an exciting character."[78] Union men charged that these rumors were the work of secessionists bent on infuriating the people of the middle states and driving them into disunion without time for reflection. "Do men think that God's eyes are closed to those proceedings," the Salisbury *Watchman* asked, "or that He will not avenge?"[79]

The governor's newspaper meanwhile was imploring the people "for God's sake, for the sake of decency," to "throw off the lethargy with which HOLDEN'S pusillanimous policy of 'Watch and wait' has seized you, and act as men who know their rights and dare maintain them."[80] Its editor, Spelman, challenged the male population of the State: "North Carolinians, are we *men*, to tamely suffer these warnings and dishonors, or are we slaves,—slaves to our fears and our blind adoration for what has become a vicious and unholy Union?" And then his pen soared:

Trembling old age and helpless infancy and tender womanhood lift up their supplicating hands to *you*, to ask for one *manly*, vigorous effort for their salvation. Freemen of North Carolina, it is a time for MEN TO ACT IN—awake from your political torpor, rouse yourselves from your moral lethargy, for this sleep into which you are sinking is the slumber of DEATH. We tell you that if you shall continue to hold your peace, the very stones of our Revolutionary soil will immediately cry out.[81]

The growing pressure of events led both factions in the legislature to agree to submit to a referendum of the people the question of a convention, whose work would be restricted to federal affairs and would be ratified by the people; at the time of the referendum, delegates to the convention, if it should be approved, were to be elected. A bill to this effect passed its final reading in both houses January 24, and the referendum and election were set for February 28. A little earlier, resolutions had been passed asking Governor Ellis to appoint five prominent North Carolinians as commissioners to represent the state at the peace conference scheduled for Washington on February 4, and three others as observers (not delegates, since North Carolina was not a member of the Confederacy) at Montgomery on the same date, when a provisional Southern government was to be formed. [82]

Holden lost no time in telling the people how to vote on the convention question. "Nominate no man—vote for no man who will not pledge himself against secession and disunion," he wrote. "BE SURE THAT YOU KNOW YOUR MEN BEFORE YOU COMMIT YOURSELF TO THEIR SUP-PORT." [83] He followed that directive a week later by saying:

Let us when the country is in danger, cast party to the winds. Let us rise above party and save the Union. Let us bury all past feuds and prejudices, and address ourselves to the great work of restoring peace to the country. We are threatened with divisions among ourselves, and with civil war. Shall we go into a war of any kind as partizans? God forbid! Let our rallying cry be, *our country first, our country last, our country all the time*.[84]

The administration's *State Journal* took the opposite tack, urging the election of "true men, who will look singly to the safety and honor of our State," men who recognized that the main question was not disunion or union, but what North Carolina should do to protect herself, for "practically the Union is now dissolved and a Southern Confederacy is now formed." [85]

In Wake County the three Union candidates for the convention were George E. Badger, Quentin Busbee, and W. W. Holden. They immediately made appointments to address the people in various parts of the county. The fight involving Holden was particularly bitter. It early led to an incident which was termed by the *Register* an "editorial fracas," the details of which that paper told with some relish:[86]

Early one afternoon small groups of men were standing, as usual, in front of the Yarborough House. Holden and Spelman were in separate groups, both conversing with friends. Governor Ellis passed down the street, and Holden remarked in a loud voice that "there goes the meanest man in North Carolina, except John Spelman."

Spelman immediately approached Holden, demanding that he repeat what he had said. In answer, Holden began pummeling Spelman with his cane, one blow causing blood "to flow very freely" from Spelman's head. Spelman drew a pistol and fired, the bullet smashing the upper part of a second-story window. Then W. H. Laughter, a clerk employed by Spelman at the *State Journal*, whipped out a gun. By this time Spelman had recovered his temper and "did not show any disposition to fire again;" a bystander told Laughter that "if he did not put up his pistol he would knock his d---d head off, when the latter very promptly complied with his request."

That ended the "fracas." The two principles were haled before the court the next day and furnished $500 bond each to appear later. If any further action in the case was taken, it was not noted in the papers. Neither Holden nor Spelman mentioned the incident in their columns at the time, although, as the *Register* said, it "occasioned, for a time, a vast deal of excitement." Nearly three years later, however, in accounting for the hatred of Spelman, Holden said in the *Standard* that "under much provocation, we on one occasion caned him publicly."[87]

The "desperate effort"[88] to defeat Holden brought another unusual occurrence. It grew out of the alleged misquotation in the *State Journal* of a speech Holden made at Rolesville, where the *Journal* reported him as saying that he was in favor of using force against the seceding states and that he would not oppose the march of federal troops across North Carolina to get to Fort

Sumter. Holden denied this promptly in a speech in Raleigh and also in the next issue of the *Standard*, declaring that he was strongly opposed to coercion.[89] His opponents apparently continued to circulate distortions, however, and just before the election he took a personal advertisement in the *Whig Register* to clarify his position. Syme, for many years his sparring partner, made a plea for Holden's election and urged the voters to back the whole Union ticket.[90] Syme's editorial and Holden's ad looked strange in the *Register*, which could not have published such items before or after. Truly, the situation was bringing extraordinary associations, not the least of which were this and the friendship with Badger, the "Whiskerando" of Holden's youthful sketches on the "Mysteries of Coondom."

The election gave the Union element a decisive victory. While the call for a convention was narrowly defeated, a large portion of the delegates elected to it—should it have been held—were Union men. The *Standard*, only slightly at variance with other papers, reported that eighty-three of the elected delegates were Unionists, while thirty-seven were for secession.[91] In Wake County Holden, Badger, and Busbee were elected by handy majorities. Since the convention itself was rejected, however, the election was meaningless except as an indication of sentiment in the state.

From the results of the referendum the *Standard* judged that a new party composed of Unionists had been formed, and it explained the stand of that party: "In speaking of the successful party as Unionists, we must not be understood as saying that they will submit to the administration of the government on sectional or black Republican principles, but that they are anxious to preserve the Union on a Constitutional basis and to obtain such guarantees as will lead to a permanent re-construction of the Union."[92]

The *Wilmington Journal*, on the other hand, did not think the vote against the convention represented the deliberate will of the people, who, Fulton said, did not understand the situation. They were led to believe that the deliberations of the Peace Congress in Washington might result satisfactorily and ought to be given an unimpeded opportunity,[93] he said.

The *Standard* noticed in the *Goldsborough Rough Notes* an item claiming that every vote cast in Tarborough and Wilson was for the convention, and that three groans were given for Lincoln and for Holden. In reply, Holden pointed to the twelve hundred majority given him in Wake County after he had been "assailed, catechized, misrepresented, pursued, maligned," and he declared himself content. "Groan, sinners, groan," he wrote. He noted also that he had been hanged in effigy in Charlotte but "attached no importance to it, for we felt sure the people of Charlotte not only had no hand in it, but disapproved of it."[94]

A little later Holden received insults closer home when members of the Southern Rights Citizens of the state, a secession faction, were returning by train from Goldsborough, where they had held a convention March 22 and 23 to make plans for combatting what Spelman had called the lethargy of the people. The *Standard* said the convention delegates approached the city depot singing "vulgar songs and abusing Raleigh and Wake County" as dens of submission.[95] One of the songs, according to the report in the *Standard*, was:

> W. W. Holden is a d---d Submissionist,
> And a d---d Submissionist is a d---d Abolitionist.

An affray between the delegates and Raleigh citizens was barely averted. The *Standard*'s report said that a Raleigh resident made "some remark, when the reply by one of the delegates was that they had been to Goldsborough to demand their rights and secure justice. The reply to that by the citizen was, that if some people got justice they would get it with a rope around their necks." The exchange soon led to an invitation to the delegate to leave the train, whereupon a number of them sprang from the cars spoiling for a fight; but "fortunately good counsels prevailed, and bloodshed was prevented. If one blow had been struck the probability is that several persons would have been killed."[96]

Meanwhile, the editors in the state had been watching with interest and apprehension the trip of Lincoln to Washington, noting his speeches and wondering what he would say in the inaugural address, which Holden was telling them to "watch and wait" for.

All of the editors, whether for union or secession, were dissatisfied with Lincoln's preliminary statements. "These speeches," the *Carolina Watchman* said, "exhibit no superior talent whatever, and a very inadequate notion of the serious nature of the disturbances which have rent the Union. Indeed, there is a degree of puerility and barrenness about them truly surprising."[97] The *Fayetteville Observer* also thought the speeches "show such a want of appreciation of the dangerous condition of the country, such an ignorance, real or affected, of the 'hurt' it has already received, to say nothing of what is imminently impending, such constant contradictions of himself, such mere twaddle in short— that it is impossible to regard him as either very well informed, very profound, or very patriotic."[98] The *State Journal* went much farther, declaring that "Lincoln has said he will subjugate the seceded States—that is, he will enforce the laws and retake the forts. This is a cowardly way of declaring war. . . ."[99]

The *Wilmington Journal* drew a contrast between Lincoln on his way to Washington, "with the Chicago platform for his gospel, and coercion for his motto," and the more inspiring scene at Montgomery, where "another native of Kentucky [Jefferson Davis], but this one a noble and chivalrous son," was inaugurated as the first President of the Confederacy.[100] Other papers also noted, most with detailed accounts, this latter "great event of the day."[101]

Both factions in North Carolina looked to Lincoln's inaugural address to strengthen their case before the people; the secession-ists, though chagrined over their convention setback, appeared as determined as before to push their program; Union men were just as resolved to hold their lines. When the address was made, the *Standard* hurried to interpret it as friendly to the South. Two days after the inauguration, it ran the paragraph: "A friend telegraphed us yesterday evening about four o'clock from Wash-ington, that Mr. Lincoln's Inaugural *is moderate and concilia-tory in its tone.* This information is reliable."[102]

By the following week, Holden and the other editors had had time to read the address themselves, and he, at least, did not see anything in it to change the secondhand opinion of the previous issue. A long editorial said in part: "So far as coercion is con-cerned, Mr. Lincoln occupies the very same ground occupied by Mr. Buchanan. . . . We cannot, as an honest man, denounce in Mr. Lincoln what we approved in Mr. Buchanan. . . . If Mr. Lincoln were mad enough to attempt to subjugate the Southern States, or even if he were disposed to do so—as his Inaugural shows he is not—he has no army at his command. . . . *It is not a war message.* . . . It deprecates war, and bloodshed, and it pleads for the Union."[103]

Every newspaper in North Carolina read the message accord-ing to its own bias, some of the wilder secessionist editors sound-ing off in tones shrill and inciting. But as the weeks went by, the *Fayetteville Observer* calculated that "the clamor over its 'war meaning' is pure humbug,"[104] and the *Carolina Watch-man* graciously remarked that "we are just beginning to find out that there is a vast deal of wisdom in Holden's motto, 'watch and wait.' "[105]

Union men felt that they were gaining strength daily when there came, on April 12, the fatal firing at Charleston of the first gun of the Civil War, its lanyard pulled by a Charleston editor, Edmund Ruffin. Governor Ellis received from Simon Cameron, Lincoln's secretary of war, the telegram, "Call made upon you by tonight's mail for two regiments of military for immediate service." Ellis promptly sent a longer telegram in reply, the substance of which was contained in a single sentence that the newspapers trumpeted: *"You can get no troops from North Carolina."*

Here was a turn of events totally unexpected in the fight against the "crazy dance of disunion."[106] Holden's forces were stunned. Up until the very last, the *Standard* had warned the people against rumors that fighting had broken out, or was about to break out, in Charleston. This caution appeared in the very issue telling of the attack on Fort Sumter and the call for troops. Holden, no doubt feeling betrayed, hardly knew how to interpret the news. On the one hand, he agreed that North Carolina could give Lincoln "no aid . . . in any effort to coerce the 'Confederate States,'"[107] and so he applauded Ellis's resolute response. On the other hand, the news had come with such swiftness that he could not at once shake off his loyalty to the Union. Lamely, in an editorial that showed that he had misjudged the significance of what was happening, he said that "the mission of the border States now is to command the peace, if possible, and to maintain their rights in the Union. If *they* cannot check and control the two extremes no other power can."[108]

Within a week, however, Holden had sorted out his options and found that, in effect, he had only one. Like other Union editors, he did not hesitate to do an immediate about-face. The call for troops resulted in every Union paper joining the clamor for early secession. Probably for the first time in the history of the state, the press was united, and on April 24, Holden, more eloquent than most, put the case for the South in an editorial entitled "We Must Fight," which was to become notable:

The proclamation of Mr. Lincoln has left the people of the border States no alternative but resistance or unconditional submission. The Southern man who would quietly submit to the doctrines enunciated in that document, is fit only for a slave. We do not propose to go behind it as long as this war shall last. We have labored for peace on honorable terms,—we would hail it now on honorable terms, with profound satisfaction; but, much as we deprecate war, *war must be encouraged*, and must be continued as long as the foot of a Federal soldier rests on our soil. . . .

One heretofore for peace and the Union comes forward to say to you that this is a just and honorable war. It is a war which could not have been avoided. It has been forced upon us . . . Fanaticism and unjust power are on one side—"God and our Native Land" are on the other.[109]

At about the same time Holden was one of several men to make "strong Southern speeches" at a rally of citizens at the Raleigh courthouse. He was appointed chairman of a committee to draw up resolutions, and these, written by Holden and adopted unanimously, denounced the Lincoln proclamation, pledged the people to resistance, and called for a State convention to take steps for the separation of North Carolina from the Union.[110]

With a number of prominent men in Raleigh, Holden volunteered to form a military company of sixty men who either were the heads of families or were too old for service in a regular army; the company was to defend Raleigh in case of need. Former Governor Bragg was elected captain, and Holden was one of the privates.

The question before North Carolina now was how she might leave the Union as expeditiously as possible. Meeting in special session on May 1, the legislature passed an act ordering another referendum on May 13 to vote on a convention that, its approval a certainty, would meet on May 20 to consider secession.

In Wake County Holden and Badger immediately announced again as candidates for membership in the convention, with Kemp P. Battle the third man on their ticket. The old-line secessionists looked upon the convention as their personal property, and they objected to the candidacies of both Holden and Badger because of their earlier Union sympathies. That element put up an opposition slate, including Bragg, and the county again was treated to a bitter factional fight. Syme, who in the previous abortive convention call had supported the candidacy of the *Standard* editor, was so opposed to him on this occasion that he challenged Holden to a duel. Holden declined, saying that he regarded the custom of duelling as "barbarous and unchristian." He said that over the years he had given the same answer to four previous challenges, one of them from Spelman.[111]

Badger, Holden, and Battle were elected, although Holden squeaked through by only five votes.

When the convention met on May 20, it was composed of members belonging to both factions, the former Union men, who for the most part held to the national theory of the Constitution and believed that the Union could be dissolved only by revolution, and the former secessionists, who upheld the compact theory and argued that the ordinance of ratification could be rescinded. Badger offered a resolution providing for withdrawal by means of revolution, without mentioning secession. Burton Craige offered another resolution abrogating the ordinance of the convention by which North Carolina ratified the Constitution in 1789.

After a test vote, to let the *Standard* tell the story,

about six o'clock P. M. the ordinance offered by Mr. Craige *was adopted unanimously, every member present voting in the affirmative*. . . . As soon as the vote was announced one hundred guns were fired on Capitol Square, and the bells of the City were rung, amid the shouts of an excited multitude. . . . Thus was the anniversary of the Mecklenburg Declaration of Independence gloriously celebrated by the delegates of the people in convention assembled. North-Carolina has been slow to act, but she has acted finally. We think she has acted wisely from first to last. Henceforth her destinies are with the States of the South; and she will make good her act of the 20th of May, 1861, with her last dollar and her last man, if such sacrifice should be required at her hands.[112]

Twenty years later, Holden remembered the scene of the convention a little differently: "I remember well, that when the act of secession was consummated, the body looked like a sea partly in storm, partly calm, the Secessionists shouting and throwing up their hands and rejoicing, the Conservatives sitting quietly, calm, depressed." [113]

Spelman wrote that the enthusiasm prevailing in the convention when the ordinance was voted "can only be conceived of by him who has studied the patient suffering of the oppressed Jews while in the land of bondage and the joys which they felt when they reached the land of promise. The persecuted secessionists—and all are secessionists now, have had glory enough for one day." [114]

The story has been printed and persists that Holden signed the ordinance of secession with a new gold pen bought for the specific purpose, and that he declared his signing was "the greatest act of my life." [115] He is said also to have stated his intention of bequeathing the pen "as an heir-loom to his posterity." No evidence to support this story can be found, however, and doubtless it is apocryphal. In any case, the pen with which Holden signed into the movement he had so long resisted has never been found.

EIGHT

THE *Standard*, which seldom did things by halves, threw it-self into the support of the enterprise that North Carolina had joined, though state politics was not entirely relegated to the background, and though Syme, Spelman, and a few other traditional opponents were treated occasionally to mild ridicule (for instance, the *Standard* of June 5, 1861, spoke of the "sopho-moric sentimentalism of the *Register*, the English dullness and Irish bald-wit and blarney of the *State Journal*"). But Holden's immediate attention was taken up largely with the war: with plans being made by the state to furnish troops and to take its place in the new federation, with counsel on the conduct of the war—advice that officials might sometimes have done well to follow, with editorials lashing the Northern government and glorifying the Southern cause.

An editorial entitled "God on Our Side" virtually admitted that in the paper's thundering against "disunion" it had been opposed to the divine will, for the Lord apparently had been guiding the southern states toward separation and was directing their fight. Holden issued a stern warning to those who still might have a lingering love for the old Union and who were not giving their all to the Confederacy. The editorial he wrote on that subject was another that was to be used against him later. It went:

There are traitors in the South, in Virginia, Kentucky, and Tennessee, but we trust there are none in North Carolina. If there are, let them beware! He that is not *for* the South in this contest is *against* it; and he who would encourage our deadly enemies in the effort they are making to trample us down and destroy us, deserves to die a traitor's death. There can be no half-way ground now. *We* have been a devoted Union man, but much as we loved the old Union, we love North Carolina more. That Union is dead. It will never revive or be restored. The Confederate States will triumph in this war and establish their independence. If there be any persons in this State who prefer the old Union to the Confederate States, let them leave at once and take their shelter under Lincoln's government. If they remain here and plot against the South, they will be visited with swift destruction.[1]

There is no reason to doubt that Holden meant all he said in this and similar editorials, and there is no evidence to suggest that his fervor was inspired, as a contemporary historian suggested, "by the desire to regain the confidence of his former friends and associates,"[2] or by the satisfaction of being back with his party, in step again with its leaders. Through all the twists and turns dictated by circumstances, Holden had been and would continue to be his own man. He had said that certain developments would lead to the secession of North Carolina, that the Union would "fall to pieces at the first touch of aggressive or coercive force," that if "Lincoln should even threaten the Southern States with sword, we would defy him."[3] These developments, in his view, had taken place, and he was wholeheartedly now in favor of the cause of the South, which was also the cause of his state. It was impossible for him to foresee that circumstances would arise to make his language inconsistent and would cause him to raise his voice in objection.

Readers of the *Standard* were greeted June 19 with a caption that was single-column only because editors then knew nothing of large headlines:

WAR NEWS!
• • •
OLD BUNCOMBE IN THE FIRST SKIRMISH.
GREAT BATTLE NEAR NEWPORT NEWS.
NORTH CAROLINA CONSPICUOUS IN THE FIRST
BATTLE OF THE SECOND REVOLUTION.
• • •
HER FIRST REGIMENT A TRUMP.
Col. Hill's Official Dispatch!
1160 Southern Troops Vanquish 4,500 Northern Hessians!!
• • •
GOD BE PRAISED!

Holden went on to write jubilantly, "We were never happier over a battle, than we were upon the reception of the telegraphic dispatch announcing the defeat of 4,500 of Lincoln's hirelings by 1160 North-Carolinians, and Virginians near Bethel Church, nine miles from Hampton, Virginia. For once in the last three months, the telegraphic wires report the news about as the official account does."[4]

Yet the *Standard* showed more reserve in reporting the skirmish than many of its contemporaries, as, for instance, the *Raleigh Register*, which declared that "never since the invention of gunpowder was there such a victory achieved."[5] In this fight, Henry L. Wyatt, a North Carolina citizen though a native of Virginia, was killed, the first Southern soldier to die in battle.

A month later Holden published an extra issue of the *Standard* to give his readers the information that the first battle of Manassas had been fought and won by the Confederates. He acknowledged his "obligations to our friend, A. E. Crutchfield, of the *Petersburg Express*," for telegraphing an account of the "greatest battle ever fought on this Continent. The Confederates achieved a brilliant victory, having routed and pursued their enemies for more than fifteen miles to Alexandria."[6]

The *Standard* not only was much less frenetic and intemperate in its language directed against Lincoln and the North than were any of the other papers in Raleigh, but Holden had a much better grasp of the nature of war and how long the one then occurring might last. From the beginning he combatted the idea of a brief and easy fight for Southern independence and urged preparation for a long drawn-out struggle. He had heard it said, Holden wrote, that the war was to be "a small affair; that at most a few battles will end it, and smiling peace will return again. We could wish success to such speculations. But let us prepare for the worst."[7] Bethel Church was not to be the only battle of consequence, he warned, and "it is absolutely necessary to give the Hessians several severe drubbings."[8] Later, "Manassas rendered Southern independence a fixed, inevitable fact," but other battles "may be necessary before an honorable peace is secured."[9] In the autumn he was ready to raise his estimate of the probable length of the war and could see "no means of ending it short of three years or the termination of Lincoln's administration."[10]

The *Standard* early promised its subscribers that they would find in the paper the war news they wanted, saying that it was making arrangements to have special correspondents represent it at the points of greatest interest. This plan never worked out. No North Carolina newspaper, in fact, dispatched its own man to any of the fighting fronts. Most editors relied in large part on accounts in Virginia newspapers, which extolled the virtue of Virginia troops to the exclusion of North Carolinians. Editors, readers, and fighting men could not understand why North Carolina, which furnished a large portion of the men in the armies in Virginia, was not given due credit.

This discrimination in the granting of public plaudits to North Carolina soldiers was one of the contributing causes to a gradual defection of the *Standard* until it ultimately was to defy the Confederate and North Carolina governments and most of the newspapers in the state by coming out squarely with a demand for peace. Most of these causes may be traced in the *Standard*'s columns from the early months of the war. Those which showed up first were:

1. The belief that the state did not receive fair treatment in the matter of (a) recognition of the achievements of its troops, (b) appointment of high army officers, and (c) provision of coastal defenses.

2. The belief that the common people, of whose rights the *Standard* regarded itself as champion, were imposed upon (a) in the army in the treatment accorded privates and (b) at home in the distribution of food and other necessities.

3. Partyism in North Carolina, leading to partisan divisions and growing bitterness.

Other causes to be added to this list in the next year or two were:

4. Objection to the centralization of authority in the hands of President Davis by his assumption of war powers.

5. Disagreement with the idea of conscript laws.

6. Appointment of a Virginian as tithingman, or tax collector.

7. Refusals to treat for a peace when it became obvious that the South could not gain all the objectives for which it was fighting and when, as Holden insisted, better terms might be negotiated than if the South persisted to the bitter end.

A principal concern of Holden's in the summer of 1861, was the defense of the coast, which, with its many inlets and sounds commanding a large area of the state, he felt should be given special consideration. The Federal forts had been seized by the state, but Holden contended that neither these nor the additional forts that were constructed on Roanoke Island and at Hatteras and Ocracoke Inlets had been sufficiently strengthened and garrisoned. He joined the editors in the eastern section in criticizing Governor Ellis and the military for the inefficient and dilatory preparations to resist attack. In almost every issue he expressed dissatisfaction with the coastal fortifications, assuring readers that his anxiety was no "needless alarm . . . mere ruse . . . or party trick,"[11] but was prompted by genuine concern. "We never expect Lincoln to fight his way through Virginia to the North-Carolina line," he said, "but a point of easy access to the enemy, without a sufficient force to repel him at the outset, is the seacoast."[12]

His warning was not amiss. In August, 1861, after the forts, the Fayetteville arsenal, the state's naval vessels, and the conduct of military operations within North Carolina had been turned over to the Confederate government, Union Gen. Benjamin F. Butler was sent with a naval force to attack Forts Clark and Hatteras at Hatteras Inlet. To oppose the 143 modern, long-range guns of the ships, the forts had between them 19 old-fashioned, smooth-bore cannon, not one of which could reach the Union fleet. The two forts, with 670 men and 1,000 muskets, were taken by the Federals. The *Standard* of September 4 contained a column-long account of the disaster, and in the same issue Holden pointed out how confident the state and Confederate governments had been that the coast could be defended and how little heed had been given warnings to prepare for a real attack.

Holden was angered by the loss, but he said he was not alarmed. With the proper fortification of Roanoke Island, he continued, "we can keep the enemy at bay until doomsday."[13]

Within a month of North Carolina's entrance into the Confederacy, the *Standard* began to express its solicitude for privates in the army and for the common people at home. Such concern the paper had been accustomed to exhibit for nearly twenty years, and the war multiplied its occasions for doing so. Following this policy, the *Standard* of June 19 ran a long article making three charges against the military and civil authorities. For one thing, the paper protested the trial and punishment by court martial of a private in the volunteer service who had not been sworn into the army "and hence was amenable only to the Civil Courts." Holden demanded to know by what authority the military kept "that man under punishment not known to our laws." At the same time, he remonstrated against the seizure "without proper remuneration" of corn shipped by people in the eastern counties, and against the impressment of a piece of land belonging to a "poor, but honest and industrious mechanic in this city," for much less than the requested price.[14] Holden asked,

> Now, if these things be true, will the free people of North Carolina submit to such despotism? Is it possible that Gov. Ellis, or the Military Board, can for a moment believe, that the Legislature, *if it could do so*, intended to convey any such powers? ... The people of North Carolina are at war with Lincoln, a military despot, for the protection and maintenance of *these very rights*. We shall and will resist him with all the force and means God has given us. But the war will be a fruitless one indeed, when we conquer, as we believe we shall, our Northern foes, if the Governors of North Carolina are to be invested with so arbitrary a power, or if they are to be allowed to exercise it so improperly, through ignorance or imbecility. We warn the people of North Carolina to look closely to your home interests—watch narrowly the conduct of your rulers.[15]

These lines are significant for several reasons in addition to the meaning that Holden intended at the time: that is, a warning against the misconduct of officials and their impositions on the common people. Three years later the columns of the *Standard* were to contain virtually the same admonition, as Holden led a bitter fight against both Confederate and state administrations; thus, the editorial forecast the paper's later unequivocal insurgency.

It also indicated something of the degree of factionalism in the state that surfaced in the first weeks of the war. It transcended the old party lines and divided the state's politicians and newspapers into two distinct coalitions: those who, in the manner of the cotton states, had early favored secession, and those who, like

Holden, had fought, until the outbreak of hostilities, for the preservation of the Union. The former Unionists had voted for secession expecting that "by-gones should be by-gones,"[16] that former differences would be forgotten during a war with a common foe; they encountered what they considered flagrant factionalism and rigid proscription by which the triumphant secessionists sought to insure organizational permanency.

Holden felt that the secessionists' Southern Rights Party, or, as he afterwards called it, the Destructives, had actually been born at the Goldsborough Convention before Lincoln's inauguration, and that the organization had since been "persistently" kept up as "a standing insult and reproach to the old Union men," and as part of an effort "to beat down, decry and ostracize the conservative men of the State, solely so far as could be seen, for the purpose of holding on to the perquisites of office, and from the mere ambition of managing the revolution."[17]

As might be expected, Holden, for one, was ready with a practical answer and a fair warning: "If the *fast* men, that is, those who were not too slow in favoring secession, *will* have it so—if they insist on proscribing all those who were reluctant to destroy the old system and launch the State on the tempestuous sea of revolution and civil war, then we are ready to meet them. In a contest of this sort before the people we shall not fear for ourself or for those with whom we may act, but we shall fear for the country. We shall not engage in it unless forced to do so in self-defense."[18]

There was, of course, very little that any party could do immediately. Governor Ellis died in July, leaving his faction without a dominating personality; he was succeeded by Henry T. Clark, speaker of the Senate, who would fill the unexpired term. The gubernatorial election was a year off. The Confederate presidential election was to come in November. Jefferson Davis was the only candidate for president, and there was only a provisional nominee running for the vice presidency, Alexander Hamilton Stephens (the Georgian who, like Holden, had held out against secession). At this time Holden strongly favored them both.

In August the *Standard* carried a statement that was to assume more significance when, within a few weeks, Holden began to feel a dislike for President Davis that was to develop into intense hatred:

Having entire confidence in the ability, integrity and patriotism of the distinguished chiefs at the head of the Provisional Government of the Confederate States, and for the further reason that as far as we can judge, *it is the will of the people*, we now, in advance of suggestions from cliques, caucuses or conventions . . . declare our readiness . . . should they continue, as we believe they will, to exhibit the same patriotic and anti-partizan spirit, which has hitherto marked their course, to give the honored name of Jefferson Davis and Alexander H. Stephens our hearty support for the chief offices in the permanent Government of the Confederate States of America.[19]

Early in October, with the election a month away, the *Standard* took further steps to wipe out party dissension, but which served to polarize the factions even further. Since no slate of electors had been proposed, Holden drew up one, which generously consisted of five men who were avowed Union Whigs until the break, four who were avid secessionist Democrats, a Union Democrat, and two who had represented middle positions.

The proposal of this ticket set off another newspaper war, to Holden's professed surprise and, no doubt, to the bewilderment of the public, which could not understand why there was so much turbulence since all the votes would go to the same candidates no matter who the electors were. The Charlotte *Bulletin* immediately countered with a rival slate, and compromise candidates proliferated in amazing abundance, as if some grand prize were to be won. Holden promoted his own choices with such assiduousness that Spelman, never at loss for hyperbole, exclaimed, "The man's run mad."[20] Holden already had been accused by the *Register* of preferring "to rule in hell rather than serve in heaven."[21]

On November 17, Holden had a fight with Syme's assistant editor, William Robinson. The latter was standing on Fayetteville Street talking with a friend when Holden approached and said, "You call me a poltroon, do you?" He struck Robinson with his walking stick, whereupon Robinson tried to stab him with a blade concealed in his cane. The *Standard* editor grabbed Robinson's arm and they grappled, finally falling with Holden on top. Friends separated them, and the next day Holden appeared before the mayor to give bond for his appearance in court.[22] He forfeited the bond, and the matter was dropped.

It is not quite incidental that the Charlotte electoral ticket, composed of eight original secessionists and four Unionists, was chosen in a very light vote. Holden explained away the reverse by saying that conservative and Union voters simply did not bother to go to the polls, so offended were they by secessionist tactics. "Clearly," he said, the result "foreshadows the doom of that partizan faction in any future contest."[23] In that statement Holden was more right than wrong. When the North Carolina members of the electoral college gathered in Raleigh in December to cast the state's vote for Davis and Stephens, they represented the last success of what Holden called "the partizan party." But Holden was to clash again and again with the spirit that bound the individuals together and would not be satisfied until they had crushed him utterly.

Early in 1862 an event occurred that marks one of the turning points in Holden's attitude toward the war. Roanoke Island was lost. The *Standard*, which had largely repressed its temper after the fall of Hatteras, lost its patience with the Confederate administration and henceforward was not to regain it. The paper had kept repeating warnings that an attack on the coast was imminent, and Governor Clark had asked that two or three North Carolina regiments in Virginia be sent back to defend their homes and that guns be furnished for some regiments without arms that were in camp in North Carolina. The Confederate government, however, thought that it could not spare troops or equipment from Virginia and left North Carolina to its own devices.

Apparently some of the people of the state did not agree that another attack would be made soon and scoffed at Holden's repeated contention that preparations for defending the coast were inadequate. "The authorities and some of the people," Holden noted, "have poo-pooed at the idea of an attack. . . . Ample time has been given for the completion of our defense, and yet we have dilly-dallied, until the enemy is at our doors."[24] He was right about the enemy being at "our doors." At the time he wrote, Gen. Ambrose E. Burnside, with a fleet of eighty vessels, was approaching the North Carolina coast, and on February 7, 1862, he attacked the raw regiments on Roanoke Island. It was only a brief time until the island was surrendered. Among those captured was Joseph W. Holden, seventeen, son of the *Standard*'s editor. (Joseph, along with the other Roanoke prisoners, was paroled and exchanged the following September; it was his earnest desire to return to the fighting, but at his father's insistence he entered the University of North Carolina to complete his studies.)[25]

The *Standard* reported with "the most painful emotions" this capture of the island "with our brave men who were placed there by the government with inefficient means to defend it." Holden was ready with his I-told-you-so: "We are deeply grieved at the result, but we are not disappointed. Our readers know that for months we have importunately warned the government of the certainty of this calamity if the most effective measures were not taken for its complete defence."[26] He said, "We think the manner in which this State has been treated by the Confederate government in relation to Roanoke Island calls for investigation both here and at Richmond."[27]

Other papers were as stirred as he by the defeat but were more hesitant to place blame; for the most part, after reflection, they took Holden's after-Hatteras attitude that the state must not give way to despair, but must meet the situation with new energy and determination. All except Spelman. He was almost prepared to jest away the incident, being "disgusted with the false accounts. ... In fact, there is no truth in one-tenth of what we have heard, and we are almost disposed to suspect that no attack has been made on the Island at all, and that Burnside may be at the devil for what we know."[28]

But to Holden it was not a matter for cynical joking or for moralizing. For one thing, he was genuinely indignant over the loss of a key to a large portion of the state, especially when the loss appeared to him to be due to gross negligence. For another, politics was stirring in the state, and the defeat furnished good campaign material. He saw in it the basis for a charge that "partizan governments made partizan appointments of persons who have proved themselves unfit for their places," and his panacea to prevent such disasters in the future was to wipe out these partizan governments, for "unless we can have less partyism in the future, and more regard for merit without regard to party, the Confederate cause itself will be endangered."[29]

Almost at once Holden began to take off the gloves in his editorial treatment of President Davis and state authorities. "Between the mismanagement of the State and the Confederate governments," he said, "things are getting no better fast."[30] He thought that Davis strangely prided himself and the country on the small amount of money spent during the first year of the Confederacy. "Better had it been double that sum, if we had the arms, munition, the men and the iron-clad steamers to show for it. Two things have gone farther to bring us to our present plight, than all things else besides. First, the fatalistic blindness, which led the Southern authors of the revolution to contend . . . that we should have no war; and then after it began, that it was to be a *short* war. Secondly, the fear of spending money *to prepare for the war* lest it might endanger the popularity of the party who claimed the right to manage it. . . ."[31] Holden admitted that President Davis "has meant well, and has done the best he could," but he felt that Davis "has not displayed that forecast, energy and wisdom which were expected of him."[32]

Spelman's *State Journal*, which imputed low motives to Holden whenever it could, announced bluntly that it saw through the strategy of the *Standard*, whose "aim, as everybody knows it to be, is to increase its popularity 'among the soldiers and the people,' by misrepresenting the conduct of the authorities."[33] Probably Spelman and those for whom he spoke really believed this. At any rate they acted upon the assumption, and it was not the least important factor leading to the turmoil in the state during the next two years.

Two other matters that added to the unpopularity of the Confederate administration began to agitate North Carolina at about this time. One was the proposal for a conscript law. The state's editors generally were opposed to it, Holden calling it "inexpedient, unnecessary, oppressive, and unconstitutional. It places the rights of the States and the liberties of the people at the feet of the President,"[34] and it would result, he warned, "disastrously to the cause." He contended that for North Carolina, at least, the law was unnecessary, because the state then was ahead of calls for troops, having been asked for thirty-eight thousand and having furnished more than seventy thousand, with at least fifty thousand then in the field. The proposition, he said, "will never receive our assent."

In the other matter also, Holden opposed Richmond. The Confederacy's need of arms led the government to send Maj. W. S. Ashe as an agent to buy, borrow, or, if necessary, impress weapons held by citizens. The move aroused much resentment,

Zebulon B. Vance, governor of North Carolina 1862–1865, 1876–1879

appearing to some even as an attempt to disarm the population not drafted into the service, and Governor Clark issued a proclamation assuring the citizens that they would be protected in preserving their private arms from seizure but requesting them to give information on all public arms. Holden called attention to the "patriotic and timely proclamation" and rejoiced "that there is still spirit enough in the 'Old North State' to crush in the egg the viper *Despotism* in all its forms and to maintain Constitutional liberty among our people in every crisis."[35]

The capture of Roanoke Island by the Federals paved the way for the loss of New Bern, which General Burnside took on March 14. In this encounter the Twenty-sixth Regiment of Col. Zebulon B. Vance made a name for itself and its commander because of its gallant fighting. The *Standard* related that at one time Colonel Vance was surrounded by the enemy. "At this juncture, we are told, his voice was heard above the roar, 'Stand firm, my men—I am with you for victory or death.'" An accompanying detachment discovered his position and "gallantly and heroically rushed to his assistance, when both regiments became fiercely engaged with the enemy."[36] Vance soon was to be selected conservative candidate for governor. In the same issue which contained the account of Vance's bravery, the *Standard* sharply attacked William Johnston, generally supported as the candidate of the party in power, because "he belongs to that order of public men who regard the Old Unionists as objects of suspicion."

Holden's problem in espousing Vance's candidacy was to get him nominated tactfully, so that he might receive the support of as many papers and voters as possible. Rather than place Vance's name before the public himself, he arranged a minor conspiracy. He explained later:

I felt that being a Democrat, and Vance a Whig, his nomination had better proceed from a Whig—for example, the *Fayetteville Ob-*

server. I wrote therefore at once to Augustus S. Merrimon of Asheville, Buncombe County, to come to Raleigh and aid me in the work of bringing Vance forward. . . . Mr. Merrimon then wrote a brief article which appeared under the editorial head of the *Observer,* marked "communicated," nominating Vance for Governor. He then returned to Raleigh by way of Kinston—Colonel Vance being at Kinston with his regiment—and obtained from him his letter of acceptance, and reached Raleigh with it.[37]

The name of Vance was put under the masthead of the *Standard* beginning with the issue of June 11.

The editors of the opposition papers were not so stupid as to fail to discern the Holden touch in the nomination of Zeb Vance. The *Wilmington Journal,* in reporting that Vance had been accepted by a "mass meeting of about fifty persons" in Raleigh, asserted that the resolutions adopted "are pretty extensive reproductions of the *Standard*'s editorials against the State and Confederate governments, and people generally who, 'for the most part, have been and are now in office.' "[38] Nevertheless, Holden's strategy worked, for it drew to the support of Vance most of the Whig papers and Whig voters, leaving only the task of corralling sufficient Democrats to swing the election.

The campaign was one of the most acrimonious the state had ever known. It was carried on entirely by newspapers, with neither candidate taking the field or sending out representatives to speak for him. Colonel Vance remained with his regiment, Mr. Johnston in his office. The editors battled in such a manner that Fulton in Wilmington soon deplored the unparalleled spectacle that he said North Carolina was presenting. "The divisions got up, the feelings excited within her borders, threaten to exceed in bitterness, if they fail to equal in diffusion, those of any canvass ever before carried on in times when mere political excitement had full swing and the amplest scope."[39] The threat he saw was fulfilled.

The issue before the voters simmered down to a decision as to which of the factions was the more patriotic, or the less traitorous. Holden urged the necessity of reform in government:

We have good Constitutions, both State and Confederate, and the framework of the government is all we could desire; but the *administration* of government must be reformed. . . . Those who have been in power for the last twelve months have shown themselves utterly incompetent to manage our affairs; or, if competent, they have been so occupied in parcelling out offices among themselves, and in proscribing the conservatives of late Union men, that they have not devoted their time and their thoughts, as they should have done, to the duties assigned them.[40]

Opposing editors largely confined their exertions to abuse of Holden, following in varying degrees the lead of Spelman in calling him an instigator, if not a leader, of a traitorous movement that was proceeding more and more openly toward rebellion against the government. Colonel Vance, whom the *State Journal* called "one of the bitterest partizans in the State, and a gentleman of but moderate abilities,"[41] was treated to a few insults, but this was a campaign not so much against him as against Holden. Spelman asserted that he had evidence that the *Standard* circulated largely in disaffected areas, that it pandered to and created discontented elements, and that its aim was to weaken confidence in the government.[42] Fulton drew a somewhat gross picture of the *Standard* bellowing "to get the public teat back again within its own lips" and forming "a bitterly proscriptive party" to aid in the attempt.[43] The *Asheville News* described the *Standard* as "a demogogical sheet, which panders to any and every feeling and passion which promises to further its base and selfish ends."[44]

The *Fayetteville Observer* maintained that "there is but one paper among those supporting Col. Vance which has indulged in any bitterness. We have seen no paper of the other side which has not been full of it."[45] Hale apparently was referring to the

Standard as the one *Vance* paper stooping to immoderate language. In fact, however, Holden was remarkably restrained in his editorials, particularly in view of the war being waged against him. He denounced the "Destructive" politicians, protested that he was no traitor, and showed how the future—in his view—depended upon the election of Vance; but his prose was more like that of a political oracle advising his people than of an editor lashing out against opponents. This tone seemed to be particularly irritating to them.

The campaign, with its bitterness leading to rash statements, attracted wide attention and presented fruitful opportunities to editors outside the state to quote from the papers, without taking the pains to try to understand the North Carolina situation or even, at times, to verify the genuineness of the articles. "When the Yankee editors wish to encourage their friends at the North with the prospect that North Carolina can be restored to the Union," the *Register* said, "they quote from the Raleigh *Standard*, in which paper they find 'old Union men' constantly arrayed against 'Precipitators' or 'original Secessionists.' "[46] It was not in the *Standard* alone, however, that the idea that the battle was one of loyalty against disloyalty might be found; some of the Johnston editors were much more to blame than Holden in creating such an impression. In efforts to defeat his candidate, they were guilty of reckless and unwarranted language—particularly when they saw that the election probably was to go against them. They intimated that Colonel Vance, whom Spelman sarcastically called the "hero and statesman,"[47] was a traitor in thinking of deserting his troops to run for office and that the great mass of his supporters were traitors who would welcome the fall of the Confederacy. Altogether, both state and nation obtained a distorted view of the election.

Syme, in his *Register*, warned the public that the election of Vance would be regarded in the North as a sign that Union sentiment was in the ascendancy in the state.[48] Holden replied, "Now,

Col. Vance will certainly be elected Governor, and the *Register* has told the Yankees in advance that he is a traitor, and that the large majority of our people are anxious to reestablish the old Union.—What is this but giving aid and comfort to the enemy?"[49] Hale protested the turn the campaign had taken, asserting that it was to be charged entirely to a few partisan papers, with little of "this detestable spirit" to be found among the people.[50] He also complained that the Johnston papers were displaying "unnecessary bitterness" toward the entire Conservative faction and its candidate simply because of their hatred of a single conservative editor.[51]

Hale also charged that Northern editors did not stop with taking extracts from North Carolina papers and drawing unwarranted deductions from them, but that to "assist them in their system of lying and deception, the Yankees have actually taken to printing bogus Southern newspapers, imitations of the genuine in appearance, but filled with matter of their own concoction. . . . The printing of spurious Southern papers accounts for some things heretofore unaccountable."[52] Holden confirmed that he had been credited with the authorship of articles he never wrote, some of them treasonous.

North Carolina editors generally resented a growing inclination of the Richmond *Enquirer* to meddle in North Carolina politics. Holden was particularly indignant. A two-column article in the *Enquirer* dealing with the Vance-Johnston campaign he regarded as attempted dictation from the Confederate capital and an effort "to prejudice and influence the North Carolina soldiers around Richmond against Col. Vance." He commented impatiently: "We say now to Virginia and South-Carolina, *let North Carolina alone!* She is not 'a narrow strip of land between' you, but a sovereign, self-governing State. She wants a Governor of her own, and not one from South-Carolina, or one dictated by Virginia politicians and the government at Richmond."[53]

Inevitably, there was talk during the campaign of suppressing the *Standard* in one way or another. There was reason to believe that some postal authorities were not handling mailed issues of the paper with normal care, and Holden received a letter from western North Carolina telling of "a great effort" there and elsewhere to have the *Standard* gagged. "They fear the *Standard*," the letter said, "because of its influence with the people. I pray you, defend the rights of the people at all hazards and at all times." Holden's editorial reply was brief: "Our subscription list was never so large as it is now, and it is constantly increasing. This is the way the *Standard* is being suppressed."[54]

When the shot and shell of the newspaper war died away on election day, Zebulon B. Vance was elected governor by a vote of 74,871 to 40, 896, an overwhelming majority of 33,975. The army went for its own nearly two to one, and Wake County, home of the *Standard*, the *Register*, and the *State Journal*, gave Vance a four-to-one margin. The *Standard* was jubilant over the result, hailing it as "the most signal political victory ever achieved in this State. It was achieved mainly by the people. The politicians had little to do with it. It was a spontaneous uprising against injustice, and in favor of reform."[55]

The *State Journal* and the *Register* naturally had different explanations. Spelman said the people had been led to believe that the election of Vance would "bring peace in thirty days, or at least be followed by the return to the State of all our North Carolina troops, whilst the conscripts were to be forthwith discharged and sent to their homes."[56] The *Register* also accused Johnston's opponents of employing "the declaration that the bare election of Mr. Vance would secure immediate peace, and the return of North Carolina soldiers to their homes and business." This kind of electioneering, it said, was carried on by word of mouth.[57]

Governor Vance took the oath of office on September 8, 1862, on the western front of the capitol, where Clay had spoken nearly two decades before. It was a moment of triumph for Holden, as had been the inaugurations of Reid and Bragg, but this occurred amid the vagaries of war, when party lines were inconstant, and there were some disturbing elements in it affecting Holden. Not the least of these was the effort, already begun, to drive a wedge between Vance and Holden and to have the new executive declare, as he did, his vigorous support of pressing the war to a successful end and in winning independence.

In the next few months, however, the *Standard* naturally assumed the tasks of the party's organ at the capital, and if Holden realized what the future might bring, he shut his eyes to it and spoke with complete authority. One thing the paper asserted was that the conservatives should be as ruthlessly proscriptive as the "original secessionists" had been, on the ground that the latter "have shown themselves unequal to the task, not only of preserving but of establishing and maintaining government on sure foundations. They must give place, *in every instance*, to wiser and better men."[58]

When the anticipated squeals arose over this policy, Holden grimly retorted:

Every head that drops in the basket falls by way of retaliation *forced* upon the Conservatives. They are acting strictly in self-defense. They desire to be spared this duty, but their opponents would have it otherwise. Every head that drops is chargeable to the Clark and Ellis administrations and to the administration at Richmond.

We trust that certain gentlemen understand now the meaning of the word "Conservative." It means reform in the government. It means that hotheads, and "peaceable" secessionists, and those who would make the military power paramount to the civil, shall go out, and men of different temperaments and views and opinions, shall go in. The people have willed it, and the Legislature has acted according-ing. Amen to it say we.[59]

Such an attitude may bring satisfaction for a time, but it is a satisfaction that usually must be paid for. Holden's retaliatory attitude was another entry in the long list his opponents—in general, those with whom he had been in open conflict since 1858—were charging to his account against a day of reckoning, which they thought would surely come. Holden's defiance of these men is to be accorded some admiration for its persistence and courage, if not for its wisdom. More and more, with both him and his growing roster of enemies, the confrontation was becoming a war in which no quarter could be asked or expected and which could end only in the complete superiority of one over the other.

With politics temporarily out of the way, the newspapers in the fall of 1862 began to give more attention to the economic hardships of the public, with prices of necessities skyrocketing higher and higher under a system of speculation and extortion, which all the editors agreed existed. In August, Holden demanded relief for privates whose "pitiful pay" he said had brought "them and their families to the door of starvation. Only think of it—$11 per month, and $50 commutation for clothing for a year, for our brave soldiers, when shoes sell at $10 to $12, shirts at $4 to $5, coats at $25 to $30, etc.; bacon at 40 cts., meal at $1.50, sugar at 60 cts., etc."[60]

In November, the *Standard* asserted that "the extortion and speculation now practiced in the South are doing more to hasten our subjugation than everything else besides,"[61] a statement to which no editor or public official took exception. At that time, Spelman reported, bacon was selling at 60 to 70 cents a pound, flour for $30 a barrel, and corn for $4 to $8 a bushel, so that the mass of people were on the verge of starvation. "Better a thousand times to at once withdraw our troops voluntarily from the field, and to give up the contest, voluntarily," he said in the *State Journal*, "than to be driven into subjugation, as a famine-stricken people, by the hated foe."[62] (Holden noted that had he himself used such defeatist language before the previous election, and had Vance lost, "we would have been arrested at once and put in prison."[63]

Syme feared that the winter would bring much suffering not only to the poorer classes but also "to those who have heretofore been enabled to live in tolerable comfort." He said that salt, not obtainable in Raleigh, was selling for more than $100 for a two-bushel sack.[64] If Congress at its recent session, Syme wrote, "instead of piddling away so much of its time discussing 'State Rights,'" had only given more attention to currency, the depreciation of Confederate money might have been checked.[65] Yet a little later he expressed surprise and regret at hearing statements that Confederate money would soon be as worthless as the old Continental currency, and he thought that such opinions amounted to "an admission that the cause of the Confederacy is hopeless."[66]

True to his sympathies with the common people, Holden charged off part of the problem to wealthy landowners:

> How dare a large slaveholder, with his cribs bursting with corn and his smoke-house crowded with meat, withhold food from the families of our soldiers, or sell it to them at famine prices? Fellow-citizens, there are the traitors—*these are the enemies of the Southern cause.* We know such men in this and other Counties of the State. Their names have been furnished us, and we will publish them in due time, unless they change their conduct. *Nine-tenths of them were original secessionists*; the cowardly wretches skulk from the war which they were so anxious to bring on, and remain at home to grow rich by grinding the faces of the poor. . . . Before God and man, we believe that if Southern independence shall be lost, it will be mainly owing to the avarice, the extortion, and the spirit of speculation prevailing among us, and which is chiefly confined to the original secessionists.[67]

Two factors besides the depreciation of the currency made for the high prices and the scarcity of food. In North Carolina a large majority of persons, especially in the west, owned no slaves, so when men who were the sole reliance of their families were conscripted into the army, their dependents, having no field hands, were faced with starvation. At the same time, railroad transportation in the state was so disrupted that when a community had a surplus of food it could not ship the excess elsewhere. This forced each community to exist largely on the supplies raised in the neighborhood and on products made at home.

Such conditions, threatening to get worse, offered fertile ground for the seeds of discontent that had been noted in the last election. Still somewhat inarticulate, doubt that the South would win final independence had been forcing itself into the minds of many people. The war had been going on for more than a year, and although the Southern troops had won important battles, and the *Standard* could now report affairs of the Confederacy "more encouraging and hopeful,"[68] final victory seemed dimmer than in the rush to glory at the beginning of the conflict. Meanwhile, North Carolina was being drained of its manhood to fight on the soil of other states, the subsistence of the masses was becoming more and more comfortless and oppressive, and in a sober reaction to the initial burst of enthusiasm, some were asking themselves why they were fighting and were finding answers that led them to compare what they had to gain with what they had to lose.

In the matter of guiding public thought, as well as in providing for the masses' physical needs, Southern statesmanship was failing. It had not, for one thing, provided for the people a battle cry, a rallying point, an emotional appeal that could make them depreciate their losses and hardships. Long after the war, Governor Vance gave this deficiency as a principal cause for the South's defeat.[69] In the North the masses were kept on fighting edge by appeals for the preservation of the Union, a war cry which could be stirring; the South had nothing comparable. Certainly the preservation of slavery provided no cause for the seventenths of the population that owned no slaves.

The *Standard*, which had always sought to pick up mutterings almost before they had been uttered, now caught the undertone of dissatisfaction, and Holden found that much of it accorded with his own feelings. In fact, the *Standard* was accused of helping to originate the discontent, so strange did the guarded thoughts look in print. But it was only that "the editor has always understood the popular mind better than anybody else and always keeps up the right sail to catch the breeze," Jonathan Worth, state treasurer under Vance, said in a letter.[70] "I do not regard the *Standard* to have created this feeling. It is merely the escape valve through which the repressed strain escapes. I think the torrent is irresistible and that any obstacle employed to correct it, will be swept away." Governor Vance, on the other hand, thought that Holden was "responsible for half this feeling, at least, if it exists; of course the driver sits behind the team and yet may be said to follow his horses."[71] Both views are perhaps prejudiced; Worth at the time agreed with Holden about peace, and Governor Vance disagreed. Probably both men, however, were correct to the extent that Holden expressed a feeling that existed, and that feeling, translated into cold type, tended to proliferate.

As Holden viewed the situation in the latter part of 1862, he could see many things he considered out of joint. For some time he had been hopeful that peace might be not far distant, believing that Southern successes on the battlefields would lead to proposals of peace by Lincoln; but now he thought that the ill-advised invasions of Maryland and Kentucky had destroyed such hopes. The North, he said, had proved its disposition and ability to fight, and although Southern soldiers could "whip the Yankees in equal or superior numbers . . . that is quite a different thing to whipping the North into a peace with us, and an acknowledgement of our rights."[72] At home he could see the sufferings of the masses, with little expectation of alleviation.

He believed he could see a steady encroachment upon the liberties of the people in the use by the Confederate administration of war powers and in military dictation to civil departments—and in the *Standard*'s lexicon there was no word for which it professed more distaste than "despotism." Holden could feel the growing animosity of the temporarily frustrated "Destructives" towards him, causing him to bristle in umbrage. He could sense the beginning of war-weariness in at least a good portion of the public, which, though it might not be able to analyze its reasons and feelings as specifically as the *Standard*, was arriving at the decision that peace was something to be yearned for and possibly to be sought.

In his first issue in November, 1862, Holden ventured "to suggest, with the utmost respect for the reverend clergy and for the sincerely Christian people whom we have among us, that prayer be made for an honorable peace. The people of this State will accept no peace that is not honorable. . . . One fervent, united prayer for peace *may* avail. The Ruler of Men and Nations *may* hear, and *may* change the hearts of our enemies. Is it not worth a trial?"[73]

The idea that a despotism was developing in the South pained him. In June he had reminded readers that he had voted for secession because of Lincoln's tyrannical, coercive policy, and had urged a vigorous prosecution of the war because of Lincoln's assumption of despotic power, which he said included "his overthrow of the liberty of speech and the press . . . his arrest of men and women and imprisoning them without a hearing . . . and his disregard of the rights of the States and of the rights of property in the Southern States." With the people of North Carolina, he said, "opposition to all such acts of tyranny is inborn. . . . They have never submitted their necks willingly to the yoke of any tyrant, and they never will."[74] Now, it seemed to him, the Confederacy was evolving a tyranny just as repugnant as that in the North, whereas North Carolina itself had been saved from one only by the last election, an election in which the Confederate administration had tried to interfere.

Remonstrances against the "military despotism" that he thought was "making great strides"[75] and talk of an honorable peace alternated in the *Standard* for some months. Holden saw in the *Wilmington Journal* a notice to conscripts that Confederate authorities had set aside an opinion by R. M. Pearson, chief justice of the North Carolina Supreme Court, that persons who had furnished substitutes above the age of thirty-five when the conscription limits extended to that age were not subject to compulsory enrollment when the age limit was raised to forty-five. The *Standard* thought the notice was "cool, conclusive and contemptuous. The opinion of the Chief Justice of our State is trampled under foot by the military and the tyrant who does so is careful to have the fact announced in a public journal. The decision of the Chief Justice, it is true, not having been pronounced in open court with the concurrence of his Associates, is not binding except in the particular cases which are brought before him; yet the decision is entitled to respect, and ought to be conclusive with the Confederate authorities."[76]

When, in 1863, he began calling for mass public peace meetings in all sections of the state, however, Holden had gotten a little ahead of some of the conservatives, including Governor Vance and Hale, the Fayetteville editor. This portion of the party, agreeing that peace was desirable and to be hoped for and that the war must be carried on vigorously meanwhile, disagreed that mass meetings should be held in the South, believing that they would delay, if not defeat, the Confederate object in the war. Nothing, Hale said, would be more encouraging to bitter enemies in the North than such movements, or more discouraging "to the great peace party at the North, which has been disposed to end the war by acknowledging our independence, satisfied as they have expressed themselves to be that subjugation is impossible, and that the people whom the Yankees have outraged in every possible way will never consent again to live with them as partners in the same government."[77]

This issue led to an open break between Holden and Vance, with Hale supporting the governor. It marked, too, the beginning of a new phase in Holden's career as a political tactician. In most of the state's affairs for the preceding two decades he had been the dominating chess player, comprehending a situation before his opponents, thinking a move or two ahead of them, dictating the play. Now, perhaps because he was absorbed in the peace question, perhaps also for some other reasons, he appeared to lose some of this ready grasp, and in the next year or two he not only allowed others to outsmart him but also failed to recognize several subtle but important movements. For instance, Holden apparently did not see immediately that Vance and Hale had turned to each other, excluding the *Standard* editor from their counsels, and working, in fact, against him. Yet in June the governor wrote Hale that "you are more nearly of my *precise stripe* politically—past and present—than any other editor in the State."[78] He adopted Hale as his public spokesman.

The *Standard*'s advocacy of peace and the mass meetings that followed, beginning with one in Wake County and numbering elsewhere up to one hundred within eight weeks, brought both protests and commendation. The former naturally were the more vociferous, and most of them demanded resolutely that some counteraction be taken.

In mid-June, 1863, Gen. D. H. Hill wrote Governor Vance from Virginia that he had seen an article in *The New York Herald* claiming, upon the authority of the *Standard*, that a reconstruction element was at work in North Carolina. Hill said:

You have no conception of the mischief that is being done by this paper and the unfortunate decision of Judge Pearson. These two cases are operating to cause desertion by the thousand, are poisoning the mind of people at home, are encouraging the enemy and giving him some show of justice in his claim of restoring the Union. They are tarnishing the glorious laurels of our soldiers now upon many bloody fields. Can nothing be done to avert this terrible evil?[79]

The Richmond *Enquirer* lost its temper and urged soldiers to hang Holden. This so incensed the editor of the *Standard* that he used perhaps the most excessive language of his career upon his rival, calling the *Enquirer*'s proprietor a "vile slanderer," a "degraded pimp" and an administration "hireling." He said North Carolina troops returning to their home state through Richmond would feel that they were "performing a service to society by hanging him."[80]

President Davis wrote Vance that he had had a letter from "one of the most distinguished citizens of your State" expressing fear that trouble was brewing and that open resistance to the government might develop. "This is not the first intimation that I have received that Holden is engaged in the treasonable purpose of exciting the people of North Carolina to resistance against their government and co-operating with the enemy. . . . The case is quite grave enough for me to consult with you on the subject."[81] Vance replied that he did not fear that the state would put itself in opposition to the general government. "Neither," he said, "does there exist any reason for taking steps against Holden, the editor of the *Standard*. On the contrary, it would be impolitic in the very highest degree to interfere with him or his paper."[82]

Vance did, however, make arrangements at once to go to Richmond for a conference with Davis. Before going, he acted upon a private suggestion from Hale to get some influential person to talk with Holden. Two days later Vance told Hale in a letter that he had sent emissaries to make representations to the *Standard* editor but that "it had done little good. He pretends and may be really of [the] opinion that four-fifths of the people are ready for reconstruction and says he is only following the people not leading them." Vance said he had himself had a long talk with Holden and, realizing that an open break was inevitable, "requested him to say in his paper that he was not my organ in this matter and did not speak my sentiments."[83]

Holden responded in good faith. In his next issue he wrote:

So far as Gov. Vance is concerned, it is proper to state that he is not responsible for the course of the *Standard*. The *Standard* is an independent Conservative paper, and it is not the organ of either Presidents, Governors, or Generals. . . . Vance . . . does not agree with us in our views on the subject of peace. He is as anxious as we are to see an honorable peace established at as early a day as possible; but he regrets peace movements among ourselves, with no overtures from the North, as premature and injudicious. That he is honest and patriotic in these views we have no doubt.[84]

On the same day this editorial appeared, Syme, with his usual inattention to details, wrote that Holden was working for the governorship for himself and would "throw Gov. Vance overboard with as much *non chalance* as he would light a cigar."[85] The reverse appears to be true; if not "thrown overboard," Holden at least was required to walk the plank.

Holden had reason for his belief that the people thought his position was a proper one. "Holden's bold position in favor of peace is hailed with joy by many," Jonathan Worth (later to be governor) wrote a friend, and he urged his correspondent, "as money is no object now," to send in two hundred new subscribers from Randolph County to the *Standard*.[86] To another friend Worth wrote that Holden's peace articles "take with nearly all classes in this region,"[87] and the *Standard* itself told of volumes of correspondence from all over the state approving its course.[88] Worth agreed that this was true, saying that "from what I can gather of popular feeling over the State, the masses, and many of the best and most intelligent citizens sympathize with the *Standard*." The paper did not create this feeling, Worth said, and those who deemed it likely to do mischief "should direct their efforts to guiding the storm, rather than arresting it.

Mere denunciation of its editor only increases the tempest." Worth, like Vance, thought that Holden and the people who supported him really were for reconstruction (rather than independence), "and while he disavows it as yet, [he] is slowly shaping his sails for this current. . . . He will be ready to ride the storm. I draw this inference, not from anything he has said, but from the fact that his worst enemies who are not stupid, accord to him superior understanding, great sagacity, and his demand for peace movements, on any other supposition, are absurd."[89]

Holden denied that his efforts were directed toward submission or reconstruction and asserted that the war should be waged with unflagging energy until peace was achieved. "It is true," he wrote, "we are for peace, but we are for it on honorable terms; and we are opposed to relaxing a single nerve, or giving back an inch before the enemy, while negotiations for peace are going on."[90] The peace advocates were "not for reconstruction, but for negotiations with the Northern people with a view to separation."[91]

Holden made no bones about his central concern. In a statement that was significant not only in the peace movement, but in his entire public career, he said, "The key which unlocks the secret—if there be any secret—to our course," was that he was primarily interested in North Carolina, and he intended to stand by the Confederacy only "as long as it is to the interest of North-Carolina to do so, and no longer. . . . While we are a true Confederate, such is our affection for North-Carolina that in comparison with the affection our attachment to the Confederate States is a mere abstraction;"[92] and if "the worst should come, we are for North-Carolina against the world."[93]

The *Standard*'s goal, supported in resolutions of county rallies of as many as five hundred citizens, was for an election of peace delegates to a convention representing the states of both the North and the South, with any "treaty or ratification" to be binding, subject to the approval of the voters of the participating states. "Is there anything unreasonable, improper, or unpatriotic in this proposition?" Holden asked. "We think not."[94]

About the first of August, 1863, Governor Vance went to Richmond for the requested conference with President Davis. Before he left, he apparently talked over with Holden the complaints which North Carolina had against the Richmond administration; and when he returned, he briefed the editor on his conversations with Davis and other officials, making a point of the fact that he had defended Holden when others impeached his loyalty.[95] But in that briefing of Holden, Vance evidently kept back much information. For several months Holden seems to have been led to believe that the governor "returned with the same sentiments and feelings with which he went there."[96] As late as November he sought to discredit a report that Vance had been offered the next presidency of the Confederacy if he would keep North Carolina strongly in line, and that Vance had agreed to become a more fervent supporter of the war. A few months later, however, when he was opposing Vance for the governorship, Holden had reached the conclusion that Vance did return to Raleigh with a greatly changed attitude. The cause of this change, Holden thought, "may have been flattery, or it may have been patriotism, or it may have been the flattering reward of the Presidency after Mr. Davis which was flashed before his vision. He went there to demand justice for his State, and he returned with his views on this subject materially modified. He went there inclined to peace, and returned a red hot war man. He went there an anti-Davis man and returned more or less a Davis man."[97]

Whatever may have happened to Governor Vance at Richmond, he apparently did come to the decision that he must definitely and irrevocably separate himself from Holden and that he must fight the peace movement. In a letter to Hale telling of his conference with the president and of Davis's promise to remove the causes of North Carolina's complaints, Vance wrote that he believed "the split with Holden is decreed of the Gods. I have made up my mind to it and am preparing for it any day. ... He is for submission, reconstruction or anything else that will put him back under Lincoln and stop the war—and I might add punish his old friends and colaborers. Pitch into them—cry aloud and spare not—my life—popularity and everything shall go into the contest." [98]

The manner of Hale, when he proceeded to "pitch into" something or someone, was far different from that of most of the other editors in the state. In a lengthy editorial, well-reasoned and notable for its civilized restraint, he set forth the views of the two opposing forces in North Carolina. At the end he said he had no intention of denouncing the *Standard* but "rather appeal to it, to its good sense, its love of country, its very feeling of humanity, to use its influence to discountenance the meetings which its friends are holding in various parts of the State. ... Some may think it beneath their dignity to appeal to the *Standard*. We do not. The peace of the State and the independence of our country are objects of incalculable value. They would have been far more likely to be secure if we had had less of denunciation and more of reason and persuasion." [99]

Hale's spirit of reconciliation unfortunately did not prevail either with the other newspapers in Raleigh or with affected elements elsewhere. A number of North Carolina officers in the army in Virginia met at Orange Court House on August 12 and drew up resolutions denouncing the *Standard* and asserting that if "true patriotism in North-Carolina has so far lost its hold upon the minds and hearts of the people as to be unable to check the course of the *Standard*, and other papers which are giving utterance to such sentiments, then the public authorities would be recreant to the cause of the country if they should fail to take measures for their suppression." [100] One of the officers attending this meeting was Lt. E. Brock Holden, half brother of the *Stan-*

dard's editor.[101] A year later he ran for the legislature on a ticket arrayed against Holden.[102]

Holden was unmoved by the officers' plaint, saying that his mail showed that the lower ranks in the army were with him, as well as many officers, and that the Orange resolutions were "thorough farces."[103] He seemed confident that he had widespread support. Indeed, in a letter to Hale dated September 7 Governor Vance wrote: "I expect the peace men have a majority to start with, but the *brains* are largely with us."[104] Later developments suggest that Holden and Vance were correct about the large following of the *Standard*, and that, whether it was due to "brains" or not, this majority was whittled away by Vance in the next year.

Accusations that the course of the *Standard* in promoting the peace meetings was in large measure responsible for "the stream of desertion" from the army in the summer of 1863, after Gettysburg, were met with impatience by Holden. It was idle, he argued, "to attribute so great a result as the melting away of the armies to an humble newspaper Editor."[105] There were, he said, other factors much more inciting, including the "ill-starred and disastrous" invasion of Pennsylvania, a refusal by the army to grant promised furloughs,[106] the bad treatment at home of the families the soldiers had left behind, and "incompetency at Richmond."[107] The peace movement, he argued, actually was doing a great deal to forestall desertions, because it gave the soldiers a "gleam of sunshine."[108] Anyhow, Holden said, "we believe there are two deserters from other States to one from North Carolina. Mississippi, the President's own State, has more deserters and more men out of the service than she has in it."[109]

A few weeks after Governor Vance was in Richmond, President Davis again became concerned about the *Standard* after seeing allusions to it in the *New York Herald*, and he asked Vance to "take such action in regard to it as your judgment may suggest."[110] Vance got together a number of leading North

Carolina citizens for a talk with Holden, but their protestations were put so subtly that Holden left the meeting believing it had been called "to consult as to the state of the country."[111] The peace movement was discussed, but no decisions were made about it. In the light of the charged atmosphere in Raleigh, however, with the *Register* and the *State Journal* constantly goading the *Standard*, Vance feared that at some point an overt act of violence would be committed. He did not have long to wait.

On the night of September 9 the *Standard*'s office was all but demolished by Georgia troops passing through Raleigh, and the next morning Holden's friends retaliated by wrecking the plant of the *State Journal*. Only the intervention of the governor saved the *Register* from a concurrent assault.

The *Standard* office was attacked by men of Gen. Henry L. Benning's Georgia Brigade, which was on its way from Virginia to Chattanooga. The matter of "mobbing the office of W. W. Holden, and taking him to Chattanooga and putting him through the lines, had been discussed that day on the train"[112] as the troops neared Raleigh, a lieutenant wrote later, denying regretfully that "the honor of doing the so much needed work" could be claimed by him. He said he thought, however, that the discussion was merely in jest "and the parties who were talking did not come to any conclusion about the matter, that I heard of."

But the soldiers' talk was in earnest. About 10 o'clock that night, according to an account in the short-lived Raleigh *Daily Progress*,

probably some fifty to one hundred men, apparently led by officers, passed up Fayetteville Street and halted at the *Standard* office. They were armed and carried torches. Some of the officers went to Mr. Holden's house and enquired for that gentleman. He appeared and invited them in, but after assuring themselves they had found his residence they withdrew and soon the attack was made on the office by the armed men. The men did not seem to be excited or to manifest any passion, but went to gutting the office as they would have commenced the performance of any camp duty, all the movements seemingly directed and carried on by officers. . . . The soldiers seemed to have no feeling in the matter, but acted the part only of machines, obeying and carrying out the orders of superiors. There was a Colonel, a Major and several officers of lower rank present, and many believe here that General Benning was privy to the whole matter, and that he concurred in the proceedings. . . .

The type were all thrown in the street or scattered about the house, some State work was destroyed, and paper, stationery &c., carried off. Neither the building or the power press were injured, and Mr. Holden expects to resume the publication of his paper in a few days. . . . Governor Vance being sent for, arrived at the scene of destruction about the time the work of gutting the office had been completed. He asked one of the officers to assemble his men as he wished to address them. The men at once formed into line and the Governor addressed them, begging them to disperse and go to their quarters, which they promised to do. . . . Someone, apparently an officer and their leader, assured him that no further violence should be perpetrated, when having given three hearty cheers for Governor Vance, they marched to their camp.[113]

There are conflicting stories about what Holden was doing while the soldiers were ransacking his office. All agree that soon after the soldiers left his residence, which was next door to the office, he went to the Governor's mansion, but there is disagreement as to the route he took and as to what he did when he got there. In the gubernatorial campaign the next spring, when Holden was running against his former ally, Vance referred to the incident, saying that when he was informed of the soldiers' action,

I went up the street, while he come (sic) down a back street, to my house, entered my bedroom, turned down the gas, sat there very much frightened. On returning home, I found my competitor sitting on a chair. He asked me for a drink of brandy—said he felt badly. Soon several gentlemen came in. Mr. Holden then said: "You and I may differ in politics, but I hope my right arm may rot off if I ever raise my little finger against you," I replied: "I have done nothing but my duty." "Why," said he, "you went in among the soldiers and the bayonets—I shall always be grateful to you." [114]

The *Salisbury Watchman*, in reporting the governor's statement, said Vance had left out the best part. At about midnight that evening, the paper said, a band drew up quietly outside the mansion to serenade the governor, beginning "with a tremendous crash of big brass horn music." The startled Holden, the account continued, thinking "the Philistines were after him ... hastily *dived* under the Governor's *bed*" and would not come out until he was assured there was no threat to him.[115]

Holden disposed of the *Watchman*'s story in two sentences: "The Editor of the *Watchman* is, we believe, a member of the church, but this does not prevent him from uttering a wilful and deliberate falsehood. We call the attention of his brother church members in Salisbury to the fact, that every word in the article ... is grossly false."[116]

Early on the morning after the attack on the *Standard* office, the news spread through Raleigh and a number of citizens gathered to view the damage. As the crowd grew, it became more excited, and soon an ugly mood developed.[117] More than one hundred persons marched on the *State Journal* office and reduced it to wreckage within fifteen minutes. Galleys of type were thrown about the building and into the street; furniture was torn to pieces; books were hurled in every direction. All the equipment that could be damaged was overturned or ruined. With one journal undone, the crowd thought of moving on to the *Register* office for a repeat performance, but Governor Vance appeared, asked the people to disperse, and they complied, cheering for both Vance and Holden.

In the aftermath, Vance had President Davis issue an order forbidding troops from passing through Raleigh. The governor used a bit of blackmail on Davis, writing him privately that "if these great outrages on the peace and dignity of the State were not promptly checked," he would recall all North Carolina troops to the protection of their own State.[118]

Greater damage was done at the *State Journal* than at the *Standard*, Spelman's press being broken while Holden's was left intact.[119] For a few days workers sifted *Standard* type out of the dust, but it was more than a month before the newspaper re-appeared. Ironically, on the very day that the *Standard* was wrecked, Syme had announced in the *Register* that he was moving to Petersburg, Virginia, where he had been assured of more support than he was getting in Raleigh.[120] Spelman was to publish only a few more issues of the *State Journal*. His paper resumed publication in early November, but two months later his equipment was bought for another journal. Spelman left Raleigh, never to figure again in North Carolina politics, and there were few who regretted his passing.

That fall Hale and Holden carried on a lively correspondence, exploring their differences, but their public break did not come until after the congressional elections in November. At that time the conservatives won a substantial majority, leading Holden to believe that most of the people favored his program[121] and causing him to break away from Hale officially. He said it was "useless to mince matters any longer in relation to the *Observer*. That paper has donned the turban and turned Turk. It has gone over to the Destructives."[122] Soon afterwards Hale began printing what he called "elegant extracts from the *Standard* of 1861 and 1863,"[123] quotations paired to show that Holden had greatly altered his views from his position pledging "the last dollar and the last man" to win independence, to that of making overtures for peace before independence had been gained or was even in sight. The journalistic conflict went on until the end of the war, when both men gave up their editorships. On the surface, however, Holden still was friendly to Vance, saying in late November, 1863, that he expected to support the governor for reelection the following year.[124] But Holden pressed his peace convention

179

plans, and as Vance was forced more and more to separate himself from them, the relationship between the two men, which had been warm personally, began to cool. Very quickly a point was reached when Holden no longer felt free to call on the governor.[125]

This breach was widened in January, 1864, when Raleigh political leaders, having as newspapers only the *Standard* and its sympathizing *Daily Progress*, made arrangements to start two other journals, one to represent Vance and the other to speak for those who held more extremist views. The latter group formed a stock company, with Bragg as president, and bought the equipment of the *State Journal* for $40,000.[126] The new paper, called the *Confederate*, with Duncan K. McRae as editor, made its appearance in early February. Vance, who felt sorely in need of a newspaper voice in the capital, induced John D. Hyman, formerly an Asheville journalist, to come to Raleigh as editor of the *Conservative*, a daily which made its bow in April.[127]

Barely rid of two old annoyances, the *Register* and the *State Journal*, Holden now had to deal with two new rivals, who evidently were also intended to make him their chief concern. He lamented that for two years he had been "an object of the bitterest and most unjust political persecution; and not only this but he [Holden] is socially assailed, and is constantly threatened with personal violence."[128] The future seemed to promise more of the same.

The future also seemed to promise harassment of a different nature, for in his issue of February 24, Holden printed a cryptic announcement: "The publication of the *Standard* is for the present suspended. Due notices will be given of the resumption of publication. Our exchanges will confer a favor by continuing their visits."[129]

Hale, speculating on Holden's sudden move, wrote: "Some have attributed it to the suspension of the *habeas corpus*, and an apprehension of arrest of the Editor if he should continue to issue the *Standard*. Others [said] that it was because the Editor was a candidate and considered it indelicate to print a paper whilst occupying that position. Others [said] that he was unwilling to be called upon to answer troublesome questions whilst a candidate."[130]

The first conjecture, of course, was accurate. In a secret session on January 21 the Confederate Congress had suspended the privilege of the writ of *habeas corpus* in cases considered treasonable. Soon afterwards, perhaps by coincidence, although it was suspected that it was with the approval of Governor Vance and was for the purpose of arresting Holden and other peace leaders in Raleigh, an army brigade was ordered to encamp near the city. Holden says in his *Memoirs* that he was advised by friends to stop publication for a time because the government, apprehensive of the influence of the *Standard*, was thought to be considering action.[131] After the war, Holden was told that President Davis had determined to have him arrested for treason but was dissuaded. [132]

Despite the suspicions of Holden's friends and despite the demands of his enemies that summary action be taken against the *Standard*, Governor Vance apparently had no intention of moving against Holden in any overt manner. He wrote Davis that "if our citizens are left untouched by the arm of military violence I do not despair of an appeal to the reason and patriotism of the people at the ballot box." He warned the president "to be chary of exercising the powers" with which the suspension of the *habeas corpus* writ had clothed him and advised him to "be content to try, at least for a while, the moral effect of holding this power over the heads of discontended men."[133]

While the *Standard*'s regular publication was suspended, two important events occurred. In a speech at Wilkesborough Governor Vance announced his opposition to a peace convention;

immediately Holden got out a special issue of his paper announcing his own candidacy for the governorship, in opposition to Vance.[134]

"It was not my wish to run for Governor," Holden wrote Calvin J. Cowles of Wilkes County, who was to be his son-in-law, "and I was led to announce for two reasons: First, the *knowledge* that Gov. Vance was gone from us, and secondly, the urgent appeals of numerous friends. It is my opinion that Gov. Vance had made up his mind deliberately to go with Davis and the Destructives ever since his visit to Richmond last August."[135]

In another special issue, on April 6, Holden published a four-column account of Vance's Hillsborough speech, interpolated with his own editorial comments, and described his own candidacy as that of a conservative "after the straitest sect." He also said that he would not stump the state making speeches in his own behalf, in part because he did not want to invite the people from their employment" or to add to the excitement then prevailing by "haranguing them" for their votes. "Let the people go calmly and firmly to the polls and vote for the men of their choice. I will cheerfully abide their decision, whatever it may be. If elected, I will do everything in my power to promote the interests and honor and glory of North-Carolina, and to secure an honorable peace."[136]

If Holden thought he would be able to dictate the terms of the 1864 election, however, he was mistaken. In 1862 he had made them play his game; now he had to play theirs. Thus the state was treated to a campaign in some respects warmer than two years before, but with one candidate making all the speeches and the editors uniting almost solidly against the other. This campaign may be regarded as completing the alienation of Holden and a large portion of the state's citizens, including its most powerful politicians.

Friends of Holden, among them Jonathan Worth, pleaded with the editor to iron out his differences with Vance, Worth arguing that reconciliation would "place yourself on higher grounds of personal popularity than you ever occupied, at the same time cementing the Conservative party and inflicting on your enemies a most fatal blow. . . . I think you might be elected our next Gov. almost by acclamation."[137]

Matters had proceeded too far for reconciliation, however, even if otherwise it had been possible and the two candidates and their supporters had desired it. It had become a struggle on the one side to crush the treason that seemed to symbolize Holden's candidacy, and on the other side to strike down an obstinate regime that appeared to be blocking the people's way to peace. Vance, proving himself an adroit competitor, swung into an active speaking campaign, making election trips as far as the encampments of North Carolina troops in Virginia and handling "the antecedents of Mr. Holden in a masterly manner,"[138] as the *Conservative* once put it. The editor-candidate used his paper and other weapons that experience had given him to deal with Vance in a manner perhaps less abusive personally, as was Holden's custom, but otherwise quite as aggressive.

A major issue came to be the question of which was the better peace advocate. The *Conservative* said that as early as December, 1863, Vance had "called the attention of President Davis to the importance of negotiating immediately for peace, and urged him in the name of humanity, religion, and a bleeding country, to propose to the enemy an amicable adjustment of our difficulties."[139] Holden responded by publishing the correspondence between Davis and Vance, calling it an attempt by those two to decide "the best means for restraining and controlling public opinion in North Carolina," with Vance asking for negotiations purely as a public relations gimmick and with Davis counselling a sterner policy in dealing with the peace partisans.[140]

His friends hailed Holden as the "pioneer of the peace movement in the South," and at a public meeting at the Raleigh courthouse on May 6 they adopted a resolution declaring that "in

W. W. Holden, our friend and neighbor, we recognize an eminent statesman and a Christian gentleman, and we feel in electing him, we shall honor ourselves and this good old State whose humble sons we are."[141] Vance followed that meeting with a rally of his own, speaking so eloquently and convincingly that a friend wrote Hale, "We hear *many* persons now say that they had determined to vote for Holden—but after hearing Vance defend and explain his position, they were perfectly satisfied, and should go for him with all their hearts."[142] The latter evaluation was not in error, because a subtle change was taking place in Wake County.

When the legislature met on May 17, Governor Vance asked it for a resolution requesting the Confederate Congress to seek peace. He said that he looked upon "any attempts to treat for peace, other than through the regular channels provided by our Constitution," as dangerous, but he asked the legislators to "lay down what you would consider a fair basis of peace, and call upon our Representatives in Congress and those to whom is committed the power of making treaties, by the Constitution, to neglect no fitting opportunity of offering such to the enemy. These terms in my judgement would be nothing less than the independence of those States, whose destinies have been fairly united with the Confederacy."[143] The legislature responded by voting resolutions urging the Confederate government, in the wake of an important victory by the army, to seek peace on the basis of independence.

Vance's peace plan, calling for negotiations by the Confederate government with the Union government, was a "practical, loyal, sensible" proposition, the *Confederate* argued;[144] conversely, Holden's program of a state convention to name commissioners to meet with Northern commissioners, if indeed it did not actually lead to the secession of North Carolina from the Confederacy and to separate state action, was called impractical, treasonable, and unconstitutional.[145]

The election, like that of 1854 which had made everybody a friend in internal improvements, tended to make all voters favor peace, as that formerly ostracized word was shouted by both parties. "Twelve months ago," Holden said, "when we commenced to urge in this paper the adoption of some plan which would lead to negotiations and a treaty of peace, we were assailed and maligned and at length mobbed on account of our sentiments. But the truth is mighty and will prevail."[146]

Those who cast their votes for Holden, the *Conservative* asserted, would show their preference for the "war" candidate—"for, as sure as there is a God in Heaven, if Holden would be elected, a Convention be called, and North Carolina should secede from the Confederacy, as advocated by Mr. Holden, *a civil war* will be the result."[147] Holden agreed that the issue was war or peace, and liberty against tyranny, but his interpretation in the *Standard* was quite different. "Those who vote for Vance and the Destructives will vote for *War* and *Despotism*," he said, warning at the same time that if he was defeated, true conservatives would be "marked for the army," or, if allowed to remain at home, would suffer "intolerable" persecutions and insults.[148]

Holden apparently thought up until the last that he had a chance of victory, believing that the masses at home and the lower grades in the army would sustain his position, even though leading editors and politicians were strongly opposed to him. He wrote a friend: "The intelligence I receive continues to be of the most cheering character. I feel sure of a decided majority in the army. The minds of the people and soldiers are made up, and nothing will change their minds."

But Governor Vance had conducted his campaign with great skill, ability, and adroit diplomacy. He had made his side, if not himself, the popular one by appealing to the public's imagination in something of Holden's old style, by his persuasive platform personality, by amassing control of newspaper publicity, and by his energy on the stump. Holden, starting with an apparent advantage, had been unable to do for himself what he had done for Reid fifteen years earlier and for Vance only two years before, that is, dramatize his own candidacy. Vance, recognizing that he was unpopular at some levels of the army, had sought to overcome this by putting his reelection on a patriotic basis and to stigmatize Holden as the candidate of traitors, thereby digging a wide gulf between the two factions, with the respectable loyalists on one side, the treasonably disloyal on the other.

The result was that Vance swamped Holden, being elected by 58,070 to the editor's 14,491.[149] Holden carried only three counties, Johnston, Randolph, and Wilkes, and those by slim majorities. He was defeated by more than 200 votes in Wake; and although he charged rather lamely that there had been rigging in both army and public balloting, the result was altogether too decisive to have been accounted for by fraud. Holden and the peace plan he had so painstakingly nourished had been rejected.

The exultation of opposition editors was almost cruel. Hale, normally quite circumspect and not given to metaphor, said that Vance's reelection "is in all its aspects the most remarkable political incident of the age" and that such a victory over Holden "is worth several victories in the field." Then his prose took on a purple tinge:

Mr. Holden, who undoubtedly exercised great influence in the State, and who profanely claimed to have the power "to kill and make alive" ... the "setter-up and pullerdown of kings" ... concluded that he was strong enough to kill Vance and make Holden alive. ... Behold the result! The imaginary Samson, who had laid his head in the lap of the Delilah, Ambition, finds himself shorn of all his strength, abandoned by even his friends, and so prostrated that he can never hope to attain that "Position" which has been the cherished aim of his latter years.[150]

Fulton of the *Wilmington Journal* wrote in a similar vein, but somewhat more pointedly: "Mr. Holden, after having tried the game of killing and making alive, has at last tried the experiment on himself, and has succeeded in committing suicide. Politically speaking, he is defunct, and may hereafter be referred to as the *late* Mr. Holden."[151]

The obituary was premature. Holden would rise again. And he would be brought down even more devastatingly.

NINE

Soon after the crushing election of 1864, Holden was forced, once more, to raise his subscription prices; the weekly issue became $20 a year and the semi-weekly $30. These prices doubled those that had been in effect for several months. The reasons Holden gave for raising rates so sharply reflect the generally inflated cost of commodities still available in the Confederate states as the war wound down. Holden was paying $2 a pound for paper, $2 a pound for ink, and $60 a week to journeyman printers. As compared with costs of 1860, he said, "we pay twenty prices for the paper on which we print—eight prices for ink—and nearly seven prices for labor," while he was receiving only five prices for subscriptions. When he went to purchase supplies for his family, he said, he paid twenty prices for a bushel of corn, sixty prices for a pound of bacon, twenty-five prices for eggs, twenty-five prices for butter, five prices for wood, and fifty prices for cloth, as compared with 1860.[1]

That publishing was still profitable, however, is proved by the fact that the proprietors of the *Conservative*, begun as a campaign paper and expected to fold after the election, decided to make it permanent because its success had been so far beyond their "most sanguine expectations."[2] Hyman retired as editor, however, and the paper was entrusted to J. B. Neathery and Company. Neathery soon stated that, while he was in accord with Governor Vance "in political sentiment and public policy," the views set forth in the paper would not necessarily be official unless they were so designated.[3]

Holden promised after the election, which neither "dismayed nor depressed" him, that he would follow his accustomed course. "Principle, and not expediency, has been my guide heretofore, as it will hereafter," he said; "and when I follow principle, I have no regrets to express at defeat so far as I personally am concerned, as I would not have exulted over anyone if I had been successful. I will never, in any event, humiliate myself at the footstool of the Destructive party, or fuse with that party." He said he would "hold 'the sword in one hand and the olive branch in the other,' the sword for the Destructives, and the olive branch for all good and true Conservatives."[4]

The sword was prominent in the next few months, for what he apparently believed the "Destructives" had done to him was not to be forgiven—reluctance to forgive, a trait that had been growing in him since the bitterness first aroused in the convention of 1858. A sharpened pen of realistic comment on Confederate affairs also was in evidence. To all except those who deliberately refused to see, and this number included almost every North Carolina editor, it was apparent that the end was near. Atlanta was in the hands of Sherman, and he was planning to join Grant to the northward, marching through North Carolina. The loss of Richmond was imminent, and Governor Vance wrote to a friend: "I have never before been so gloomy about the condition of affairs. . . ."[5]

In his discussion of the demoralization of the South in that private letter, Vance made a confession that would have ruined him had he uttered it in his campaign against Holden: "It shows what I have always believed, that the great *popular heart* is not now and has never been in the war! It was a revolution of the *politicians* not the people; was fought at first by the natural inclination of our young men, and has been kept going by State and sectional pride assisted by that bitterness of feeling produced by the cruelties and butcheries of the enemy."[6]

This private feeling was something like the opinions the *Standard* had been expressing publicly, since it spoke, Holden still thought, for the "great popular heart"; but the paper, while it wanted the war carried on as vigorously as possible, continued to contend that this would not end the conflict and that a resolution should be sought in some other way. In the next few months, as he closely watched the shifting fortunes, Holden himself appeared to change: he grew more pessimistic, or perhaps more realistic, in his views of Southern military prospects, and his hatred of the Richmond administration and his desire for peace seemed to increase until he was ready to make almost any concession to obtain relief from the "despotism" and the war.

The *Standard* noticed a statement that the *Conservative* was thankful for the belated praise that President Davis was bestowing on North Carolina. "No State has been as much abused by President Davis and his special friends as North Carolina," the rival paper said in a surprising echo of *Standard* sentiment, "and yet the President now says she stands a head and shoulder above the rest."[7] Holden observed that it could "make no difference *now* what Mr. Davis may think or say of her; but it is a little singular that he did not discover her merits and commence to eulogize her publicly, until one of his friends was chosen (?) a second time to be her Governor."[8]

Along with other North Carolina newspapers, the *Standard* was appalled at a suggestion made at a meeting of Southern governors in Atlanta that slaves be armed and put into Southern service. "Such a course would not only degrade the Southern people to a level with their Northern enemies who have been employing slaves as soldiers, but it would sow broadcast the seeds of insurrection and massacre in our midst," he thundered. "The proposition is unreasonable, ridiculous, short-sighted, foolish, desperate, ruinous, horrible."[9] In repeated editorials on the subject he used up a lot more adjectives.

As the legislature met in November, 1864, the peace advocates again urged the necessity for early negotiation with the North. The *Standard* used the reelection of Lincoln as a text for an editorial on the subject, arguing that it meant that a vast majority of the people of the North stood determined to prosecute the war for the next four years, if necessary.[10] The paper hailed "with much satisfaction" resolutions introduced on November 24 in the state Senate calling for the election by the General Assembly of five commissioners to act with similar representatives from other southern states in negotiating for peace and providing that whenever any five states had appointed commissioners, President Davis should be asked to seek a conference with the Union government to work out a peace through commissioners.[11] Holden said this proposal accorded with his own views, and he was indignant when the Senate voted to lay the resolutions on the table in a parliamentary maneuver that precluded debate. He called the action "an act of gross discourtesy—the Davis Destructives and Vance Destructives refuse to discuss the question of peace!"[12]

The *Conservative* asked the *Standard* to lay aside "all declamations about this 'cruel war,' and all pretensions to superior philanthropy" and to state explicitly what it wanted by way of negotiation, "with whom it is going to negotiate, what it is for, and what it will take."[13] Holden's reply admitted for the first time that in the desperate circumstances then prevailing he favored separate state action. "We would negotiate with the government of the United States, and we would obtain the best terms we could for North Carolina. We would reserve the right, as a citizen, to say whether we would 'take' the terms agreed upon by the commissioners. Any terms that might be agreed upon ought to be submitted to the people for their acceptance or rejection."[14]

He also conceded another point that he would not have accepted a year earlier, his willingness to accept reconstruction. "For our part—and we believe we utter the sentiments of a large majority of our people—as anxious as we have been for Confederate success, we would prefer a restoration of the old government to the subjugation of the South, if such an alternative should be presented. . . . We would rather live with than under the Yankees. If forced to it, we would cut off an arm or a leg to save the body." And in that admission he was particularly prescient, saying that slavery "as a permanent institution" was doomed.[15]

From these admissions, he turned to the ever recurrent topic of negotiation for peace. If the South lost, he said, the conquerors would have the right to dictate and impose terms. "But is it sound reason to wait, before we make terms, until the heel of the conqueror is on our necks? If there is a strong probability that, in the end, we will be overrun, and subjugated and held down by our enemy at his mercy, would it not be wise to avoid that unspeakable evil by compromising our difficulties at once, on the best terms that can be obtained?"[16]

Governor Vance declared in a forceful proclamation issued February 14, 1865, that negotiation schemes such as were being clamored for were wishful thinking, citing the report of Vice President Stephens and two other commissioners who had met with President Lincoln on January 28 at Hampton Roads that no treaty would be granted the Confederates States or any separate state unless restoration to the Union were assured. "Thus you see," Vance said, "that neither terms nor conditions were spoken of in the interview, but only subjugation offered us, the mere details of which they proposed to settle." He depicted the evils of subjugation and exclaimed, "Great God! Is there a man in all this honorable, high spirited, and noble Commonwealth so steeped in every conceivable meanness, so blackened with all the guilt of treason, or so damned with all the leprosy of cowardice as to say: Yes, we will submit to all this; and whilst there yet remains half a million men amongst us able to resist."[17]

Holden's comment on this document as he published it was that it was not "destitute of a certain species of rude eloquence, which characterizes nearly all of Gov. Vance's state papers; but though we may accord to the Governor sincerity of purpose and some vigor in the use of language, we regret we cannot add that he is truthful or accurate in his statements."[18] Concurrent with Vance's exhortation there actually were editors remaining in North Carolina who believed that the stricken Southern armies would rise up in one great final fling and rout the enemy on all fronts. As Sherman advanced on Fayetteville, Hale wrote that he was confident that Gen. Robert E. Lee would make good his word that Sherman, who had left Georgia in ashes, "can and will be defeated."[19]

Holden belittled such blind bursts of faith. "The people," he said, "expect the truth in this paper, and they shall have it as far as we are able to tell it."[20] And so there were no schoolboyish declamations on whipping the enemy, no rhetorical advice against despondency. The *Standard* discussed the size of Sherman's army, his probable plans in North Carolina, and the efforts to stop him. It calculated that Sherman's march on Raleigh would be "rapid and successful," although it was conceivable that the Union general, confident of easy victory, might "encounter defeat and disaster."[21] At that time, Holden was accused of wishy-washiness, of trying to find a position that would offend neither blue nor gray. There is some truth to this charge, because Holden did appear to follow a middle-ground, noncommittal, safe policy.

When it was obvious that Sherman would not be stopped, he undertook in fatherly language to quiet the fears of readers and to prevent a panic:

We say to the people of all classes and parties, remain at your homes and be calm as possible. Let us not add to the dangers of our situation and to our inevitable deprivation, by flight, or by panic or alarm.

When a brave people have done all in their power to defend their homes, there is no dishonor in waiting calmly whatever may be in store for them. . . . So far as we are concerned, though there may be animosities against us, we have no wish to see the war diverted from its legitimate channel to the injury of any man's person or estate. After all, we are fellow-countrymen of the same blood and stock, and are all more or less responsible for the action of North-Carolina in this war, however we may have differed among ourselves on questions of party policy. . . . Let us, then, as a community and as a people stand together, and do the best we can to mitigate the calamities of war.[22]

The *Standard* of March 29 was printed on a half-sheet, "owing to the difficulties encountered in printing at this time, and the general uncertainty of events."[23] The issue of April 5, the last *Standard* with subscription rates quoted in Confederate money, increased the prices to $40 a year for the weekly issue and $60 a year for the semiweekly.

The following week, after Union troops had occupied Raleigh, Holden began publication of a daily—a plan that he had had in mind for several years. The price was quoted as 10 cents a copy in "federal money." He promised that "as soon as mail communication is restored, we shall commence again the publication of our weekly edition, and will give the terms for the future of our Daily and Weekly."

Simultaneously with the publication of this daily, there began to appear in the columns of the *Standard* some of the pent-up bitterness against the now crushed "Destructives," who had thwarted efforts at peace, who had dashed his expectation of being governor, and who were linked in his mind with the "aristocrats" that had defeated him in 1858 and seemingly had oppressed him since. He had said that if he had been successful the year before, he would not have exulted over anyone; but now that he had the whip hand, as one who had originally fought secession and had increasingly fought the Confederate administration and the continuation of the war, a vindictive quality crept into his editorials. This attitude was probably human, but it was unfortunate and in the long run made his downfall more assured.

Holden wrote no editorial on the death of Lincoln and carried no original article on the assassination, contenting himself with copying an article from the *Philadephia Inquirer* and reprinting editorial comment from other papers. Sandwiched in with these items was a paragraph greeting President Johnson and expressing for Raleigh the pride felt in the fact that he was born there. "We expect," Holden said, "to give his administration a cordial and active support, and we feel sure that in all essential respects he will fully meet in his new position the expectations of his warmest friends."[24]

The next day Holden cracked the whip at his late opponents in the city, the "secessionists and Vanceites," saying to them "once for all, that we have been very forbearing in our tone towards them since the Union forces occupied this place, and we have no wish to see them personally injured; we warn them that a swift and terrible retribution will follow any betrayal by them of Union men into the hands of Confederate guerrillas."[25] If there seemed to be in this editorial a self-serving note, there was also a warning spoken for his own personal defense. There had been a plot to hang Holden before the Union troops arrived.[26]

The *Standard* actively fought a movement to have Vance continue as governor. "He has proved himself utterly unfit to be ruler of a free people," Holden said in a bitter two-column attack. "Let him go, never to return in his capacity of Governor."[27] Federal soldiers, who once had been called "Lincoln hirelings," were eulogized for their "glorious work" in bringing peace, "the greatest of earthly blessings," and also in wiping out the despotism of President Davis.[28] The issue containing this panegyric also carried the *Standard*'s last war story, and it is interesting to compare the captions, at least, with those on the first story of four years earlier:

PEACE! PEACE!

· · ·

CAPITULATION OF THE ONLY REMAINING REBEL ARMY THIS SIDE OF THE CHATTAHOOCHEE! !

· · ·

GENERAL JOHNSTON SURRENDERS TO GENERAL SHERMAN!

· · ·

TROOPS TO GO HOMEWARD!

· · ·

GREAT REJOICING OF SOLDIERS AND PEOPLE

Perhaps more interesting is the absolutely vitriolic story of the reported escape of President Davis:

Our opinion is that this great sectional imposter and robber has struck for the seacoast, and that his purpose is to make his escape on a small vessel to some of the West India Islands. . . . We trust he may yet be caught and brought to justice. Here is a man who, to gratify his own wicked ambition, involved his country in war, and for four long years . . . dragged his subjects through seas of horrors; and at last, having exhausted even hope itself, he makes his escape like a convict with millions of treasure. . . . He escapes and carries with him this treasure coined from the blood and tears of his country men, much of it the voluntary contributions of misguided men, and women and children who thought they were making a patriotic sacrifice when they poured it into his lap. First a traitor, then a tyrant, then a flying robber! May his gold perish with him![29]

Davis and the "secessionists" also were attacked by Holden in a speech the editor made at a Union mass meeting in Raleigh's Capitol Square a few days later. Resolutions adopted at that meeting expressed confidence in the "ability, integrity and patriotism" of President Johnson and made this urgent plea: "In the event of an election for the office of Governor, which we believe should soon be held, we cheerfully recommend, as the first choice of the PEOPLE therefore, W.W. HOLDEN—their great Confederate champion—whom they should delight to reward and honor."[30]

The invectives against Davis, the leadership the *Standard* had taken in speaking for the Union, the bitterness against the "Destructives" and "Vanceites," and the resolutions forwarding Holden's name for the governorship, were the forerunners of—even if not the decisive elements in—an announcement in the *Standard* of May 15 that the editor would be absent "for some ten days on important business."[31] The notice did not give any reasons for the absence, but rumors and guesses probably did hint at an explanation. At any rate, Holden had received a summons from President Johnson calling him to Washington, and he must have understood what the message portended. With a group of close friends, he made the trip to the White House and was joined there by another group of North Carolinians, headed by former Gov. David L. Swain, called in by Johnson for consultation. The result was a decision by the president to appoint Holden provisional governor, with duties beginning on June 5, 1865.[32]

Thus W. W. Holden had at last achieved the governorship. He had perhaps dreamed of it as a Whig—vaguely, in the nebulous manner of ambitious youth. He had sought the nomination for it as a Democrat and perhaps would have made an excellent executive, especially if the personal bitterness of the 1858 convention had been avoided. He had run for it as a conservative amid the excitements and rancors of civil war. Now he was appointed to it as, possibly, a Republican, to try to lead his state out of chaos back into the Union and a more peaceful routine.

The *Standard* for June 5 published the proclamation of President Johnson appointing the provisional governor for the state and printed the president's announcement of his policy for reorganization.

The following day Holden announced that he was turning over the editorship of the paper to his son, Joseph W. Holden, and to Joseph S. Cannon. In the *Standard* of June 7, the name of W. W. Holden, after twenty-two eventful years, was replaced in the masthead by other names, and Holden's editorial days were temporarily ended. He had entered upon another phase of his career, the only part most southern historians seem to care about. It was a phase, it may be added, that he probably had in mind when he remarked nearly twenty years later of his chief editorial contemporary: "Mr. Hale has shown his good sense in that he never sought or held public office."[33]

Holden was to pay a huge price to learn the wisdom of that statement.

TEN

WHEN Holden took office as provisional governor of North Carolina in June, 1865, the task he faced would have dismayed a less energetic man. Government in the state was utterly disorganized; all offices were vacant. The state was without money and without any means of collecting taxes. City and county officers had to be appointed, courts set up, and the entire machinery of government rebuilt to direct affairs until the people could hold the convention needed under President Johnson's plan to frame a constitution that would entitle the state to readmission to the Union.

A week after he assumed his duties, Holden issued a proclamation assuring the public that the convention would be called soon and would provide for the election of a governor, congressmen, and legislators; the state legislature thus constituted would select two United States senators. In the meantime, the state was to be served by appointed officials. Holden urged the people to abandon disloyal sentiment, now that the war was over, and to take an active interest in public affairs again.

In little more than a month the new governor appointed more than three thousand officials, including an entire set of state authorities, mayors and commissioners for the towns, magistrates for the county courts, directors and overseers for various institutions, and numerous other persons to fill vacancies.[1]

J. G. deRoulhac Hamilton, a historian and author of the

account in the *Dictionary of American Biography*, said that Holden's designation as provisional governor "was a most unfortunate one. Holden had played fast and loose with all parties, factions, and classes, and had in consequence lost the confidence of nearly every responsible leader of opinion in the State. In addition, he had won the bitter enmity of a very large and influential class. Not less important in determining the character of his administration, he was consumed with ambition and was certain to try to use his position for the punishment of his opponents and for contributing to his own advancement."[2] But of this six-week period of feverish activity in which the expenses were borne by the War Department, Hamilton wrote: "Leaving out of consideration all questions of motive or of his action in some individual cases, his work was well done. He was far less proscriptive than his enemies or even his friends had expected."[3]

In the middle of July Holden wrote President Johnson that his preliminary work was done and that he was prepared to issue a proclamation for a convention to meet, possibly in October. "It could be called sooner," he said, "but in so important a matter I think I ought to proceed deliberately and carefully."[4]

In addition to the aforementioned matters of pure government, Holden had to receive and pass on to the president, with favorable or unfavorable recommendations, applications for pardon from those whose conditions cast them outside the general amnesty Johnson had already proclaimed. (That proclamation excluded executive and diplomatic officers of the Confederacy, governors of the seceded states, those who had left Union military service to join the Confederate forces, the highest ranking secessionist army and naval officers, and Southerners holding property in value exceeding $20,000 who voluntarily took part in the war.) In seven months Holden received and made notations on more than twelve hundred such applications, marking only four for outright rejection. There were also many details of office to be attended to, perplexing questions to be decided, and "not less than seventy-five" visitors to see daily. "I was robust and in good health when I entered on my duties," he said years later, "but at the close of them I was thin and sallow and weak, so intensely had I labored, as I thought, for North Carolina."[5]

On August 8, when sufficient time had elapsed for citizens to take the federal oath of allegiance, Governor Holden ordered the election of delegates to the convention. The balloting was set for September 21, and the date of the convention was fixed for October 2. Despite the exhortations of Holden, many former supporters of the Confederacy stubbornly stood aside and refused to vote. Nevertheless, some outstanding men were elected, including Bartholomew F. Moore, Bedford Brown, Alfred Dockery, Thomas Settle, John Pool, Robert P. Dick, Judge Edwin G. Reade, and a number of others who had served either in the legislature or in previous conventions. Judge Reade was chosen to preside over the sessions.

Two major problems confronted the convention: the renunciation of secession and the disposition of the debt contracted by the state during the war. A resolution offered by Nathaniel Boyden stating that the ordinance of secession "is now and hath been at all times null and void," thus agreeing with President Johnson's view that the state had never been out of the Union, brought a protest from the minority. Dennis D. Ferebee offered a substitute providing merely for the repeal of the act of May 20, 1861. This substitute was defeated 96 to 19, and the Boyden resolution then was passed 105 to 9.

A more embarrassing question concerned the state debt. The Washington administration wanted it repudiated, but there naturally was strong opposition in the state to this action, and Holden at first appeared to agree with this sentiment. Jonathan Worth, whom Holden had appointed state treasurer, insisted that repudiation was unthinkable and moreover was not within the jurisdiction of the convention. A telegram, however, from President Johnson (Holden's enemies said he had inspired it) asking for repudiation was decisive with the convention, which acceded to the wishes of the president.

This matter brought a rupture in relations between Worth and Holden, and Worth announced his candidacy for governor in elections provided for by the convention. Holden already had received a letter signed by fifty members of the convention urging him to be a candidate so that "restoration should be completed by one under whose guidance it has been so auspiciously begun."[6] In acquiescing, Holden replied that whatever the decision of the voters, "I shall always possess the consciousness that I am a faithful and devoted son of our dear old State, and that I have labored with zeal, and with what success my poor faculties could command, to improve the condition of her people, and to restore her to her appropriate and natural position in the Union." As provisional governor, he said, "I have known no party but the sincere friends of the Union. I am neither a Democrat nor a Whig. Both these parties were buried in the grave of the rebellion. All I can say is I am a North Carolinian, heart and soul."[7]

In the brief time before the November 9 election neither candidate made any speeches. It was urged by Holden's friends, however, that President Johnson desired his success as ratification of his appointment and would be displeased with the state if Worth was chosen. Worth's friends harped on the idea that Holden had favored repudiation, which had forced every bank in the state into liquidation and had impoverished thousands of people who held now worthless bonds. The election gave Worth 31,643 votes to 25,704 for Holden, and for the third time the boy from Hillsborough had been denied the office he wanted. Holden attributed his defeat not only to the debt issue, in which he said he had only followed presidential orders, but also to the animosity of old secessionist Democrats.[8] Wake County, incidentally, voted for Holden 1,702 to 453.

Holden, after protesting to President Johnson against recognition of the election and being directed to give way to Worth, turned the state's seal over to his successor on December 28 and retired, apparently having made a generally satisfactory executive. He was assured that the president appreciated his work and that it would "in no case be forgotten."[9] In the summer of 1866 Holden accepted an appointment as minister to El Salvador but was rejected by the Senate, which could not yet bring itself to favor rewards of any kind to Southerners.

He turned back to state politics and to the *Standard*'s editorship; but it was a different Holden and a different *Standard* from before, for neither became the force of former years. Worth, whose first election had been for a partial term, announced his candidacy for reelection to a regular term, and the problem was to find an opponent for him. After several draftees had declined, the nomination was offered to Alfred Dockery, who declined, but not so explicitly as to be convincing. Holden and other friends worked for him but failed to arouse any enthusiasm for his half-way candidacy. Worth was reelected with a majority of almost 20,000 votes.

Holden then became interested in the Union League, a political organization established in the North in 1862. After the Civil War it quickly spread to the South, gathering into its membership the emancipated slaves. Albion W. Tourgee, an Ohioan known to state historians of the period as a notorious carpetbagger, was the first president of the North Carolina league. He was succeeded by Holden in 1867. Union league lodges were organized and were bound together in a statewide organization that the historian Hamilton says in "its very name has remained a symbol of all that was evil in Reconstruction."[10] The reason it became the symbol, he says without offering proof, is that it was a terrorist organization. "Although there was nothing objectionable, the meetings, under the influence of evil and designing leaders became the hot-beds of violence and crime. Labor was disbanded by it, larceny, assault, riot, arson, murder, and rape were [its] products. . . . The Ku Klux Klan movement was the logical result."

Hamilton's version is a myth popularized in the South to excuse the later excesses of the Klan, after whose appearance, Hamilton says, the atrocities of the league became "beautifully less." While there was assuredly exploitation of the former slaves by self-serving whites, both native to North Carolina and alien to it, it cannot be shown that men of Holden's caliber would have countenanced a policy of pillage.

Concurrent with his activities in the Union League, Holden was a dominant figure in the formation of the Republican Party in North Carolina, when delegates from fifty-six counties met in Raleigh in March, 1867, about the time the Reconstruction Acts were passed. These laws replaced President Johnson's plan for restoring the Confederate states to the Union that Holden had followed when he was provisional governor, granting amnesty, convening a state constitutional convention, and holding the subsequent elections. Holden said he accepted the new laws in good faith as the next best plan, since they promised the restoration of all the states to the Union.[11]

The Reconstruction Acts put the Confederate states back under military command, and Brig. Gen. Daniel E. Sickles, the North Carolina commander, issued an order continuing the civil government under Governor Worth but declaring it provisional and making plain that it existed at the sufferance of the military authorities. Sickles, however, was removed after a confrontation with the United States District Court in Wilmington, to be succeeded by Maj. Gen. E. R. S. Canby, who, Worth wrote, "was much more esteemed by Holden & Company."[12]

On July 4, 1867, members of the Union League paraded to the grove behind the Governor's Mansion, where a program was given, with Holden among those speaking. Letters were presented from Charles Sumner, B. F. Butler, and others, the Declaration of Independence was read by Joseph Holden, and resolutions were adopted "pledging support to the Republican party . . . and appealing to that party to relieve the people of the State from the present civil government."[13] A committee was appointed to go to Washington to present this matter. Another resolution expressed "the utmost confidence in the loyalty, integrity, and statesmanship of Ex-Governor W. W. Holden . . . ."[14]

Registration of voters, ordered by the Reconstruction Acts, was begun in August, and General Canby declared it complete on October 18, when the tally showed 106,721 whites and 72,932 Negroes qualified to vote. The general set November 12 and 20 as the days for those voters to elect delegates to a convention that was to frame a new state constitution that would accord with the ideas of Congress. Republicans won 107 seats in the convention, while Worth's adherents, known as conservatives for lack of an official name, took 13 places. Calvin J. Cowles, Holden's son-in-law, whom Hamilton describes as a man "of unimpeachable honesty but of only fair ability" and otherwise "entirely under the influence of Holden and the carpet-baggers,"[15] was elected president of the convention, and Tourgee was prominent in the deliberations.

In two months a new constitution, known as the "Canby Constitution," was completed and the convention adjourned March 17, 1868. Some of the new provisions were received with ill grace by the state's conservatives. Among them were the extension of the term of governor to four years, the creation of the offices of lieutenant governor, superintendent of public works, and auditor, renaming as the House of Representatives the lower house of the General Assembly, known for a hundred years as the House of Commons, declaring all men equal, guaranteeing to all the privilege of an education, and abolishing of property qualifications for holding legislative office. By today's standards these do not seem revolutionary or unjust innovations; to those North Carolina whites still clinging to the ideals of the Old South, they were anathema.

This new document was to be submitted to the voters in April, and at the same time there was to be another election for governor, the third within two years.

Holden was nominated as the candidate of the Republicans, who held their convention in Raleigh in February; Tod R. Caldwell was the candidate for lieutenant governor. The conservatives selected as Holden's opponent Thomas S. Ashe, the well-dressed college youth whom Holden had encountered in Hillsborough nearly forty years before. The campaign brought more than the usual vituperation and personal abuse, with Holden bearing the brunt of it, and was in part a battle between the Union League and the Ku Klux Klan, which was making its first political appearance in North Carolina and accompanied its debut with this notice:[16]

K. K. K.

Attention! First Hour! In the Mist!

At the Flash! Come. Come. Come ! ! !

Retribution is impatient! The grave yawns!

The sceptre bones rattle!

Let the doomed quake!

The chief issue before the voters, other than prejudice for or against the candidates and their supporting organizations, was whether the constitution should be ratified. The election, the first in which Negroes had voted for governor, resulted in the sanctioning of the new constitution, 93,084 to 74,015, and the election of Holden as governor, 92,235 to 73,594. Holden had kept the vow he was said to have made as a ragged newsboy.

Again Holden gave up the editorship of the *Standard*, selling it to N. Paige & Co., and announcing that he and his son, Joseph W., were relinquishing all connection with the paper,[17] although two years later Joseph W. Holden did become editor again for a time.

A typical post-Civil War costume of the Ku Klux Klan

REMEMBER THE

6

These degenerate sons of the white race who control the republican machine in this county, or those whose positions made them influential in putting negro rule on the whites, will suffer the penalty of their responsibility for any disturbance consequent on the determination of the white men of this county to carry the election at any cost.

REMEMBER THE

6

A typical Klan election warning

Congress approved the new North Carolina constitution on June 25 and provided for the admission of the state's senators and representatives as soon as North Carolina approved the Fourteenth Amendment. It directed Holden to summon the legislature at once, and the governor-elect called a special session for July 1. Governor Worth was notified on June 30 that the oath of office would be administered to Holden the next day. When it was intimated that in protest against the special election and Congressional Reconstruction policies Worth might refuse to give up the office, a military order was issued ejecting him. Still declaring that he did not recognize the validity of the election,[18] Worth surrendered his chair to Holden, who was inaugurated on July 4, 1868. The Fourteenth Amendment had been ratified on July 2, the day after the legislature convened. At once General Canby ordered military interference with the civil government to cease.

In his inaugural address, Governor Holden urged the people to obey the laws and thus let peace and tranquillity once more rule the state. He cited two types of disturbing influences. It was known, he said, that some regarded the Reconstruction laws as unconstitutional, "and it may be that this may lead, if not to open resistance, to a forcible denial in some localities of the rights guaranteed by the Constitution of the State. . . . It is also known that a disposition exists, among no inconsiderable portion of our population, to oppress the poor whites and the colored race on account of their political opinions." He warned the public that a purpose to subvert the government would "be narrowly watched and promptly checked on the first manifestation of any overt act on the part of those cherishing such purpose."[19]

In addition, he pleaded:

Fellow-citizens, let us come out of the caverns of the past, and forgetting what is not worthy to be remembered, let us resolve to do our duty in our day and time, as North Carolinians, as Americans. In a climate and with a soil for which Providence has done so much, let us resolve to do something for ourselves and our children. Let us devote ourselves to the arts of peace. . . . Prejudices growing out of nativity, or out of the rebellion, are not worthy to be cherished. Let us discard such prejudices. We are once more Americans—all.[20]

It was a mild speech, but it was ahead of its time. With the "aristocrats," whose scorn Holden had withstood for decades, the "prejudices" of the "rebellion" were not dead. They lamented the lost cause of the Confederacy most grievously. The way of life they had enjoyed in antebellum years had vanished; they resented the newfound freedom of the erstwhile slaves, whom they had regarded as subhuman; and they would never treat them as equals, no matter what the law specified. Against the blacks, except as the Klan provided a convenient front, they could not act en masse; and all of the shame and humiliation they felt was concentrated ultimately upon one man—the Reconstruction governor of North Carolina. On him they could work their revenge.

Two matters connected with Holden's administration need to be noted: the Reconstruction frauds perpetrated by the legislature and the deadly confrontation with the Klan, as the agent of white supremacy, which led directly to his impeachment.

Corruption probably reached its peak in the legislative session of 1868–69, the principal frauds being connected with the issuance of railroad bonds for state aid in the construction of the Western Division of the Western North Carolina Railroad. In a program pushed by Milton Littlefield, who had been a Federal officer and had come to Raleigh as a carpetbagger after the war, the legislators authorized $27,850,000 in railroad bonds, of which $10,190,000 were not issued and $4,345,000 were returned to the state, leaving $13,315,000 added to the state's debt. Some of these bond issues were initiated by George W. Swepson, president of the Western Division, in accordance with a state promise to subscribe two-thirds of the stock for building the road. Littlefield, as a reward for shepherding the issue through the legislature, is said to have obtained a commission of ten percent; he also was charged with obtaining additional bonds for other roads and with being involved in other frauds which strongly affected the state's credit.

Holden, it should be noted here, was never seriously accused of benefiting personally in the wave of looting and speculation—which had its roots in the election to the legislature of men unschooled in the law, no doubt unqualified for office and certainly ill-equipped to cope with lobbyists and crooks. Nevertheless, in the eyes of many, Holden as governor was fraternizing with and protecting men who were plundering the treasury. There was considerable feeling that he might have prevented much of the fraud, although he insisted that he was innocent of connivance and was acting for the public good in the matter of providing internal improvements—something in which he had been interested for years.

Several years later, in his first public defense of himself against suspicions of fraud, Holden said:

I solemnly declare that I never performed any act while Governor, or signed my name, with a view to reward or the hope of reward; and I never received a bribe from any one for any of my acts while Governor. There could have been no motive to bribe me to sign my name, even if I could have been bribed, for every paper, or document, or bond which I signed was signed strictly in accordance with law. I had no veto power as Governor. I did not pass the bills to issue the bonds. I never appealed in person to any member of the Legislature to vote for these bills.[21]

There is no reason to believe that Holden here was trying merely to exculpate and whitewash himself. If any evidence existed connecting him with the frauds in any way, it would have been presented at his impeachment trial; yet when an article was introduced in the bill of indictment charging him with complicity in issuing bonds, it was quickly dropped because Swepson, the railroad executive, telegraphed the committee from New York that the charge was false and that if it were pressed he would return to Raleigh and personally prove Holden innocent of the accusation.[22]

In his war with the Ku Klux Klan Governor Holden's intentions were more admirable than his political astuteness, for he allowed his opponents to create a situation that led to an impasse. The Klan, fed by opposition to the Reconstruction Acts and an attempt to reinstitute white supremacy, grew rapidly in 1868 and 1869 until it reached a membership, by Holden's estimate, of 40,000 in North Carolina. No one disputes that figure. Klan ideology consumed even some very good and otherwise honorable men, despite the governor's pleas for peaceable acceptance of the laws and despite several remonstrating proclamations to curb Klan activity.

The first of these proclamations was issued within three months after Holden's inauguration; it argued for the constitutionality of the established government and warned against outrages. On April 16, 1868, Holden issued another warning that bands of masked and armed men must cease going about at night creating fear and doing violence. On October 20, another proclamation noticed in more detail various crimes and misdemeanors for which the Klan was blamed and attempted to arouse public opinion to aid in suppressing the disorders.[23]

The conservative public was in no mood to respond to the governor's pleas, perhaps feeling much more acutely the sentiment to which the historian Hamilton gave voice a half century later in defense of the Klan. He wrote that by its actions

heart had been put into the despairing whites and a revolution had been wrought through its operations, or to be more exact, the results of a revolution had been overthrown and a form of government, wickedly, illegally, and unconstitutionally imposed upon the people, had come into the hands of the class best fitted to administer government, and the supremacy of the white race and of Anglo-Saxon institutions was secure. . . . Its chief work in the State and in the South in addition to the protection it furnished, was in restoring heart and courage to the white people who at first seemed overwhelmed by the immensity of their misfortunes.[24]

In December, 1869, Holden recommended to the legislature the enactment of a law whereby the governor would be empowered to declare counties in a state of insurrection and to place them under martial law to suppress violations of the Constitution and the laws of the state. The legislature responded with the Shoffner Act, which not only allowed the governor to declare counties in insurrection and to send in militia to restore order, but also allowed blacks to be recruited as militiamen.

John W. Moore, the historian, gives a vivid impression, surrealistic in its factual basis, of the result:

The Negroes, like children with fresh toys, were enraptured with the opportunity of appearing as soldiers in the villages and cross-roads of their vicinity. The hottest and longest day did not abate their military ardor. Through clouds of dust and stifling heat, from sunrise till dark, amid the discord of tortured drums, they marched and countermarched at the inexorable commands of their sable captains. In such uproar village life became almost insupportable, for the Africans, with their admiring females in attendance, generally considered their duties but half performed with the setting sun, and were too apt to make night hideous with a continuation of the maddening and ridiculous noise.[25]

Moore was not inclined to dampen rhetoric with factual citations.

The Shoffner Act, which resulted in its author fleeing the state with the Klan yapping at his heels, did not immediately halt Klan activity. On March 8, 1870, Holden issued a proclamation giving the details of hangings and whippings by the Klan and urging the public to assist in restoring order. Without public announcement he had enlisted the aid of sober-minded conservatives in bringing about peace in some of the less-infected areas. But on the night of February 26, 1870, Wyatt Outlaw, Negro leader of the Union League in Alamance County, was taken out and hanged as a substitute for Shoffner. In Klan reasoning Outlaw deserved what he got, because he had organized the blacks of Alamance to vote Republican in 1868. In Caswell County, in the months of April and May, the Klan killed Robin Jacobs, a Negro, and, in broad daylight in the Caswell County Courthouse, before numerous witnesses, shot Republican State Senator John W. Stephens to death. At that time, the senator who has gone down in North Carolina history as "Chicken" Stephens, was trying to collect evidence of Klan activity for Governor Holden. Twenty-one other persons in Caswell, black and white, were whipped or scourged by the Klan. In June the governor listed thirteen murders committed since February, 1870, and he deprecated, at the same time, the retaliations that he said had begun against the Klan: he offered rewards for both classes of offenders.[26]

"There is no doubt now," according to Cortez A. M. Ewing, a careful student of this period, "that the Conservative leaders hoped to provoke Holden to the point at which he would declare martial law. Then he could be lambasted as a tyrant, and North Carolina was, and for that matter still is, inherently fearful of governmental tyranny. Holden's was a Hobson's choice. By curling up, he would procure nothing but contempt from his adversaries; by fighting the menace, he would seal the fate of his own political future as well as that of the party."[27]

In March Holden took the plunge that was to prove fatal. He declared Alamance County in a state of insurrection and informed President Grant of his action and his reason for it, sending a pamphlet containing testimony of witnesses on conditions in the county.[28] The civil government was not displaced by military rule, however, and the move resulted in no improvement of conditions.

In June, acting both on the advice of U.S. Senator John Pool and on the basis of a large number of depositions relating outrages in the county, he decided on stronger measures and determined to send in troops. Pool wrote from Washington that he had learned that Gen. Bedford Forrest, reputed head of the Klan, was roaming Alamance and Caswell in disguise. He suggested that a stern judge and a fearless prosecuting attorney be sent in with the troops.[29]

In his *Memoirs*, published posthumously in 1911, Holden tells about the considerations that compelled him to meet force with force, and in the process recreates the anarchic conditions brought about by the Klan's utter contempt for the law.

"For the space of twelve months," he wrote,

while the laws were thus being set at naught, and while grand juries were failing to find bills, or, if they were found, petit juries refused to convict, I was most constantly importuned by letters, and in person, by many of the victims of these outrages, and was urged to adopt some means of protection to society, and especially to the victims of the secret combinations referred to [the Klan klaverns].

These combinations were at first purely political in their character, and many good citizens were induced to join them. But gradually, under the leadership of ambitious and discontented politicians, and under the pretext that society needed to be regulated by some authority outside or above the law, their character was changed, and these secret Klans began to commit murder, to rob, whip, scourge and mutilate unoffending citizens . . .

The members were united by oaths which ignored or repudiated the ordinary oaths or obligations resting upon all other citizens to respect the laws and to uphold the government; these oaths inculcated hatred by the white race against the colored race. The members of the Klan . . . met in secret, in disguise, with arms, in a dress of a certain kind intended to conceal their persons and their horses, and to terrify those whom they menaced or assaulted.

They held their camps, and under their leaders they decreed judgement against their peaceable fellow citizens, from mere intimidation to scourgings, mutilations, the burning of churches, school houses, mills and in many cases to murder.

This organization, under different names, but cemented by a common purpose, is believed to have embraced not less than 40,000 voters in North Carolina.

It was governed by rules more or less military in their character, and it struck its victims with such secrecy, swiftness and certainty as to leave them little hope either for escape or mercy. The members were sworn to obey the orders of their camps even to assassination and murder. They were taught to regard oaths administered before magistrates and in Courts of Justice, as in no degree binding when they were called upon to give testimony against their confederates. They were sworn to keep the secrets of the order—to obey the commands of the chief—to go to the rescue of a member at all hazards, and to swear for him as a witness and acquit him as a juror.

. . . There are, at least, four Judges and four Solicitors in the State who will bear witness to the fact, from their own experience, that it was very difficult, if not impossible, to convice [sic] members of this Klan of crimes and misdemeanors. I have information of not less than 25 murders committed by members of this Klan, in various Counties of the State, and of hundreds of cases of scourging and whipping. Very few, if any, convictions have followed in these cases. The civil law was powerless.

One State Senator (Stephens) was murdered in the open day in a County Court-house, and another State Senator (Shoffner) was driven from the State, solely on account of their political opinions. A respectable and unoffending colored man (Outlaw) was taken from his bed at night, and hanged by the neck until he was dead, within a short distance of a County Court-house. Another colored man (Puryear) was drowned, because he spoke publicly of persons who aided in the commission of this crime. No bills were found in these cases.

A crippled white man, a native of Vermont, was cruelly whipped because he was teaching a colored school. No bill was found in this case. The Sheriff of a County was waylaid, shot and killed on a public highway. . . . A County jail was broken open, and five men taken out and their throats cut. Another jail was broken open, and five men taken out and shot, one of whom died of his wound. Another jail was broken open and a United States prisoner released. No punishments followed in these cases.

The members of this Klan, under the orders of their Chiefs, had ridden through many neighborhoods at night, and had punished free citizens on account of their political opinions, and had so terrified many of them by threats of future visitations of vengeance that they fled from their houses, took refuge in the woods, and did not dare to appear in public to exercise their right of suffrage. Some of these victims were shot, some of them whipped, some of them were hanged, some of them were drowned, some of them were tortured, some had their mouths lacerated with gags, one of them had his ear cropped, and others, of both sexes, were subjected to indignities which were disgraceful not merely to civilization but to humanity itself.[30]

Through behind-the-scenes persuasion, sometimes employing political foes who, nevertheless, were dedicated to the preservation of legality, Holden succeeded in restoring order over most of the state, but the counties of Caswell and Alamance still were hotbeds of violence. Because of continuing outrages there, the governor declared the two counties in a state of insurrection and under the authority granted by the Shoffner Act, moved to organize a military counterforce.

Holden had been reluctant to take such drastic action and had, in fact, shown remarkable restraint, considering the authority the legislature had given him. No doubt he felt repugnance to the idea of using troops to control his own people, and he must have had some hint of the political repercussions, magnifying across the state, that would accrue. But he had issued five proclamations within a year and a half, and he had telegraphed or written to members of Congress, to North Carolina's senators, to President Grant, and to military officers informing them of the situation in the state and asking their aid in finding a solution to the vexing problem which he thought "threatened the stability of all government, and the peace, if not the very existence, of society."[31] The employment of troops, despite the probability that it would affect the state legislative elections in August, appeared in the end to be the only answer.

Two regiments were organized. One was commanded by Col. W. J. Clarke, who had been one of Holden's companions on the stagecoach in 1836. It was to remain in Raleigh and would play no conspicuous role in the events ensuing. The other regiment was commanded by Col. George W. Kirk, a native of Tennessee who had served during the Civil War as leader of a band of Federal guerrillas that harried the country in western North Carolina and eastern Tennessee. Kirk bore an unenviable reputation among former Confederates as a desperado and bushwhacker and in the white supremacy histories is remembered to this day as "Cut-throat" Kirk. Choosing him was probably unfortunate, although Holden thought his reputation would be an advantage in subduing the counties more expeditiously than if he were not so well known. That, at least, is how Holden later explained it. "I sent Col. Kirk to those counties . . . because I believed that the name of terror which Kirk bore (whether justly or not) would prevent resistance and bloodshed; and the result proved in this I was right."[32]

Holden distributed five hundred handbills calling on Kirk's old regiment, the Third North Carolina State Volunteers, "to aid in enforcing the laws, and in putting down disloyal midnight assassins." Kirk recruited most of his 670 troops, black and white, in Tennessee. The occupation of Alamance and Caswell began on July 15, after Holden had made a quick trip to Washington to explain his course to the president and members of Congress and to obtain suggestions from them. Kirk at once began to arrest men who he had reason to believe were leaders of the Klan. Nineteen men in Caswell County and eighty-two men in Alamance were picked up and clapped into prison. A writ of *habeas corpus* was obtained from Chief Justice Richard

M. Pearson to effect the release of A. G. Moore, of Alamance, but Kirk refused to honor it, saying that he would surrender his prisoners, for whom bail was denied, only upon the order of Governor Holden. The Shoffner Act did not authorize the suspension of the right of *habeas corpus*, but, as the historian Ewing comments, "In a brilliantly written defense of his policy, Holden informed Pearson that the prisoners would be held beyond the reach of the civil power until peace and order were restored in Alamance County."[33] After hearing arguments of counsel, Pearson admitted the right of the governor to impose martial law on the counties but denied that the privilege of *habeas corpus* could be abrogated, though at the same time confessing the inability of the court to enforce the writs. Holden replied that the civil and judicial authorities had shown themselves unable to deal with the insurgents and that, as the situation demanded a remedy, he had been forced into his action, by which he was trying to restore, not subvert, the judicial processes in the counties.

In Yanceyville, the county seat of Caswell, several of the men in detention had been arrested by Kirk on suspicion of murdering Senator Stephens. These arrests occurred only two weeks before the August 4 elections for Congress and the state legislature. Holden's enemies accused him of using force to influence the balloting, totally disregarding the activities the Klan had undertaken for the selfsame purpose. The Klan had, in fact, goaded Holden into taking reprisal measures, hoping that the net result would be a conservative advantage, and in that strategy the night riders were successful.

Coupled with the expected backlash of the military operation, the Klan had been so assiduous in its intimidation of Republican voters, both black and white, that 12,000 of them had made up their minds not to go to the polls.[34]

The day before the election, which Holden fully expected his party to win,[35] the governor performed one of those rash acts

Josiah Turner, editor of the *Raleigh Sentinel*

that he, as a journalist, should never have allowed himself to be stampeded into. He arrested Josiah Turner and sent him to jail in Yanceyville. Turner was editor of the Raleigh *Sentinel*, a man described by Hamilton as having

positive genius for political warfare, sparing not and caring little where he struck. Quick-witted, ingenious in putting an opponent on the defensive and keeping him there, and at the same time ignoring a counter attack, gifted with a keen sense of humor, he saw the ridiculous side of everything and employed it as a means to an end, realizing that in politics a dangerous enemy is often rendered harmless by laughter and ridicule. . . . He was the inspiration of the Conservative party in its deepest gloom, and to him more than any other man belongs the credit for the speedy overthrow of Reconstruction in North Carolina.[36]

There is a little bit more to this story than Hamilton tells. In 1865, as provisional governor, Holden had opposed a pardon for Turner because he judged Turner's imbedded opposition to the Union, as evidenced by his editorials, treasonable beyond redemption.[37] Turner never forgave Holden. In the thick of the Klan war, known to Southern apologists as the "Holden-Kirk War," Turner dared Holden to arrest him. On August 2 he wrote a brief editorial that read:[38]

LIES LIKE A THIEF

The governor has been lying on us for twelve months; his profligate son and organ lies on us to-day by calling us a Ku Klux. If we are, why don't the pumpkin-faced rascal arrest us? We defy and dare him to arrest.

The following day Turner wrote an open letter.[39]

TO GOVERNOR HOLDEN

Gov. Holden:—You say you will handle me in due time. You white-livered recreant, do it now. You dare me to resist you; I dare you to arrest me . . . Your ignorant jacobins are incited . . . by your lying charges against me that I am King of the Ku Klux. You villain, come and arrest a man. . . .

Yours with contempt and defiance—*habeas corpus* or no *habeas corpus*.

Thus harassed, Holden obliged Turner, although as a sometime gadfly himself he should have recognized one when he saw one and let the insults pass. (There is an interesting footnote to this incident related by Ewing. Turner applied to Judge E. W. Jones of the Second Judicial District for a writ of *habeas corpus* and was turned down. After Holden was impeached, the House of Representatives, "lusting for another Republican victim to send to the impeachment chamber," adopted an impeachment resolution charging Judge Jones with public drunkenness. Before the trial, Jones was allowed to resign.)[40]

The day after Turner's arrest, the conservatives swept the election, electing five of the state's seven members of Congress and gaining large majorities in both houses of the legislature. In each house they failed by a few seats of electing a two-thirds majority—which they would need in the days ahead—and they promptly remedied that oversight of the voters by unseating three Republicans in each house, declaring them ineligible to hold office.

Hard on the heels of the election, counsel for Kirk's prisoners, acting in the belief that their rights were protected by the Fourteenth Amendment, applied to United States District Judge George W. Brooks in Elizabeth City—whose jurisdiction was debatable—for writs of *habeas corpus*, and Brooks, repairing to Raleigh, ordered Kirk to bring the prisoners before him. In desperation Holden telegraphed President Grant to intervene, but Grant instead instructed Holden to obey the writs. Brooks freed all the prisoners.[41]

That the handwriting was now on the wall is not only a cliché but an understatement. Holden was in midterm. He was coupled with a legislature not only outraged by his attempts to curb Klan hostilities, but also remembering with deep bitterness the power that Holden had wielded as an editor, his criticism of state and Confederate authorities during the war, his "treasonous" efforts to bring about peace, and that consideration which was never very far from the minds of the North Carolina "aristocracy": Holden's "humble" birth.

As soon as the election results became clear, impeachment talk began, although it was largely desultory. The legislature met on November 24, 1870, and on the next day received from Holden a message defending his employment of troops. After reciting the story of many outrages, he said:

In fine, gentlemen, there is no remedy for these evils through civil law, and but for the use of the military arm, to which I was compelled to resort, the whole fabric of society in the State would have been undermined and destroyed, and a reign of lawlessness and anarchy would have been established. The present State government would thus have failed in the great purpose for which it was created, to-wit; the protection of life and property under equal laws; and, necessarily the national government would have interfered, and, in all probability, would have placed us again and for an indefinite period under military rule.[42]

That message, an honest accounting of Holden's views, was considered by Holden's enemies an attempt to forestall impeachment, and they at once determined on action. They were further spurred to retaliate by an editorial in the *Standard*, then edited by Holden's son, Joseph, which dared them to give substance to the mutterings widely heard. "We demand a trial at the bar of the Senate," Joseph wrote. "Innocent or guilty, let us have a verdict. If the Democratic members of the Legislature fail to make good the charges made by them during the campaign, they are worse than the Governor and Chief Justice if we admit they are as bad as the Democrats say they are. Fail to impeach, and you stand before the people convicted of slander and perjury.

Such will be the opinion that the people will entertain of every man who preached impeachment, and fails to vote to arraign the accused parties before the Senate."[43]

Thus unmistakably challenged, the House Judiciary Committee set the wheels in motion, aiming to bring down not only Holden but Chief Justice Pearson. The jurist, who had admitted Holden's right to occupy Alamance and Caswell and whose writs of *habeas corpus* had been ignored by the governor without his seeking further remedy, had expected to be charged and had gone so far as to employ legal counsel. But he had former students in the legislature who blocked moves against him, and, Hamilton writes, Pearson "thus escaped a fate he richly deserved."[44]

Holden had no college chums to come to his aid, and on December 14, 1870, at the favorable recommendation of the judiciary committee, the House of Representatives adopted the following resolution by a vote of 60 to 46:

"That William W. Holden, Governor of the State of North Carolina, be impeached of high crimes and misdemeanors in office."[45]

The lad from Hillsborough, in a way that he had never anticipated, had become the chief business of the state.

ELEVEN

THE TENOR of the charges against Governor Holden is shown in the Judiciary Committee report sent to the House floor along with the impeachment resolution. Because it conveys the heart of the case, as far as legislators chafing to undo Holden were willing to put it into print, it is reproduced in full here:

That William W. Holden, Governor of North Carolina, unmindful of his oath of office, did in July last organize, arm and equip a military force not recognized by, but in subversion of, the Constitution of the State of North Carolina; which military force, so unlawfully organized, was not kept under subordination to and governed by civil power, but was by the order of the said William W. Holden, Governor as aforesaid, made paramount to, and subversive of the civil authority.

That the said William W. Holden, Governor as aforesaid, did, in the month of July and August last, without lawful warrant and authority, and in defiance and subversion of the Constitution, arrest and imprison many of the peaceful and law-abiding citizens of the State, depriving them of their liberties and privileges, and certain of said citizens, so unlawfully arrested and imprisoned, did cause to be subject to cruel and unusual punishment.

That the said William W. Holden, Governor as aforesaid, denied to citizens unlawfully restrained of their liberty by his authority, all remedy to enquire into the lawfulness thereof, and in defiance of the Constitution, the laws and the process of the courts, he suspended the privileges of the writ of *habeas corpus*, claiming that he was governed

William Woods Holden, editor of the *North Carolina Standard* and governor of North Carolina, 1865, 1868–1871, the only governor ever to be impeached and convicted

by a "supreme law" whereby he could deny the privileges of the said writ, when, in his opinion, the safety of the State required it.

In the view of the matters herein set forth, combining historical facts with statements contained in public documents, and the records of the public departments and the courts, the undersigned members of the committee, who are a majority thereof, are of the opinion, that William W. Holden, Governor of the State of North Carolina, be impeached of high crimes and misdemeanors.[1]

When the House accepted that recommendation, it then faced the task of adopting articles of impeachment. The charges speedily settled upon, eight in number, have been described by Ewing as "long, rambling, political canards, poorly drafted, inaccurate, and, in all, fine illustrations of shysterism in investigatorial workmanship."[2]

In brief, the articles of impeachment contained the following charges:[3]

Article I. Unlawfully declaring the County of Alamance in insurrection and raising bodies of "armed, desperate and lawless men" who arrested and detained eighty-two citizens, when in fact there was no insurrection and civil authorities were in full exercise of all their functions.

Article II. Unlawfully taking the same action, in the same manner, against the County of Caswell, where eighteen men were arrested.

Article III. Unlawfully ordering "evil disposed persons" to arrest the editor Josiah Turner, Jr., in Orange County.

Article IV. Unlawfully arresting and detaining John Kerr, Samuel P. Hill, William B. Bowe, and Nathaniel M. Roane in Caswell County, four men whose names had already been included in Article II.

Article V. Unlawfully refusing to obey a writ of *habeas corpus* in the case of Adolphus G. Moore of Alamance County.

Article VI. Unlawfully refusing to obey a writ of *habeas corpus* in the case of nineteen citizens arrested in Caswell County.

Article VII. Unlawfully recruiting and arming five hundred men and more, "many of them most reckless, desperate, ruffianly and lawless characters," and placing them under the command of George W. Kirk, "a notorious desperado"; unlawfully arresting and imprisoning many men; hanging by the neck William Patton, Lucien H. Murray, and others; thrusting Josiah Turner into a "loathsome dungeon"; and illegally drawing more than $70,000 from the state treasury to pay the troops.

Article VIII. Unlawfully causing the state treasurer to disregard an injunction that would have restrained him from making the money for the troop payments available.

The Senate court of impeachment was organized on December 23, after some study as to how the trial should be conducted, conservative leaders believing that they were making history with the first impeachment proceeding against an American governor. Actually similar steps had been taken in 1862 against Gov. Charles Robinson of Kansas;[4] he was acquitted of the charges.

As the Senate got ready for the trial, Lieutenant Governor Caldwell withdrew as presiding officer and assumed the duties of the governorship, from which Holden was automatically removed pending resolution of the case against him. Chief Justice Pearson, who had anticipated his own impeachment, took over the president's chair in the Senate. The historian Moore, writing closer to the event, gives a somewhat more compassionate view of the judge than Hamilton does. Moore wrote that Pearson presided "with great learning and propriety through the long trial," adding to "his fame as a great jurist. No man has surpassed him in our history in his knowledge of the law. He did not possess elegance of language or literary grace seen in other great judges, but in the grasp of his thought and extent of legal knowledge, he was among the foremost jurists then living."[5]

Thomas Sparrow, manager of the prosecution for the House, employed as counsel, at fees of $1,000 each, two former governors, Thomas Bragg and William A. Graham, who were assisted by A. S. Merrimon. Holden had been associated with them all before and, of course, had been instrumental in Bragg's attainment of the governor's seat. Holden's battery of defense lawyers, to whom he paid $2,500 out of his own pocket,[6] had equal reputation in the state. They were headed by Richard C. Badger, son of the senator with whom Holden had had a long acquaintance; the others were J. M. McCorkle, descendant of a noted Presbyterian minister; Nathaniel Boyden, a Northerner who had been a judge in the western part of the state; Edward Conigland, an Irishman described by Moore, as possessing "a noble integrity, cultivated tastes and singular power at the bar";[7] and W. N. H. Smith, a judge of considerable reputation.

Holden asked for time to formulate an answer to the charges and was given thirty days, the court adjourning until January 23, 1871, while the governor's lawyers got together the necessary papers and pleadings. This exercise was in large part lost motion, because in the light of the mood of the General Assembly, no answer Holden could have given, however well fortified by facts, would have satisfied his accusers.

By this time quite aware that the cards were stacked against him, Holden nevertheless dignified the impeachment charges by responding to them in lengthy detail. Throughout, his theme was that as governor of North Carolina, lawfully seated, he had a constitutional and statutory obligation to preserve law and order in all parts of the state;[8] he had been legally authorized to raise troops and to send them into areas of distress, the arrests following were within his authority, and his failure to obey court orders was within the interests of peace. He made it clear that he considered the Ku Klux Klan the principal agent of the state's unrest, and he asserted, with verifiable truth, that officers charged with enforcing the law had, in fact, connived with the Klan, sometimes as members, in its illegal activities. He argued with equal logic that if he had the power to arm troops, which he believed he had, he also had the concomitant authority to draw on state funds to pay them.

Some of Holden's arguments should be noted here. At the outset he quoted a letter from Jonathan Worth, whom he had succeeded as governor, in which Worth said that he did not consider Holden's election valid, that Holden could be installed only because he had the support of the United States Army, and that Worth would resist eviction right up to the Supreme Court if there was any hope of reversal there.

Holden said he at first felt that Worth was speaking only for himself, in personal protest, but that the former governor's opposition to him was taken up by the newspapers and converted into a weapon intended to subvert gubernatorial authority. Very early, he said, he "became officially cognizant of a settled design, existing in various parts of the State, through the aid of secret combinations of a political character, of which he believes the aforesaid protest was the nucleus, practically to render null and void the Reconstruction Acts, and to set at naught those provisions of the Federal and State constitutions which secure political and civil equality to the whole body of the people, without respect to race, color or previous condition."

To avert the "evil consequences" of the designs of the secret orders and, in particular, to protect the rights of black citizens, Holden said, he issued a proclamation on October 12, 1868, enjoining all magistrates, sheriffs, and other peace officers to be "vigilant, impartial, faithful and firm in the discharge of their duties . . . ferreting out offenders, protecting the weak against the strong who may attempt to deprive them of their rights, to the end that the wicked might be restrained . . . and the government perpetuated on the basis of freedom and justice to all."

His directives, he said, were to no avail, and the white brotherhoods that came to be known collectively as the Ku Klux Klan "continued to gather strength. The members thereof met in secret, selected the victims to be punished, and perpetrated out-

229

rages in the dead of night, through disguised parties, on quiet and unoffending citizens, chiefly colored persons, and always of the Republican party." It was to check their activities, he continued, that the legislature on April 12, 1869, passed an act making it a felony to go about masked, disguised, or painted with the intent to "terrify or frighten" any citizen of any community.

Holden then reviewed his message of November 22, 1870, to the General Assembly in which he told in detail of the illegal activities of the Ku Klux Klan and of the powerlessness or unwillingness of local law enforcement authorities to check them. He recalled that on October 20, 1869, he had cited the breakdown of security in four counties—Lenoir, Jones, Orange, and Chatham—and that he had ordered the violations of the law to cease, failing which he would declare the counties in a state of insurrection and would take steps "to protect every citizen without regard to his antecedents, his color or his political opinions."

In defiance of his warnings, Klan activities spread into Alamance and Caswell counties with redoubled atrocity, and the stories of terror were so common that the legislature on January 29, 1870, gave him explicit statutory authority to put down insurrection through the use of militia and to call upon federal authorities for assistance if state controls were not sufficient to restore order. It was in compliance with the law, then, he said, that on March 7, 1870, he declared Alamance County in a state of insurrection. As to Caswell, he offered a reward of $500 for information leading to arrests in half a dozen murders, including those of Outlaw, Stephens, and Puryear, and when that step was unavailing, he declared Caswell in insurrection on July 8, 1870.

Directing himself to the articles of impeachment, Holden said that he did, indeed, declare Alamance and Caswell in insurrection, as alleged; that he did, indeed, send in troops; that he supported the arrest of suspects as a measure necessary to restore peace; but that he did not know of or authorize the maltreatment of any person taken into custody. His actions, he said, were perfectly legal under the powers given him as chief executive.

With respect to Josiah Turner, Holden said that the editor by his writings and speeches had contributed to the outbreaks in Alamance and Caswell and that he was encouraging the white citizens of the two counties not only to resist but to attempt to eject Holden's peace force. He had reason to believe, Holden said, that Turner was himself a member of the night riders. "Moreover, the said Josiah Turner, Junior, under a morbid craving for notoriety, a desire to advance his political prospects, and a hope to increase his patronage as a citizen and editor amongst his political friends, did resort to various ways and means to procure his own arrest, and to that end frequently challenged and dared this respondent to make the same, expressing his purpose to protect himself by force of arms and declaring that he should be arrested only over the dead bodies of such as might attempt the same." Holden said that he had ordered Turner's arrest to take place in either Alamance or Caswell and that if he had been arrested in Orange, it was contrary to the governor's directives.

As answers to the succeeding charges, Holden relied in large part on the lengthy responses already summarized, maintaining throughout that he had acted legally, that his motive in all instances had been to preserve order, and that nothing that he did was malicious or could in any way be honestly characterized as misconduct in office.

The trial itself began on February 2, 1871, and lasted forty-four days. During that time, Moore writes, "the wit and wisdom of the State were upon the floor of the Senate chamber, while from the galleries the eyes of many beautiful women gazed in absorbing interest upon the strange spectacle of a Governor of North Carolina answering as a criminal for a violation of his sworn duty as Chief-Magistrate of the Commonweath." For two centuries "no ruler of the State had become so personally obnoxious to his lieges as to incur either violence or legal prosecution."[9]

In the long trial the prosecution called 57 witnesses and the defense 113. In large part Holden's accusers tried to establish that there was no trouble in either Alamance or Caswell that could be regarded as an insurrection, and most of their witnesses had never heard of secret terrorist organizations. Those who had been detained by Kirk were innocent of all wrongdoing and, almost to a man, had never been members of night-riding bands. A few admitted to minor associations and even to a whipping or two, but according to their testimony, they were only responding to black assaults, and the retaliation they took was relatively trivial.

The House managers attempted to block the introduction of witnesses by Holden's attorneys, but at length defense testimony was allowed, with whites and blacks recounting tales of Ku Klux outrages. Their testimony takes up more than one thousand pages in the official three-volume transcript, which runs to more than twenty-five hundred pages, not counting appendices. After eighteen days Holden, sensing the mood of the Senate, stopped attending the sessions and went to Washington.[10]

Former Governor Graham, summarizing the evidence for the prosecution, found Holden blatantly guilty of every crime ascribed to him and concluded:

Senators, the last bulwark against oppression by public agents or abuse of official authority is found in the constitution of this high court of impeachment. While no personal or political prejudice should be for a moment permitted to influence your determination against the respondent, I trust that no personal appeal . . . nor any consideration of the consequences that may result from a just discharge of your duty will weigh with you for his acquittal. A fair and impartial but at the same time a fearless judgement, is alike due to yourselves and your country.[11]

Before Holden's counsel was allowed to make its final appeal, the Senate was asked to allow the normal payment of fees to certain of the governor's witnesses who had been on call for days but who had not been sworn. They were mostly black, and although they had been required to sacrifice both time and money to stand in waiting, the Senate refused to authorize payment to them.[12]

Nathaniel Boyden, initiating the final appeal for Holden, tended to dismiss the charges against him as frivolous and succeeded in making the Senate laugh good-naturedly at the text describing the dire plight of some of Holden's "victims," especially Josiah Turner, who had so diligently courted arrest.[13] "I desire," Boyden said,

frankly and candidly to express here the sentiments I entertain. I come here not as the friend or partizan of the respondent. That he and I have usually been at points upon the great questions before the country is probably known to every senator here. . . . I am here, as I said before, to express my genuine thoughts and views upon the points in this case. I know that my days are but few. I am near the foot of the hill. I look about me and see the great men of North Carolina, with whom I have been associated at the bar for many years, have all passed the bourne from which no traveller returns. It is with these sad memories crowding upon me, and with a deep sense of the responsibility resting upon me, that I have addressed this learned high court of impeachment on behalf of the respondent, and urged that in my judgement the cause of truth and justice requires your acquittal of the charges preferred against him.[14]

Judge Smith, continuing the argument for Holden, said flatly that his conviction would be an act of "official profligacy," because Holden was only doing his duty.[15]

These appeals were, of course, unavailing.

On March 22, 1871, the forty-fourth day of the trial, the Senate gave its verdict, with a two-thirds majority required for conviction. On Article I, concerning the declaration of insurrection in Alamance County and the arrest there of a number of citizens, Holden was acquitted, the opposition failing by three votes to gain the necessary margin (voting guilty, 30; not guilty, 19).[16] On Article II, relating to Caswell County, Holden escaped conviction by one vote (Voting guilty, 32; not guilty, 17)[17] On all of the other six charges he was convicted in a straight party-line vote.[18]

Immediately after the decision was final, the Senate, by a vote of 36 to 13, passed a resolution removing Holden from the office of governor and disqualifying him from ever again holding "any office of honor, trust or profit under the State of North Carolina."

And so was written, in utterly partisan spirit, the end to the political career of the boy from Hillsborough who had risen from an obscure byway and an unmentionable origin to positions of formidable power in North Carolina journalism and North Carolina politics.

No governor, no editor, before or since, has been so raucously ousted from polite society.

TWELVE

T HE REMAINING score of years of W. W. Holden's life were very different from the earlier days of striving, learning, getting acquainted with power, wielding it, and for a time bestriding the political stage of his native state. Hurt, subdued, chastened by the turn of events, he lived quietly and peacefully, more concerned with being a good neighbor and exemplary Christian than with keeping tabs on political affairs. He no longer wanted, in fact, to be in the heat of the battle. Ever hanging over him, he admitted, was the fact that his state had declared him unfit to hold office. The stigma attached to his name he felt with deep sensitivity.

After his impeachment he remained in the national capital, for a time taking a position on the Washington *Chronicle*. Several times he called at the White House to confer with President Grant, but apart from this and his writing, he maintained a low profile. "I will not humble myself here to be recognized by any," he wrote his second wife. "*They say* I have saved the country in 1872, and from a terrible civil war, *but that is all*. I simply meant to do my duty to the oppressed without regard to party."[1]

Holden's interests, however, did not lie in Washington or in activities there; he was unhappy in the national capital and wanted to return to Raleigh, where he had left his family and friends. After some months he did return, and in 1873 he was appointed postmaster in Raleigh, with reappointment following in 1877 at the instance of President Hayes. Four years later a renewal of the appointment was blocked by Raleigh Republicans, who complained to President Garfield that Holden was apathetic toward party affairs and that he had discriminated against blacks in post office employment.[2] Holden denied the charges, saying that he had done everything in his power to bolster the Republican Party and that his refusal to appoint certain Negroes as mail clerks was due not to racial discrimination but to the fact that they were not qualified for the jobs they sought. His letter to the president did no good.

As time brought a moderation of the acrimony connected with the impeachment, and as death claimed some of the leading actors in the drama, efforts were made to remove the legal disabilities imposed on Holden upon his impeachment, denying him state office. W. J. Yates, editor of the *Charlotte Democrat*, who had opposed Holden during and after the war but had maintained friendly personal relations with him, took a leading part several times in attempts to wash away the stigma, but there were always some politicians who remembered with too much bitterness and who could not find it within themselves to be forgiving.

Edward Conigland wrote to Thomas Clingman when an ordinance to remove the disability was to be discussed in the constitutional convention of 1875 that he knew Holden "was rarely, if at all, the instigator of any of the measures for which he stood impeached." He added:

Men in public position are but the exponents of the party to which they belong, and a true analysis of Mr. Holden's conduct proves that he was no worse than those who placed him in power, and was, in fact, made the scape-goat for their sins. Of the men who, when he was in office, took an active part in the government of the State he was, in my opinion, in all respects the best. Yet many, if not most of them, deserted him in his hour of need, although if he had not been restrained by his sense of honor, he could easily have proved on his trial, that he often resisted their counsel, and that the measures which he adopted and which brought his difficulties upon him, were the result of their persistent urging. His errors were of the head and not of the heart.[3]

One factor that perhaps helped to keep legislators from acting was that Holden himself was too proud to ask for pardon and the removal of his disabilities. He wrote the editor of the Raleigh *News*: "I think I did nothing in 1870 which deserved impeachment. I feel that I was unjustly convicted, and to ask pardon would be to confess my guilt."[4] He also insisted to friends that any action must be taken graciously and without wrangling. In 1885 he requested Senator H. A. Gudger of Buncombe County to drop efforts in his behalf because, although Gudger had obtained a list of a majority of senators pledged to vote favorably, one man, Judge H. G. Conner, had threatened to speak against any act of compassion.[5]

And so relief was never voted. Perhaps the attitude of some was expressed by the Raleigh editor Walter Hines Page when he wrote in the *State Chronicle* that he hoped even the talk of restoring Holden's rights would cease.

That punishment should stand forever in our history as a warning. If he committed high crimes against the State, the State, in this respect unlike an individual, should not hold its forgiveness so easy. The Commonwealth cannot afford to make an apology to any man. Mr. Holden ought to be allowed to die with the forgiveness of all individuals for private injuries; but the State must hold her honor so high that the punishment for disregarding it shall be lasting. The willingness of some men to remove his disabilities does credit to their hearts, but hardly to their judgment of the greatness and dignity of the Commonwealth.[6]

Meanwhile Holden, although he had been reared in the Methodist faith, joined the Baptist denomination under the persuasion of the Rev. M. A. B. Earle, an evangelist who conducted a revival at the First Baptist Church. This entered Holden into religious activity which, with charitable work among the common people he loved, was to claim more and more of his time in later years. "Even Aunt Abby House, his old-time foe who wished the water to be boiling when he was baptised, came, in her last years, to bless him for his personal ministrations and his generous aid," the historian S. A. Ashe wrote.[7] Holden became prominent in the denomination as a layman, but as age overtook him he wanted to get back into the church of his early days. In the summer of 1886 he rejoined the Edenton Street Methodist Church,[8] and when its new church building was completed the following year, he wrote the dedicatory hymn.

In these years he also was in demand as a writer and occasional speaker, usually on religious or historical subjects. He wrote a religious column for Raleigh's Sunday *News and Observer*, and he turned out one on state history for the Charlotte *Democrat*. One of his more important talks was made in June, 1881, when he was invited to make an address on the history of journalism in North Carolina at Winston. That invitation, he told his audience, brought him "equal surprise and gratification."[9]

At that meeting was a young newspaperman, Josephus Daniels, who was seeing Holden for the first time and who "never watched a man with so much curiosity." He had tried from early boyhood, Daniels wrote, to conceive what kind of man Holden was:

I had heard him denounced on the stump as the meanest of men and worst of Governors and except now and then a feeble apology for his course by Republican speakers, in whose statements I put little credence. I had heard nobody say a good word of him. I imagined—drawing upon the story of Bluebeard and other famous characters with which children early become acquainted—that Gov. Holden was a man of powerful build, of stiff grizzly beard with a stern, commanding eye and that one would be awed by his very appearance. ... When he began to read his speech I noticed with surprise that his voice was low and not at all harsh; that he spoke most kindly and warmly of the great men who in other days controlled journalism of North Carolina; and particularly was I impressed with the thread of profound reverence for things sacred and allusions to duty to God, that ran through the entire address. "What," thought I, "can this be the man who has been an enemy to North Carolina?"[10]

In 1883 Holden wrote a letter to the *News and Observer* announcing that he had left the Republican Party because it advocated a high tariff, Negro equality, and sectionalism in government. "I am," he said, "a 'Holden man.' The old people of the State will know what this expression means. If I shall vote hereafter, I will vote independently for good men and proper measures." Older persons probably did understand, and for the younger he explained, "I am perhaps the most independent man politically in the state."[11]

Within a year after Holden retired as postmaster, he suffered a paralytic stroke. A few years later he began dictating his memoirs to his daughter, Mrs. C. A. Sherwood of Raleigh. These *Memoirs* show a remarkable absence of any vindictive feelings. With a benignity and a charity that are in contrast to some of his own earlier writings, Holden discussed the events and the men that came to his mind. He was innocent, he said, of any purpose to do injustice to anyone:

"I cherish no resentment towards any person for what has occurred in the past. I am at peace, or would be, with all men. My life has been a somewhat stormy one, but it is well nigh over. I wish to die with no earthly or heavenly ban on me, and I would accept the Golden Rule of the Divine Master, 'Do unto all men as ye would they should do unto you.' I am now walking quietly and serenely on the shore of the 'great ocean I must sail so soon.' "[12]

Holden approached three friends for assistance in the revision and editing of his manuscript, but none of them would undertake it.[13] His *Memoirs* were not published, in fact, until 1911, almost twenty years after his death. One of those he sought out, former Governor C. H. Brogden, nevertheless shed some retrospective light on the situation prevailing when Holden was governor, revealing conditions that had been dismissed as unfounded rumor at his trial. Brogden wrote, "The impeachment trial proved that the Ku Klux Klan were so numerous that no one could deny their existence. It was shown in Alamance County a majority of the voters belonged to the order, and that Albert Murray, the Sheriff of the County, was a member of it, and was chief of a Ku Klux camp near his residence, and there were ten Ku Klux camps in Alamance County. You were charged falsely...."[14]

The morning after his manuscript was completed in 1890, Holden again was stricken with paralysis, and he did not recover. For the last year of his life, his memory was failing.

He died on March 1, 1892. In a kind of ironic apology the state flags next day were flown at half mast on the capitol and city hall in Raleigh. Printers in Raleigh came forward to testify that he was a kind employer, looking to the interests of his men, with always a kind word for them.[15] The Raleigh Typographical Union No. 54, of which he had been an honorary member, attended his funeral on March 3 in a body.[16] The Edenton Street Methodist Church was filled for the service, with the highest officials of the state government in the congregation. At the request of the family, the pastor, the Reverend J. N. Cole, did not pay an extended tribute but spoke of the "exemplary Christian character which illumined the sunset of the life of the ex-Governor and of the love and affection which all the members of his church and all Christian people who knew him, bore for him."[17] At the close of the service the body was borne to Raleigh's Oakwood Cemetery, where today a tall, plain monument marks the grave.

Among the printed eulogies generally sympathetic toward him was that of the Raleigh *Daily Evening Visitor*, which predicted that "history will doubtless do his memory justice."[18] History has remembered principally his changes of party affiliation, presumably for the sake of raw ambition, and his ignominious impeachment by a two-thirds majority of the North Carolina Senate.

When studied closely, though, history does have a way of laying bare old secrets. Twelve years before Holden's death the chronicler John W. Moore wrote in his history that "the case of Governor Holden, like the murder of John W. Stephens, will always be a puzzle to the latest investigators of historical truth."[19] The murder of "Chicken" Stephens is no longer "a puzzle." It happened exactly as Holden alleged.

In 1919, at the request of the North Carolina Historical Commission, Captain John G. Lea left a nine-page typed deposition giving the details of Stephens' death. The sealed statement was opened after Lea's death in 1935. In it Lea said that he had helped organize the Ku Klux Klan in Caswell County when whites became apprehensive that Stephens was stirring up the Negroes against them. After a number of burnings allegedly instigated by Stephens, the Klan gave the culprit "a fair trial" in absentia and condemned him to death. On a day when the county Democrats were holding a convention at the Yanceyville courthouse, about a dozen robed Klansmen, Lea among them, set upon Stephens in a secluded room, disarmed him, put a rope around his neck and stabbed him repeatedly. With Stephens dying, the door was locked and the key thrown away.[20]

Lea showed no remorse in his account and boasted proudly for posterity that it never was proved that a Klan klavern existed in Caswell County.

While the excesses of the post-Civil War Klan and its modern imitators have long been recognized as the devices of desperate men to circumvent the law of the land, contemporary historians have yet to concede generally that Governor Holden was the victim of his era rather than its primary villain. It was Holden's great tragedy to be born in the time and in the locality which fate had chosen for him. Despite his success as an editor and his undoubted love for his state, he possessed a broad conception of democracy which always seemed slightly out of place in North Carolina's antebellum society. His contemporaries—before the war, during it, and after—never quite understood him, and what they could not understand, they conspired to suppress. In a western state, or at a later time, class consciousness might not have been raised against him to arouse the bitterness of the patricians.

There are probably three keys to an understanding of Holden's career, not counting the mental capacities that he derived from sources impossible to determine.

The first is, as he described it, his "unpretending" origin. This gave him a handicap that he struggled mightily to overcome but still left him a social misfit. It also gave him a feeling of kinship with the common people that made him attempt to lead them and speak for them.

The second is his love for his own state, which caused him to consider most national affairs from a North Carolina viewpoint, gave him a distrust of strong central government and a belief in state's rights, and drove him to pour out his energies to "leave his impress for good on her history."[21]

The third is the fact that he did not clearly discern when his own interests were involved and on such occasions apparently placed too great reliance on the advice of friends.

The great pity is that his contemporaries did not understand him and did not use to fullest advantage for the state the fine talents that even his bitterest enemies were quick to acknowledge. And equally piteous is the fact that the crowning acts of his career had to take place in an atmosphere that no one man, no legislature, no congress, no president, could control. In that respect he was a victim of his times.

W. W. Holden was not only a colorful, arresting personality, not only North Carolina's preeminent editor of the nineteenth century, not only its shrewdest political strategist; he was also one of the outstanding intellectual men in the state's history, and in his own way, as far as his contemporaries would let him be, one of the most public-spirited of her native sons. His plain monument bears no inscription other than his name and the dates of his birth and death, but it might fitly bear a sentence he once wrote: "Unpretending as was my origin, I thank God that He has given me a disposition to love my State, and my whole State, with the affection of a son; and though others have served her with far more efficiency and ability than I have, yet none has laid upon her altar the offerings of a more loyal and patriotic heart."[22]

CHRONOLOGY

1818 Holden born, November (exact date uncertain).

1820/21 Missouri compromises maintain equal number of free and slave states.

1822 Monroe Doctrine enunciated.

1824 John Quincy Adams elected president; National Republican (later, Whig) and Democratic Republican (later, Democratic) parties begin to emerge.

1824/25 Holden moved to father's house.

1825 North Carolina State Literary Board and Fund established to provide public education.

1827/28 Holden apprenticed to Dennis Heartt at *Hillsborough Recorder*.

1828 Andrew Jackson elected president.

1836 Holden moves to Raleigh; employed at *Star*.

1837 "Gag rules" established in Congress to dampen contention over slavery.

1838 Holden fails in attempt to buy *Star*; takes up study of law. Texas petitions for annexation.

1840 North Carolina's first public school opened.

1841 Holden gets law license, opens practice in Raleigh; marries Anne Young.

1842 Holden attends Whig convention as delegate.

1843 Holden purchases *North Carolina Standard*; named to Democratic state executive committee. Nativist American (later, Know Nothing) movement appears.

1844 *Standard* calls on Henry Clay to clarify his stand on Texas, which Clay does in his Raleigh Letter.

1845 Texas admitted to Union.

1846 Oregon boundary dispute with England settled. Holden elected to North Carolina House.

1850 Free suffrage amendment approved by North Carolina legislature.

1852 Anne Young Holden dies.

1854	Kansas-Nebraska Act makes Popular (Squatter) Sovereignty national policy. Republican Party formed by coalition of antislavery elements.
1855	Holden marries Louisa Harrison.
1858	Holden loses bid for Democratic nomination for governor to John W. Ellis after North Carolina's first preconvention campaign.
1859	John Brown's raid at Harpers Ferry alarms South.
1860	Abraham Lincoln elected president. South Carolina secedes.
1861	Confederacy organized. Civil War begins. North Carolina secedes.
1862	Federal forces capture part of coastal North Carolina. Holden calls for prayers for peace. Zebulon B. Vance elected governor of North Carolina with Holden's support.
1863	Emancipation Proclamation declares slaves freed. Holden endorses call for peace convention.
1864	Holden runs for governor as peace party candidate, loses to Zebulon B. Vance.
1865	Lee surrenders to Grant. Lincoln assassinated. Thirteenth Amendment, abolishing slavery, ratified. Federal forces capture Fort Fisher; Sherman occupies Raleigh. Holden named provisional governor, turns *Standard* over to son. North Carolina's secession repealed.
1866	Ku Klux Klan founded.
1867	Reconstruction Acts put Confederate states under martial law. North Carolina Republican Party organized.
1868	North Carolina adopts new constitution and is readmitted to Union. Holden elected governor as Republican. President Johnson impeached.
1869	Shoffner Act empowers North Carolina governor to impose martial law.
1870	Holden puts Alamance and Caswell Counties under martial law.
1871	Holden impeached and removed from office.
1873	Holden appointed Raleigh postmaster.
1875	Civil Rights Act outlawing racial discrimination passed.

1877	Reconstruction ends. Troops withdrawn from South.
1881	Holden loses postmastership.
1890	Holden completes *Memoirs*, is stricken by paralysis.
1892	Holden dies March 1.

NOTES

CHAPTER ONE

1. William P. Randel, *Ku Klux Klan* (New York, 1965), pp. 4-5. Randel's third chapter, "The Klan Impeaches a Governor," is particularly relevant to this study.

2. *Ibid.*, p. 50.

3. *Impeachment Trial of W. W. Holden* (Raleigh, N. C., 1871), pp. 9-18. This is the official record of the proceedings in Holden's impeachment trial (hereafter cited as *Transcript*).

CHAPTER TWO

1. "Recollections of W. W. Holden," Margaret Holden Murdock, 1930, unpublished manuscript in possession of the authors.

2. *Ibid.*

3. *Hillsborough Recorder*, Aug 21, 1835, et al.

4. Murdock manuscript.

5. W. W. Holden, editorial in the *North Carolina Standard* (Raleigh), Oct. 20, 1858 (hereafter this newspaper is cited as *Standard*).

6. *Ibid.*

7. "Memoranda of W. W. Holden," Fred G. Mahler, 1932, unpublished manuscript in possession of the authors.

8. Murdock manuscript.

9. *Standard*, Oct. 21, 1846.

10. Holden, "Address on the History of Journalism in North Carolina," delivered at the ninth annual meeting of the Press Association of North Carolina, June 21, 1881, at Winston, N. C. (hereafter cited as "History of Journalism in North Carolina").

11. *Ibid.*

12. *Ibid.*

13. *Ibid.*

14. W. K. Boyd, "William W. Holden," *An Annual Publication of Historical Papers*, Historical Society of Trinity College, Series III, 1899, Durham (hereafter cited as "Holden"). The story was also related to the authors by S. A. Ashe, the North Carolina historian who

was a member of the legislature that impeached Holden. It was said to have been a favorite of Holden's in later years.

15. *Standard*, Feb. 5, 1862.

16. Boyd, "Holden." Historical Society of Trinity College.

17. *Standard*, Feb. 5, 1862.

18. *Raleigh Register and North Carolina Gazette*, Apr. 15, 1842 (hereafter cited as *Register*).

19. *Standard*, Feb. 5, 1862.

CHAPTER THREE

1. Boyd, "Holden."

2. Holden, *Memoirs of W. W. Holden* (Durham, N. C., 1911), p. 150 (hereafter cited as *Memoirs*).

3. Holden, letter to editor, *Raleigh Christian Advocate*, May 25, 1887.

4. M. N. Amis, *Historical Raleigh* (n.d., n.p.), pp. 73-74.

5. Holden, "History of Journalism in North Carolina."

6. *Wilmington Journal*, quoted in *Standard*, Jan. 29, 1845.

7. *Raleigh Christian Advocate*, May 25, 1887.

8. *Standard*, June 28, 1854.

9. Holden, *Memoirs*, p. 94.

10. Holden to Ruffin, Feb. 3, 1841, *The Papers of Thomas Ruffin*, I: 192.

11. *Raleigh Star*, Apr. 6, 1842 (hereafter cited as *Star*).

12. *Ibid.*, Apr. 22, 1843.

13. *Ibid.*, July 14, 1841.

14. *The Rasp* (Raleigh), July 17, 1841.

15. *Star*, Aug. 12, 1842.

16. *Register*, Feb. 25, 1842.

17. *Star*, Jan. 19, 1842.

18. S. A. Ashe, *History of North Carolina*, II: 367.

19. *Standard*, July 1, 1840.

20. *Ibid.*, Nov. 8, 1837.

21. *Star*, Feb. 17, 1841.

22. *Standard*, May 5, 1841.

23. *Ibid.*, Feb. 5, 1845.

24. Holden, *Memoirs*, p. 97.

25. *Mecklenburg Jeffersonian*, Jan. 24, 1843.

26. *Standard*, Feb. 8, 1843.

27. *Ibid.*, Apr. 5, 1843.

28. *Star*, Jan. 18, 1843.

29. *Standard*, Jan. 18, 1843; Feb. 8, 1843.

30. *Ibid.*, May 10, 1843.

31. Boyd, "Holden."

32. S. A. Ashe, *Biographical History of North Carolina*, III: 186, et al. Despite the popularity of the story, no documentary basis for it can be found.

33. Boyd, "Holden."

34. *Standard*, Sept. 30, 1857.

35. *Ibid.*, Aug. 9, 1843.

36. Holden, *Memoirs*, p. 97.

37. Boyd, "Holden."

CHAPTER FOUR

1. *Standard*, May 31, 1853.

2. *Ibid.*, June 7, 1843.

3. *Ibid.*, June 14, 1843 ff.

4. *Register*, June 2, 1843.

5. Holden, *Memoirs*, p. 97.

6. Josephus Daniels, article in *State Chronicle*, Sept. 9, 1886. Holden apparently recognized the truthfulness of the information, because he saved that issue of the *Chronicle*.

7. *Highland Messenger*, Sept. 15, 1843.

8. *Standard*, Aug. 9. 1843.

9. *Register*, July 21, 1843.

10. *Fayetteville Observer*, July 12, 1843.

11. *Standard*, Sept. 27, 1843.

12. *Ibid.*, Nov. 22, 1843.

13. *Ibid.*, Dec. 20, 1843.

14. *Ibid.*, Apr. 10, 1844.

15. Holden, letter to editor, *State Chronicle*, Apr. 30, 1886.

16. *Fayetteville Observer*, June 26, 1844.

17. *Ibid.*, Apr. 23, 1845.

18. *Standard*, May 7, 1845.

19. *Ibid.*

20. Holden, "History of Journalism in North Carolina."

21. *Fayetteville Observer*, June 19, 1844.

22. *Standard*, Nov. 13, 1844.

23. *Ibid.*, Sept. 10, 1845.

24. *Ibid.*

25. *Ibid.*, Nov. 5, 1845.

26. *Register*, Mar. 20, 1846.

27. *Standard*, Dec. 17, 1845.

28. *Standard*, Aug. 12, 1846. The term is used in resolutions adopted by Democrats in Northampton County.

29. *Standard*, Aug. 12, 1846.

30. *Ibid.*, Aug. 6, 1845.

31. Holden to Reid, Dec. 8, 1847, David S. Reid Papers, II, 1845–50.

32. *Standard*, Jan. 19, 1848.

33. *Ibid.*, Dec. 8, 1847.

34. *Ibid.*, Mar. 1, 1848.

35. Holden to Reid, April 19, 1848, Reid Papers, II, 1845–50.

36. *Standard*, July 5, 1850. Article by Reid.

37. *Ibid.*, July 6, 1850.

38. *Star*, June 19, 1850.

39. *Ibid.*

40. *Standard*, July 6, 1850.

41. *Ibid.*, July 5, 1850.

42. *Register*, May 10, 1848.

43. *Standard*, May 24, 1848.

44. *Ibid.*, June 7, 1848.

45. Holden to Reid, Reid Papers, II, 1845–50.

46. *Register*, May 27, 1848.

47. *Ibid.*, June 7, 1848.

48. *Star*, May 24, 1848.

49. *Standard*, July 13, 1848.

50. *Standard*, July 12, 1848.

51. *Ibid.*

52. *Register*, June 21, 1848.

53. Holden to Reid, Aug. 1, 1848, Reid Papers, II, 1845–50.

54. *Ibid.*, June 1, 1850.
55. *Register*, Aug. 13, 1848.
56. *Standard*, Nov. 15, 1848.
57. Holden, letter to *News and Observer*, Aug. 31, 1883.
58. *Fayetteville Observer*, Aug. 8, 1864.

CHAPTER FIVE

1. Holden, *Memoirs*, pp. 97–8.
2. *Standard*, Apr. 10, 1850.
3. *Ibid.*, Mar. 2, 1853.
4. *Ibid.*, Nov. 8, 1848.
5. *Ibid.*, Mar. 27, 1850.
6. *Ibid.*, Feb. 7, 1849.
7. *Ibid.*, May 31, 1843.
8. *Ibid.*, Nov. 7, 1849.
9. *Ibid.*, Dec. 26, 1849.
10. *Star*, May 15, 1850.
11. Holden to Reid, June 1, 1850, Reid Papers, II, 1845–50.
12. *Standard*, Feb. 20, 1850.
13. *Wilmington Journal*, May 17, 1850.
14. Holden, *Memoirs*, p. 7.
15. *Standard*, June 12, 1850.
16. Holden to Reid, June 1, 1850, Reid Papers, II, 1845–50.
17. Paul C. Cameron to Joseph B. G. Roulhac, Aug. 8, 1850, *The Papers of Thomas Ruffin*, II: 298.
18. *Standard*, Aug. 7, 1850.
19. *Ibid.*, Dec. 2, 1857.
20. *Star*, Oct. 23, 1850.
21. *Standard*, Nov. 9, 1850.
22. *Register*, Aug. 2, 1851.
23. Jonathan Worth to B. S. Hedrick, April 20, 1866. *The Correspondence of Jonathan Worth*, I: 550.
24. *Standard*, Jan. 13, 1864.
25. *Ibid.*
26. *Ibid.*, Apr. 9, 1851.
27. *Ibid.*, Jan. 15, 1851.
28. *Ibid.*, Nov. 13, 1850.

29. *Star*, Nov. 13, 1850.

30. *Standard*, Feb. 26, 1851.

31. *Ibid.*, June 18, 1851.

32. *Ibid.*, Nov. 27, 1850.

33. *Ibid.*, Jan. 22, 1851.

34. *Ibid.*, June 2, 1852.

35. Holden to Reid, Aug. 10, 1852, Reid Papers, III, 1850–56.

36. K. F. Lilly to E. J. Hale, Sept. 22, 1852. Willie P. Mangum Papers, 1850–59.

37. *Standard*, July 2, 1853.

38. Holden, "History of Journalism in North Carolina."

39. *Warrenton News*, quoted in *Register*, Aug. 3, 1853.

40. *Standard*, July 30, 1853.

41. *Ibid.*, Aug. 20, 1853.

42. *Ibid.*, Mar. 3, 1858.

43. *Goldsborough Tribune*, quoted in *Standard*, Mar. 3, 1858.

44. *Wilmington Journal*, Apr. 28, 1854.

45. *Standard*, Sept. 13, 1854.

46. *Ibid*.

47. *Ibid.*, May 16, 1855.

48. *Ibid.*, June 6, 1855.

49. *Fayetteville Observer*, Jan. 31, 1856.

50. *Greensborough Patriot*, Mar. 17, 1855.

51. *Ibid*.

52. *Standard*, May 23, 1855.

53. *Ibid.*, May 26, 1855.

54. *Register*, July 18, 1855.

55. *Standard*, Aug. 1, 1855.

56. *Ibid*.

57. *Standard*, Jan. 19, 1856.

58. *Ibid.*, Sept. 5, 1860.

59. *Ibid.*, Dec. 15, 1858.

60. *Register*, Nov. 11, 1857.

61. *Greensborough Patriot*, Nov. 20, 1857.

62. *Standard*, Dec. 30, 1857.

63. *Ibid.*, Sept. 30, 1857.

64. *Register*, Nov. 18, 1857.

65. *Ibid.*, Mar. 10, 1858.

CHAPTER SIX

1. *Standard*, Jan. 23, 1856.

2. *Democratic Pioneer*, Sept. 23, 1857.

3. *Ibid.*, Oct. 20, 1857.

4. R. H. Whitaker, article in *News and Observer*, Mar. 19, 1905.

5. *Democratic Pioneer*, Sept. 23, 1857.

6. *Register*, Sept. 30, 1857.

7. *Greensborough Patriot*, Dec. 4, 1857.

8. *Ibid.*, Dec. 11, 1857.

9. *Standard*, Jan. 13, 1858.

10. *Democratic Pioneer*, Jan. 19, 1858.

11. *Register*, Nov. 11, 1857.

12. *Standard*, Feb. 17, 1858.

13. *Wilmington Journal*, Feb. 24, 1858.

14. *Goldsborough Tribune*, quoted in *Wilmington Journal*, Mar. 12, 1858.

15. Governor's Papers, Thomas Bragg, Jan. to June, 1858.

16. *Fayetteville Observer*, Mar. 15, 1858.

17. *Register*, Apr. 14, 1858.

18. *Greensborough Patriot*, Feb. 12, 1858.

19. *Standard*, Apr. 17, 1858.

20. *Register*, Apr. 21, 1858.

21. These and other details not otherwise credited are taken from the reports in the *Western Democrat*, the *Standard*, and the *Wilmington Journal*, all of which are in agreement.

22. *Western Democrat*, Apr. 20, 1858.

23. Mordecai himself had been elected to the Legislature as a Whig in 1854.

24. *Wilmington Journal*, Apr. 16, 1858.

25. *Fayetteville Observer*, Apr. 26, 1858.

26. *Standard*, Apr. 21, 1858.

27. Ashe, *History of North Carolina*, II: 516.

28. Whitaker, *Reminiscences*, Raleigh: Edwards & Broughton Printing Co., 1905, p. 10.

29. *Standard*, Apr. 21, 1858.
30. *Ibid.*
31. *Ibid.*, Nov. 24, 1860.
32. *Register*, Aug. 14, 1858.
33. *Ibid.*, July 28, 1858.
34. *Greensborough Patriot*, May 14, 1858.
35. *Western Democrat*, Apr. 27, 1858.
36. *Greensborough Patriot*, May 14, 1858.
37. *Register*, Apr. 14, 1858.
38. *Standard*, Apr. 21, 1858.
39. *Wilmington Journal*, Apr. 24, 1858.
40. *State Chronicle*, Mar. 2, 1892.
41. *Register*, Apr. 21, 1858.
42. *Confederate*, June 29, 1864.
43. *Standard*, Apr. 17, 1858.
44. *Ibid.*, Apr. 21, 1858.
45. *Carolina Watchman*, Apr. 20, 1858.
46. *Standard*, Apr. 21, 1858.
47. *Register*, Apr. 21, 1858.
48. *Fayetteville Observer*, Nov. 18, 1858.
49. *Standard*, Oct. 20, 1858.
50. *Wilmington Journal*, Oct. 29, 1858.
51. *Fayetteville Observer*, Oct. 25, 1858.
52. *Ibid.*, Oct. 28, 1858.
53. *Register*, Oct. 28, 1858.
54. *Standard*, Nov. 3, 1858.
55. *Fayetteville Observer*, Nov. 18, 1858.
56. *Greensborough Patriot*, Nov. 19, 1858.
57. *Wilmington Journal*, Nov. 22, 1858.
58. *Standard*, Dec. 1, 1858.
59. *Fayetteville Observer*, Nov. 25, 1858.
60. *Greensborough Patriot*, Dec. 3, 1858.
61. *Fayetteville Observer*, Nov. 20, 1860.

CHAPTER SEVEN

1. *Wilmington Journal*, Nov. 15, 1858.
2. *Carolina Watchman*, June 1, 1858.

3. *Standard*, Sept. 4, 1858.
4. *Ibid.*, Apr. 6, 1859.
5. *Ibid.*, Apr. 20, 1856.
6. *Fayetteville Observer*, Nov. 18, 1858.
7. *Standard*, Apr. 13, 1859.
8. *Ibid.*, Feb. 8, 1859.
9. *Ibid.*, Sept. 7, 1859.
10. *Ibid.*, Jan. 5, 1859.
11. *Ibid.*, Aug. 31, 1859.
12. *Ibid.*, June 8, 1859.
13. *Ibid.*
14. *Ibid.*, Oct. 26, 1859.
15. *Ibid.*, Nov. 9, 1859.
16. *Greensborough Patriot*, Nov. 4, 1859.
17. *Standard*, Dec. 7, 1859.
18. *Ibid.*, Nov. 30, 1859.
19. *Ibid.*
20. *Ibid.*, Dec. 7, 1859.
21. *Ibid.*, Nov. 30, 1859.
22. *Ibid.*, Dec. 14, 1858.
23. *Register*, Dec. 21, 1859.
24. *Wilmington Journal*, Nov. 12, 1859.
25. *Standard*, Jan. 25, 1860.
26. *Ibid.*, Jan. 28, 1860.
27. *Ibid.*, Mar. 10, 1860.
28. *Ibid.*
29. *Ibid.*, Mar. 28, 1860.
30. *Ibid.*, Jan. 13, 1864.
31. Holden, *Memoirs*, pp. 10–12.
32. *Standard*, May 16, 1860.
33. *New York Times*, May 3, 1860.
34. *Ibid.*
35. *Standard*, May 9, 1860.
36. *Ibid.*, May 23, 1860.
37. *Standard*, May 30, 1860.
38. *Ibid.*

39. *Democratic Press*, quoted in *Standard*, Aug. 22, 1860.

40. *Standard*, June 9, 1860.

41. *Ibid.*, June 13, 1860.

42. *Ibid.*, May 23, 1860.

43. *Ibid.*, June 2, 1860.

44. *Ibid.*, June 13, 1860.

45. *Ibid.*, July 4, 1860.

46. *Ibid.*

47. *Ibid.*

48. *Ibid.*, July 7, 1860.

49. *Ibid.*, July 11, 1860.

50. *Ibid.*, July 18, 1860.

51. *Ibid.*, Sept. 5, 1860.

52. *Ibid.*

53. *Ibid.*, Oct. 17, 1860.

54. *Ibid.*, Oct. 31, 1860.

55. *Ibid.*, Nov. 7, 1860.

56. Holden, article in *Charlotte Democrat*, Feb. 11, 1881.

57. Worth to —— (probably J. J. Jackson), undated, *Correspondence of Jonathan Worth*, I: 125–6.

58. *Standard*, Nov. 24, 1860.

59. *Wilmington Journal*, Feb. 26, 1861.

60. *Standard*, Nov. 28, 1860.

61. *Ibid.*, Dec. 5, 1860.

62. *Greensborough Patriot*, Nov. 22, 1860.

63. *Standard*, Sept. 5, 1860.

64. *Ibid.*, Dec. 5, 1860.

65. *Ibid.*, Sept. 14, 1864.

66. *Wilmington Journal*, Nov. 15, 1860.

67. *State Journal*, Dec. 5, 1860.

68. *Register*, Dec. 5, 1860.

69. *Standard*, Dec. 8, 1860.

70. *Ibid.*, Dec. 12, 1860.

71. *Standard*, Jan. 2, 1861.

72. *Standard*, Jan. 2, 1861.

73. *Ibid.*, Jan. 23, 1861.

74. *Wilmington Journal*, Dec. 17, 1860.
75. *Standard*, Dec. 19, 1860.
76. *Ibid.*, Jan. 9, 1861.
77. *Ibid.*, Jan. 2, 1861.
78. *Fayetteville Observer*, Jan. 7, 1861.
79. *Carolina Watchman*, Jan. 29, 1861.
80. *State Journal*, Jan. 16, 1861.
81. *Ibid.*, Jan. 9, 1861.
82. *Standard*, Jan. 30, 1861.
83. *Ibid.*, Feb. 6, 1861.
84. *Ibid.*, Feb. 13, 1861.
85. *State Journal*, Feb. 13, 1861.
86. *Register*, Feb. 6, 1861.
87. *Standard*, Dec. 9, 1863.
88. *Register*, Feb. 27, 1861.
89. *Standard*, Feb. 20, 1861.
90. *Register*, Feb. 28, 1861.
91. *Standard*, Mar. 20, 1861.
92. *Ibid.*, Mar. 6, 1861.
93. *Wilmington Journal*, Mar. 16, 1861.
94. *Standard*, Mar. 27, 1861.
95. *Ibid.*, Apr. 3, 1861.
96. *Ibid.*
97. *Carolina Watchman*, Feb. 21, 1861.
98. *Fayetteville Observer*, Feb. 25, 1861.
99. *State Journal*, Feb. 27, 1861.
100. *Wilmington Journal*, Feb. 21, 1861.
101. *State Journal*, Feb. 27, 1861.
102. *Standard*, Mar. 6, 1861.
103. *Ibid.*, Mar. 13, 1861.
104. *Fayetteville Observer*, Mar. 20, 1861.
105. *Carolina Watchman*, Mar. 26, 1861.
106. *Standard*, Apr. 3, 1861.
107. *Ibid.*, Apr. 17, 1861.
108. *Ibid.*
109. *Ibid.*, Apr. 24, 1861.

110. *Ibid.*, Feb. 5, 1862.
111. *Ibid.*, May 22, 1861.
112. *Ibid.*
113. Holden, *Memoirs*, p. 17.
114. *State Journal*, May 22, 1861.
115. Ashe, *Biographical History of North Carolina*, III: 193. Boyd attributes to Holden the words "the proudest moment of my life": Boyd, "Holden."

CHAPTER EIGHT

1. *Standard*, July 24, 1861.
2. Samuel S. Cox, *Three Decades of Federal Legislation* (Providence: J. A. and R. A. Reid, 1885).
3. *Standard*, Dec. 25, 1861.
4. *Ibid.*, June 19, 1861.
5. *Register*, June 19, 1861.
6. *Standard*, July 24, 1861.
7. *Ibid.*, May 29, 1861.
8. *Ibid.*, July 3, 1861.
9. *Ibid.*, Aug. 7, 1861.
10. *Ibid.*, Oct. 30, 1861.
11. *Ibid.*, June 19, 1861.
12. *Ibid.*, June 12, 1861.
13. *Ibid.*, Sept. 11, 1861.
14. *Ibid.*, June 19, 1861.
15. *Ibid.*
16. *Ibid.*, July 3, 1861.
17. *Ibid.*, May 14, 1862.
18. *Ibid.*, Sept. 4, 1861.
19. *Ibid.*, Aug. 21, 1861.
20. *State Journal*, Oct. 30, 1861.
21. *Register,* May 29, 1861.
22. *Standard*, Dec. 11, 1861.
23. *Ibid.*, Dec. 4, 1861.
24. *Ibid.*, Feb. 5, 1862.
25. Ida Holden Cowles, preface to *Hatteras and Other Poems* by

Joseph William Holden (Raleigh: Edwards & Broughton Printing Co., 1925).

26. *Standard*, Feb. 12, 1862.
27. *Ibid.*, Feb. 19, 1862.
28. *State Journal*, Feb. 19, 1862.
29. *Standard*, Mar. 5, 1862.
30. *Ibid.*, Mar. 19, 1862.
31. *Ibid.*, Mar. 5, 1862.
32. *Ibid.*, Apr. 2, 1862.
33. *State Journal*, Mar. 5, 1862.
34. *Standard*, Apr. 23, 1862.
35. *Ibid.*
36. *Ibid.*
37. Holden, *Memoirs*, pp. 19–20.
38. *Wilmington Journal*, June 12, 1862.
39. *Ibid.*, July 3, 1863.
40. *Ibid.*, May 28, 1862.
41. *State Journal*, June 25, 1862.
42. *Ibid.*, Mar. 12, 1862.
43. *Wilmington Journal*, July 3, 1862.
44. *Asheville News*, July 17, 1862.
45. *Fayetteville Observer*, Aug. 7, 1862.
46. *Register*, July 30, 1862.
47. *State Journal*, Aug. 20, 1862.
48. *Register*, July 23, 1862.
49. *Standard*, July 30, 1862.
50. *Fayetteville Observer*, July 28, 1862.
51. *Ibid.*, June 30, 1862.
52. *Ibid.*, July 17, 1862.
53. *Standard*, July 2, 1862.
54. *Ibid.*
55. *Ibid.*, Aug. 20, 1862.
56. *State Journal*, Aug. 13, 1862.
57. *Register*, Sept. 10, 1862.
58. *Standard*, Oct. 29, 1862.

59. *Ibid.*

60. *Ibid.*, Aug. 27, 1862.

61. *Ibid.*, Nov. 5, 1862.

62. *State Journal*, Oct. 28, 1862.

63. *Standard*, Nov. 5, 1862.

64. *Register*, Nov. 19, 1862.

65. *Ibid.*, Nov. 5, 1862.

66. *Ibid.*, Nov. 19, 1862.

67. *Standard*, Feb. 23, 1863.

68. *Ibid.*

69. Walter Clark, *North Carolina Regiments* (Goldsboro: Nash Brothers, 1901; Published by the state), V: 476-7.

70. Jonathan Worth to John M. Worth, August 9, 1863, *The Correspondence of Jonathan Worth*, I: 254.

71. Vance to Hale, July 26, 1863, E. J. Hale Papers, III, 1863-67.

72. *Standard*, Oct. 29, 1862.

73. *Ibid.*, Nov. 5, 1862.

74. *Ibid.*, June 18, 1862.

75. *Ibid.*, May 1, 1863.

76. *Ibid.*, Feb. 11, 1863.

77. *Fayetteville Observer*, Aug. 24, 1863.

78. Vance to Hale, June 10, 1863, E. J. Hale Papers, III, 1863-67.

79. D. H. Hill to Vance, June 15, 1863, Z. B. Vance Papers II, 1863.

80. *Standard*, July 1, 1863.

81. Jefferson Davis to Vance, July 24, 1863, Z. B. Vance Papers, II, 1863.

82. Vance to Davis, July 26, 1863, *The War of the Rebellion*, Official Records of the Union and Confederate Armies, Series I, Vol. II, Part II: 740.

83. Vance to Hale, July 26, 1863, E. J. Hale Papers, III, 1863-67.

84. *Standard*, July 29, 1863.

85. *Register*, July 29, 1863.

86. Jonathan Worth to Jesse G. Henshaw, July 23, 1863, *The Correspondence of Jonathan Worth*, I: 245.

87. Jonathan Worth to A. G. Foster, Aug. 1, 1863, *Ibid.*, I: 247.

88. *Standard*, July 8, 1863.

89. Jonathan Worth to John M. Worth, Aug. 9, 1863, *The Correspondence of Jonathan Worth*, I: 253-5.

90. *Standard*, Aug. 19, 1863.

91. *Ibid.*, Aug. 12, 1863.

92. *Ibid.*

93. *Ibid.*, Aug. 19, 1863.

94. *Ibid.*, Aug. 12, 1863.

95. *Ibid.*, Jan. 4, 1865.

96. *Ibid.*, Nov. 4, 1864.

97. *Ibid.*, Jan. 4, 1865.

98. Vance to Hale, Aug. 11, 1863, E. J. Hale Papers, III, 1863-67.

99. *Fayetteville Observer*, Aug. 17, 1863.

100. *Standard*, Aug. 19, 1863.

101. Mahler Manuscript.

102. *Raleigh Confederate*, June 20, 1864.

103. *Standard*, Aug. 19, 1863.

104. Vance to Hale, Sept. 7, 1863, E. J. Hale Papers, III, 1863-67.

105. *Standard*, Sept. 9, 1863.

106. *Ibid.*, Aug. 19, 1863.

107. *Ibid.*, Sept. 9, 1863.

108. *Ibid.*, Aug. 19, 1863.

109. *Ibid.*, Sept. 2, 1863.

110. Davis to Vance, Aug. 22, 1863, Z. B. Vance Papers, III, 1863-64.

111. *Standard*, Jan. 4, 1865.

112. W. D. Howard, letter to the *Spirit of the Age*, quoted in *Standard*, Nov. 25, 1863.

113. *Daily Progress*, Sept. 11, 1863.

114. *Standard*, May 18, 1864.

115. *Ibid.*

116. *Ibid.*

117. *Daily Progress*, Sept. 11, 1863.

118. Vance to Hale, Sept. 11, 1863. E. J. Hale Papers, III, 1863-67.

119. Jonathan Worth to A. M. Tomlinson, Sept. 10, 1863, *The Correspondence of Jonathan Worth*, I: 261-2.

120. *Register*, Sept. 9, 1863.

121. *Standard*, Dec. 2, 1863.

122. *Ibid.*, Nov. 18, 1863.

123. *Fayetteville Observer*, Nov. 30, 1863.

124. *Standard*, Nov. 25, 1863.

125. Vance to Hale, Feb. 4, 1864, E. J. Hale Papers, III, 1863–67.

126. *Standard*, Apr. 6, 1864.

127. John D. Hyman to Vance, Apr. 20, 1863, Z. B. Vance Papers, III, 1863–64.

128. *Standard*, Feb. 10, 1864.

129. *Ibid.*, Feb. 24, 1864.

130. *Fayetteville Observer*, Apr. 11, 1864.

131. Holden, *Memoirs*, p. 112.

132. *Ibid.*, p. 43.

133. Vance to Davis, Feb. 9, 1864, *The War of the Rebellion*, Official Records of the Union and Confederate Armies (Washington: Government Printing Office), Series I, Vol. II, Part II: 818.

134. *Standard*, Mar. 3, 1864.

135. Holden to C. J. Cowles, Mar. 18, 1864, Holden Papers in Duke University Library.

136. *Standard*, Apr. 6, 1864.

137. Jonathan Worth to Holden, Apr. 23, 1864, *The Correspondence of Jonathan Worth*, I: 306–8.

138. *Conservative*, May 18, 1864.

139. *Ibid.*, Apr. 27, 1864.

140. *Standard*, June 15, 1864.

141. *Ibid.*, May 18, 1864.

142. A. M. Gorman to Hale, May 18, 1864, E. J. Hale Papers, III, 1863–67.

143. *Standard*, May 25, 1864.

144. *Confederate*, May 4, 1864.

145. *Ibid.*, June 1, 1864.

146. *Standard*, June 22, 1864.

147. *Conservative*, July 20, 1863. It should be noted that North Carolina editors never referred to the conflict then in progress as a "civil war."

148. *Standard*, July 27, 1864.

149. These and the figures following are taken from the official vote published in the *Standard*, Oct. 19, 1864.

150. *Fayetteville Observer*, Aug. 8, 1864.

151. *Wilmington Journal*, July 30, 1864.

CHAPTER NINE

1. *Standard*, Sept. 14, 1864.

2. *Conservative*, Aug. 17, 1864.

3. *Ibid.*, Oct. 5, 1864.

4. *Standard*, Aug. 17, 1864.

5. Vance to D. L. Swain, Sept. 22, 1864, Z. B. Vance Papers, V, July–Oct., 1864.

6. *Ibid.*

7. *Standard*, Oct. 12, 1864.

8. *Ibid.*

9. *Ibid.*, Feb. 15, 1865.

10. *Ibid.*, Nov. 16, 1864.

11. *Ibid.*, Nov. 30, 1864.

12. *Ibid.*, Dec. 21, 1864.

13. *Standard*, Jan. 18, 1865.

14. *Ibid.*

15. *Ibid.*

16. *Ibid.*

17. *Ibid.*, Feb. 22, 1865.

18. *Ibid.*

19. *Fayetteville Observer*, Mar. 6, 1865.

20. *Standard*, Mar. 1, 1865.

21. *Ibid.*

22. *Ibid.*, Mar. 22, 1865.

23. *Ibid.*, Mar. 29, 1865.

24. *Ibid.*, Apr. 26, 1865.

25. *Ibid.*, Apr. 27, 1865.

26. Mrs. Calvin J. Cowles of Wilkesboro, N. C., a daughter of Holden, recalled in conversation with the authors that on the night before Federal troops arrived in Raleigh, Holden's dinner with two Confederate officers was interrupted as a Southern cavalry officer

came in to say that he had been sent by his superiors to warn the editor that he was to be hanged that night. Guards stationed about the house turned away men bent on carrying out the threat.

27. *Standard*, Apr. 28, 1865.

28. *Ibid.*, Apr. 29, 1865.

29. *Ibid.*, May 1, 1865.

30. *Ibid.*, May 12, 1865.

31. *Ibid.*, May 15, 1865.

32. Holden, *Memoirs*, pp. 44-5.

33. Holden, "Address on the History of Journalism in North Carolina.

CHAPTER TEN

1. Ashe, *History of North Carolina,* II, 1020. Ashe, whose sympathies were not with Holden, says, "In the main Holden's appointments were good."

2. J. G. deRoulhac Hamilton, *History of North Carolina* (New York: Lewis Publishing Co., 1919) III: 59-60.

3. *Ibid.*, 63.

4. Holden to Andrew Johnson, July 17, 1865, Holden Papers, Duke University.

5. Holden, *Memoirs*, pp. 57-63.

6. *Ibid.*, pp. 64-5.

7. *Ibid.*, pp. 66-7.

8. *Ibid.*, pp. 68-9.

9. William H. Seward to Holden, Nov. 21, 1865, Holden Papers in Duke University Library.

10. Hamilton, *History of North Carolina*, III: 99.

11. *Weekly Constitution*, Raleigh, Oct. 26, 1876.

12. Jonathan Worth to B. G. Worth, Oct. 25, 1867, *The Correspondence of Jonathan Worth*, I: 1061.

13. *Register*, July 12, 1867. This paper had been revived by Daniel R. Goodloe.

14. *Ibid.*

15. Hamilton, *History of North Carolina*, III: 102-3.

16. *Ibid.*, p. 111.

17. *Standard*, July 15, 1868.

18. Jonathan Worth to Holden, July 1, 1868, Holden, *Memoirs*, pp. 110–2.

19. Holden, *Memoirs*, p. 102.

20. *Weekly Standard*, July 8, 1868.

21. *Weekly Constitution*, Oct. 26, 1876.

22. *Ibid.*, Aug. 26, 1876.

23. These orders are part of the impeachment record.

24. Hamilton, *History of North Carolina*, III: 136–9.

25. John W. Moore, *History of North Carolina* (Raleigh: Alfred Williams & Co., 1880), II: 340–1.

26. In the Holden Papers in the Duke University Library there are many letters and depositions detailing outrages, including murders, rape, beatings, and other atrocities, causing in some instances the closing of schools, especially those for Negroes, and creating chaotic conditions generally.

27. Cortez A. M. Ewing, "Impeachment of Governor Holden," unpublished manuscript in the possession of Dr. Ewing at the University of Oklahoma.

28. Holden papers, Duke University.

29. John Pool to Holden, June 22, 1870, *Ibid.*

30. Holden, *Memoirs*, pp. 138–41.

31. *Weekly Constitution*, Oct. 26, 1876.

32. *Ibid.*

33. Ewing, "Impeachment of Governor Holden."

34. Randel, *Ku Klux Klan*, p. 56.

35. *Standard*, August 5, 6, 1870.

36. Hamilton, *History of North Carolina*, III: 130–2.

37. Randel, *Ku Klux Klan*, p. 54.

38. *Ibid.*

39. *Ibid.*

40. Ewing, "Impeachment of Governor Holden."

41. *Ibid.*

42. *Weekly Constitution*, Oct. 26, 1876.

43. *Standard*, Dec. 6, 1870.

44. Hamilton, *History of North Carolina*, III: 156.

45. *Transcript*, p. 1.

CHAPTER ELEVEN

1. *Transcript*, pp. 1–2.
2. Ewing, "Impeachment of Governor Holden."
3. *Transcript*, pp. 9–18.
4. Ewing, "Impeachment of Governor Holden."
5. Moore, *History of North Carolina*, II: 383.
6. Holden, *Memoirs*, p. 149.
7. Moore, *History of North Carolina*, II: 384.
8. *Transcript*, pp. 29–54.
9. Moore, *History of North Carolina*, II: 385.
10. Holden, *Memoirs*, pp. 165–6.
11. *Transcript*, p. 2311.
12. *Ibid.*, pp. 2312–4.
13. *Ibid.*, p. 2363.
14. *Ibid.*, 2365–6.
15. *Ibid.*, pp. 2369–2438.
16. *Ibid.*, p. 2539.
17. *Ibid.*, p. 2541.
18. *Ibid.*, pp. 2542–58.
19. *Ibid.*, pp. 2559–60.

CHAPTER TWELVE

1. Holden to Louisa Harrison Holden, May 1, 1871. Holden Papers, Duke University.
2. Holden Papers, Duke University.
3. Edward Conigland to Thomas Clingman, Sept. 21, 1875, Holden Papers, Duke University.
4. Raleigh *News*, Oct. 4, 1878.
5. Holden, *Memoirs*, p. 181.
6. *State Chronicle*, Sept. 15, 1883.
7. Ashe, *Biographical History of North Carolina*, III: 205.
8. *State Chronicle*, Sept. 8, 1886.
9. Holden, "History of Journalism in North Carolina."
10. *State Chronicle*, Sept. 9, 1886.
11. *News and Observer*, Aug. 31, 1883.
12. Holden, *Memoirs*, pp. 182–3.
13. Boyd, Introduction to Holden, *Memoirs*.

14. Holden, *Memoirs*, p. 172.
15. *State Chronicle*, Mar. 2, 1892.
16. *Ibid.*, Mar. 3, 1892.
17. *Ibid.*
18. Raleigh *Daily Evening Visitor*, Mar. 1, 1892.
19. Moore, *History of North Carolina*, II: 370.
20. Cited in Randel, *Ku Klux Klan*, pp. 57–8.
21. John Nichols, article in *News and Observer*, June 6, 1907.
22. *Standard*, Oct. 20, 1858.

BIBLIOGRAPHY

SOURCES IN MANUSCRIPT

North Carolina Historical Commission, Raleigh:
  Letters of Thomas Bragg.
  Governor's Papers of Thomas Bragg.
  William A. Graham Papers.
  E. J. Hale Papers.
  William W. Holden Papers.
  Willie P. Mangum Papers.
  David S. Reid Papers.
  Swain Manuscripts.
  Z. B. Vance Papers.
  North Carolina Letters from the Van Buren Papers, 1824–58.
Duke University, Durham:
  W. W. Holden Papers.
Mary Sherwood, Raleigh:
  W. W. Holden Letters and Papers.
Ellis Knowles, New York:
  Personal Papers of John W. Ellis, 1846–61.

SOURCES IN NEWSPAPERS

Asheville News, Asheville, 1854–62.
Carolina Watchman, Salisbury, 1854–64.
Democratic Pioneer, Elizabeth City, 1854–59.
Democratic Signal, Raleigh, 1843–44.
Fayetteville Observer, Fayetteville, 1843–65.
Greensborough Patriot, Greensborough, 1843–65.
Greensborough Times, Greensborough, 1856–61.
Hillsborough Recorder, Hillsborough, 1833–65.
Mecklenburg Jeffersonian, Charlotte, 1843.
New Bern Daily Delta, New Bern, 1859.
New Bern Weekly Journal, New Bern, 1854–56.
North Carolina Republican, Goldsborough, 1854.
North Carolina Standard, Raleigh, 1835–65.

Raleigh Confederate, Raleigh, 1864–65.
Raleigh Conservative, Raleigh, 1864–65.
Raleigh Daily Progress, Raleigh, 1863–65.
Raleigh Register and North Carolina Gazette, Raleigh, 1840–65.
Raleigh Star, Raleigh, 1836–52.
State Journal, Raleigh, 1860–64.
Wadesborough Argus, Wadesborough, 1859–65.
Western Democrat, Charlotte, 1854–65, sometimes called *Charlotte Democrat*.
Western Sentinel, Winston, 1851–65.
Wilmington Journal, Wilmington, 1844–65.

Also the following papers for the dates cited in footnotes:

Charlotte Democrat, for articles written by Holden, 1880–86.
Charlotte Observer, Charlotte.
Christian Advocate, Raleigh.
Danville Register, Danville, Virginia.
Daily National Republican, Washington, D. C.
Highland Messenger, Asheville.
New York Times.
News and Observer, Raleigh.
Raleigh News, Raleigh.
Raleigh Register (a different paper begun in 1867). Raleigh.
Raleigh Sentinel, Raleigh.
Raleigh Times, Raleigh.
Raleigh Visitor, Raleigh.
Southern Citizen, Asheborough.
State Chronicle, Raleigh.
The Rasp, Raleigh.
Warrenton News, Warrenton.
Weekly Constitution (a Republican campaign newspaper), Raleigh.
Wilmington Messenger, Wilmington.
Wilson Mirror, Wilson.

Also a scrapbook kept by Holden in his later years and containing principally newspaper clippings. In the possession of Mary Sherwood of Raleigh.

DOCUMENTARY SOURCES

The Correspondence of Jonathan Worth, I. Edited by J. G. deR. Hamilton. Raleigh: Edwards & Broughton Printing Co., 1909.

Impeachment Trial of W. W. Holden. Raleigh: *Sentinel* Printing Office, 1871.

Journals of the Senate and House of Commons, 1845–65. Raleigh.

Memoirs of W. W. Holden. Edited by W. K. Boyd. The John Lawson Monographs of the Trinity College Historical Society. Durham: The Seaman Printery, 1911.

"Memoranda of W. W. Holden." Fred G. Mahler, Raleigh, 1932. Manuscript in possession of authors.

The Papers of Thomas Ruffin, 4 vols. Edited by J. G. deR. Hamilton. Raleigh: Edwards & Broughton Printing Co., 1913–20.

"Recollections of W. W. Holden." Margaret Holden Murdock (a half-sister), Hillsboro, N. C., 1930. Manuscript in possession of authors.

United States Census Reports, 1850, 1860.

The War of the Rebellion, A Compilation of the Official Records of the Union and Confederate Armies. Washington: Government Printing office.

Whitaker, R. H. *Reminiscences*. Raleigh: Edwards & Broughton Printing Co., 1905.

BULLETINS, PAMPHLETS, PUBLICATIONS
OF SOCIETIES, ETC.

Boyd, W. K., "William W. Holden." *An Annual Publication of Historical Papers*. Series III. Durham, 1899. Published by the Historical Society of Trinity College, 1899.

Crittenden, Charles C., *North Carolina Newspapers Before 1790*. The James Sprunt Historical Studies. Chapel Hill: The University of North Carolina Press, 1928.

Ewing, Cortez A. M., "Impeachment of Governor Holden." Unpublished manuscript in possession of Dr. Ewing at the University of Oklahoma.

———. "Impeachment of Judge E. W. Jones." Unpublished manuscript in possession of Dr. Ewing.

Hamilton, J. G. deR., *Party Politics in North Carolina, 1835–1860.* The James Sprunt Historical Studies. Chapel Hill: The University of North Carolina Press, 1916.

Holden, W. W., "Address on the History of Journalism in North Carolina." Raleigh: *News and Observer* Book and Job Print, 1881.

———— "Address to State Educational Association in 1857." Raleigh: Holden and Wilson, 1857.

STATE HISTORIES AND OTHER SECONDARY WORKS

Amis, M. N., *Historical Raleigh.* Raleigh, 1913.

Ashe, S. A., *History of North Carolina,* II, 1783–1925. Raleigh: Edwards & Broughton Printing Co., 1925.

The Biographical History of North Carolina, I–VIII. Edited by S. A. Ashe and others. Greensboro: Charles L. Van Noppen, 1905.

Bleyer, Willard G. *Main Currents in the History of American Journalism.* Cambridge, Mass.: Houghton Mifflin Co., 1927.

Bowers, Claude. *The Tragic Era.* Cambridge, Mass.: Houghton Mifflin Co., 1929.

Boyd, W. K. *History of North Carolina,* II, 1783–1860. Chicago and New York: The Lewis Publishing Co., 1919.

Clark, Walter. *North Carolina Regiments, 1861–65, V.* Published by the State. Goldsboro: Nash Brothers, 1901.

Connor, R. D. W. *North Carolina, Rebuilding an Ancient Commonwealth, I.* Chicago and New York: American Historical Society, Inc., 1929.

Cox, Samuel S. *Three Decades of Federal Legislation.* Providence: J. A. and R. A. Reid, 1885.

Hamilton, J. G. deR. *Reconstruction in North Carolina.* New York: Columbia University Press, 1914.

————. *History of North Carolina,* Vol. III. New York: Lewis Publishing Co., 1919.

Helper, Hinton Rowan. *The Impending Crisis.* New York: Burdick Brothers, 1857.

Holden, Joseph W. *Hatteras and Other Poems,* with a biographical preface by Ida Holden Cowles. Raleigh: Edwards & Broughton Printing Co., 1925.

Hudson, Frederick. *Journalism in the United States*, from 1690 to 1782. New York: Harper & Brothers, 1873.

Moore, John W. *History of North Carolina*, Vol. II. Raleigh: Alfred Williams and Co., 1880.

———. *School History of North Carolina*. Raleigh: Alfred Williams and Co., 1893.

Norton, Clarence C. *The Democratic Party in Ante-Bellum North Carolina*. Chapel Hill: The University of North Carolina Press, 1930.

Olmsted, F. L. *A Journey in the Seaboard Slave States*, 2 vols. New York: Dix and Edwards, 1856.

Randel, William P. *The Ku Klux Klan*. New York: Chilton Press, 1965.

Spencer, Cornelia Phillips. *The Last Ninety Days of the War in North Carolina*. New York: Watchman Publishing Co., 1886.

Stem, Thad, Jr. *The Tar Heel Press*. Charlotte: The North Carolina Press Association, 1973.

INDEX

279

Library of Congress Cataloging in Publication Data

Folk, Edgar Estes.
    W. W. Holden, a political biography.

    Biography: p.
    Includes index.
    1. Holden, W. W. (William Woods), 1818–1892.
2. Reconstruction—North Carolina.
3. Impeachments—North Carolina. 4. North
Carolina—Politics and government—1775–1865.
5. North Carolina—Governors—Biography.
6. Journalists—North Carolina—Biography.
I. Shaw, Bynum. II. Title.
F259.H74   1982   975.6'041'0924   [B]   82–12780
ISBN 0–89587–025–8